THE
DAILY
COCKTAIL

Text © 2006 Fair Winds Press
First published in the USA in 2006
by Fair Winds Press, a member of
Quayside Publishing Group
33 Commercial Street
Gloucester, MA 01930

10 09 08 07 06   2 3 4 5

ISBN 1-59233-186-6

Library of Congress Cataloging-in-Publication Data

Design by Laura McFadden Design, Inc.

Photography by Allan Penn

Printed and bound in China

DALYN A. MILLER AND
LARRY DONOVAN

THE
DAILY
COCKTAIL

365
INTOXICATING
DRINKS
AND THE
OUTRAGEOUS
EVENTS
THAT INSPIRED
THEM

FAIR WINDS
PRESS
GLOUCESTER, MASSACHUSETTS

CONTENTS

INTRO

READY, SET, DRINK!

Dear Drinker,

Congratulations on your brand new cocktail book! Hopefully, you will find the drinks to be exactly what you were thirsting for, and the information that goes along with each good enough to get you a few pieces of that pie next time you're shooting to best your socially-awkward-yet-freakishly-smart Aunt Mildred at Trivial Pursuit. We believe most of the trivia in here is correct, but really, how should we know? We were drinking when we wrote it.

In this first section, our goal is to arm you with all of the basics you will need before you start your year of great drinking. We really feel obligated to do this; otherwise, it would be like sending a skydiver out without his chute, a policeman out without his donuts, or a New York City cab driver out without his surly disposition. Read carefully—you'll thank us for it later.

WHAT YOU DRINK IT OUT OF

The first thing you want to get down right is the glasses. The drinks in this book use five basic glasses, with a few more thrown in here and there. They are:

The Old-Fashioned

Also known as rocks glasses or tumblers,

these are those short, round glasses with wide mouths and thick bottoms, much like the previously mentioned Aunt Mildred. A good one will have a thick base and feel much heavier than you first expect it to. These tend to be the first glasses hurled across the room during a drunken brawl. Take care to avoid those: these little babies pack a mean punch.

The Collins

Also known as the highball, these are the taller, slightly more slender glasses. You use these for tall or long drinks. Don't try to fit a drink meant for an old-fashioned into a Collins glass because you think it holds more booze; that's a desperate road that you don't really want to start down (and it's also not true; they hold about the same amount). Stick with the glass parameters we give you and you'll do okay.

The Champagne Flute

The Champagne flute is long with a stem. It can taper in or out. These are popular for drinks such as mimosas and bellinis and, of course, good old Champagne. Note: The Champagne saucer, by contrast, is a broad and shallow glass with a stem, very similar to the margarita glass. It's not good for much else and will make a great substitution if you don't have a margarita glass.

The Cocktail

Also known as the martini glass, the cocktail glass is short with a stem. Its sides slope sharply upward. These are the glasses for the small but strong drinks. Do yourself and your guests a favor: don't buy the monster-sized cocktail glasses that are out there these days. The smaller cocktail glass is better for two reasons: you can get through a drink before it gets too warm, and you won't get crocked on just one.

The Shot

All bets are off when it comes to the shot glass! Although the glass itself is not too much bigger than a thimble, your guests will know you mean business when this bad boy comes off the shelf. It's the tiny glass that only holds a few ounces. You use it for, well, shots. There are plenty in here, so have the shot glass at hand. It'll be easy to find—it will be the one with the logo of a Vegas casino or the Hard Rock Café or your favorite college bar on the side.

The Others

We've also used a beer mug upon occasion. Do we really need to tell you what that is? It's tall, fat, and heavy and has a handle. The margarita glass is a Champagne saucer with a few more curves. And the parfait glass is tall, has a stem, and sort of swerves its way upward—it's the same thing as a piña colada glass.

HOW YOU PUT IT TOGETHER

This part is where we tell you what those vague terms such as "shake," "mix," or "blend," which we use throughout the book, actually mean. No, we don't think you were born yesterday, but remember we've had all of these drinks and we understand how a simple reference guide will come in handy after you've had a few. Trust us.

Stirring

A drink that is stirred instead of shaken stays clear: it doesn't get muddled with ice chips or become opaque. Many think martinis should be stirred and not shaken. We disagree, but that's where we give you license to make your own decisions. Just don't come crying to us if you decide to make it your way and then you don't like it. The goal of stirring your drinks is to just mix all the ingredients together. Remember, you're trying not to dilute the drink. "Dilute" rhymes with "pollute," and nobody wants that. When stirring, stir gently; you're not mixing paint for the bathroom.

Shaking

Instead of stirring, you can shake a drink. You're going to need a shaker for this, of course: it's the metal cylinder with a tight-fitting lid that has a built-in strainer in the top. We're very fond of this method because it's easier to do and much more dramatic. Sure, you lose some of the clarity of the liquor as everything gets so thoroughly shaken together, but what are you planning to do with your cocktail, frame it or drink it? Shaking is good for thicker ingredients, such as cream, fruit juices, and eggs. Shake vigorously; it makes you feel all-powerful and will impress your guests.

Blending

This one is easy. First things first: you will need a blender in order to blend. This method is all about the frozen drink. Remember: ice first, then ingredients. We suggest you use the pulse button and hold that lid on tight. We're still cleaning lime juice and tequila off of our kitchen ceiling. Oops.

Layering

The idea here is to keep the ingredients in the drink in separate layers that do not mix with the others. The easiest way to layer one liquor on top of another is to use a demitasse spoon (stay with us here, a regular spoon will work just fine), holding it over the glass and slowly trickling the liquor over the back of the spoon. Also a crowd-pleaser, we promise you.

Muddling

Muddling is mashing, simple as that. It's used for mint and other herbs. This is going to be a big one with the mojitos later in the book, and, of course, the classic mint julep. You can use a wooden "muddler" or a bar spoon with a muddler on the end. A mortar and pestle or the end of a wooden spoon also works great. Crush the herb in the glass until the leaves look dead and the juices have seeped out. Trust us, it tastes better than it sounds!

Frosting

To frost a glass, first dip it in water and then put it in the freezer for 15 to 30 minutes. This is especially great for drinks in cocktail glasses, as you tend to want those to stay icy cold from the first sip to the last.

Rimming

Rimming a glass is easy. Turn it upside down, dip just the edge in water or juice or liquor, then run the rim through the spices or flavoring that will make your drink sing, such as salt, celery salt, or sugar, to coat.

So that's about it. Making a cocktail isn't rocket science, thank God, or we'd have a society of very unhappy sober people. Remember to enjoy the year, try all the drinks, and . . . Who are we kidding, you're not going to remember anything! Enjoy!

JANUARY
1

> "There can't be good living where there is not good drinking."
>
> —BENJAMIN FRANKLIN

You were cavorting with your friends last night, having a great time. Time passed. Two a.m.? Hey, it's still early. Three a.m.? It's not even midnight in Hawaii! Four a.m.? Who are you kidding? You couldn't even read a clock by 4 a.m. So clear that foggy feeling by indulging in the Bloody Mary recipe below! After your first sip, consider this: You wouldn't even be that hung over if it weren't for Julius Caesar. He changed the calendar in 45 b.c.e. so that January 1 was the first day of the year. Voilà! A drink fest is born.

BLOODY MARY (OF COURSE!)

- 1 1/2 oz vodka
- 3 oz tomato juice
- 1 dash lemon juice
- 1/2 tsp Worcestershire sauce
- 2–3 drops Tabasco sauce
- 1 lime wedge

Mix all the ingredients in a Collins glass with ice (except the lime wedge, you hungover bastard!). Add salt and pepper (not the early '90s female hip-hop group, you hungover bastard!) and the lime wedge. Drink until the cobwebs fade away.

2

Ah, the '70s. Sex and drugs and rock 'n' roll, baby! (Never mind the hideous hair, clothes, and avocado-colored appliances.) But by the end of the decade, the partying times took their toll. Just think about poor Sid Vicious, née John Simon Ritchie. Bass player for the Sex Pistols, one of the greatest and best-known punk bands, he fell in love with Nancy Spungen. They had sex. They did drugs. They were rock 'n' roll! Unfortunately, all good things come to an end. Just ask Nancy. You see, in a drug-induced haze, Sid stabbed her. To death. He went on trial on this date in 1979. While out on bail, he died of an overdose of heroin. Have a drink—the Red Hot Lover, described below—and be thankful you are comfy in your flannel pj's and well-chosen investment portfolio.

RED HOT LOVER

    2   shots vodka
    2   shots peach Schnapps
    I   dash grenadine
    3   oz strawberry juice
    3   oz orange juice

Throw it all into a shaker, do your thing, and pour Into a hurricane glass filled with ice. Finish the whole thing, ya nancy!

3

Howard Carter unraveled a discovery of tremendous historical significance on this day in 1923 when he and his ragtag team of archaeologists cracked the tomb of Egypt's Pharaoh Tutankhamen, known to the rest of us simply as King Tut. A young and impetuous ruler in a time of civil unrest, Tut wasn't long for the throne and died at age 18 of mysterious causes. The moral of his story: Don't allow yourself to become entombed in the politics that surround you and wrapped up in other people's problems, or you too might find yourself all alone in a bind. Today, try wrapping yourself around The Mummy in honor of King Tut, who lived and died long before a minimum-age requirement for drinking went into effect.

THE MUMMY

    2   oz vodka
    I   oz Triple Sec
    I   tbsp lemon juice
        club soda

Mix vodka, Triple Sec, and lemon juice in an old-fashioned glass half-filled with ice. Top off with club soda. Stir.

4

You know when your younger sibling or less-well-off best friend finally makes it big? You know how you are "happy" for your loved one at the time, but secretly you are ashamed that you aren't the big honcho anymore? Now try being a whole continent and feeling that way! You see, on this date in 1999, the "euro" (clever nomenclature, no?) became the single currency for eleven European nations and 290 million citizens. It seems Europe didn't like being the "little" sister to the huge American economy. "We want to have a say in how things happen on the planet." Can't you just hear the whining?! Dry your tears and enjoy the drink below.

EUROPEAN

- 1 oz gin
- $^1/_2$ oz cream sherry
- $^1/_2$ oz vermouth
- $^1/_2$ tsp Grand Marnier
- 1 maraschino cherry

Add ice to an old-fashioned glass and pour the liquids in, stirring well. Add the cherry and salute unity!

"Work is the curse of the drinking classes. "

—OSCAR WILDE

15

5

If you are older than 21 (if you aren't, then why are you reading this book?), then you have to admit to the following: At one point in your life you were getting ready to go out with friends, blow-drying the hair you wish you still had, and listening to Bruce Springsteen cranking on the old hi-fi. (If you can't admit to that, then you're probably a Mormon and you shouldn't be reading this, either.) On this date in 1973, "Greetings from Asbury Park, N.J." was released by Bruce Springsteen, a.k.a. The Boss. We think you should relive old times by trying the Who's the Boss drink recipe below. And then thank us that we aren't using a Tony Danza/Judith Light reference!

WHO'S THE BOSS

  1 oz rum
  2 oz sour apple liqueur
  1 oz vodka
  1 oz lemonade

Combine the ingredients with ice and pour into a highball glass. Do not drive down Thunder Road after this one!

6

On this date in 2001, Congress certified George W. Bush as the winner of the 2000 presidential election. How does Congress decide such a thing? Florida's race was too close to call due to some malfunctioning ballots. Chads, the things we didn't even know about till 2000, were to blame. It seems that many voters just didn't have the physical strength to push a chad out of its slot on the ballot. Thousands of votes were deemed invalid; recounts were undertaken, but the Supreme Court put a stop to them. This, in essence, gave Florida's electoral votes to Bush, and Congress ratified the election results. Bush defeated Al Gore and became the new president, and the rest is history.

FLORIDA SPECIAL ❱

  1 1/2 oz rum
  1/4 oz Triple Sec
  1/4 oz maraschino liqueur
  3/4 oz orange juice

Mix all of the liquids with ice; strain into a cocktail glass. Garnish with some unpunched chads. (Kidding!)

7

In the late 1990s, American citizens began looking at cigars differently, thanks to a young, vivacious White House intern named Monica Lewinsky. Among other acts, President Bill Clinton had used a cigar as a sort of tobacco phallus. His affair became publicized after Lewinsky was recorded admitting to the dalliance to a one-time coworker. At first, President Clinton proclaimed his innocence. Congress didn't buy it and began impeachment hearings on this date in 1999. We especially love that the drink below, the Dirty Dog, is served in a Mason jar, in honor of our beloved Bubba president!

DIRTY DOG

1	oz cognac
1 1/2	oz vodka
5	oz chilled orange juice
1	oz chilled cranberry juice

Everything goes into a shaker; work it "something good," and serve in a Mason jar. Hillary loves these!

8

It's all in a name . . . or maybe a nickname? You see, William Randolph Hearst, America's most powerful media tycoon in the nineteenth and early twentieth centuries, allegedly had an affair. Her name was . . . well, that's not the point. It's the alleged nickname for her, um, how do we put this delicately . . . the nickname for her "delicates" that got the attention: Rosebud. Eventually, news of the alleged affair got out, and a movie was made that included this and other unflattering information about Mr. Hearst. Anyhoo, *Citizen Kane*, written, produced, directed by, and starring Orson Welles, has since been deemed by a majority of film critics as the best movie ever made.

ROSEBUD

2	oz grapefruit juice
2	oz vodka (can be a citrus-flavored one)
1/2	oz Triple Sec
1	oz lime juice

Pour the grapefruit juice over ice into a Collins glass. Shake the remaining ingredients in a shaker and add to the glass.

9

Nothing says "circus" like the word flaming! Okay, well, maybe flaming has other connotations these days, but seriously, can't you picture Fifi the Flying Poodle diving through the burning hula hoop when you think of a circus? On this date in 1768, Philip Astley established the first modern circus, not to be confused with the Roman days of putting people to death. (Gives flaming a whole new meaning, no?) So, sit back, sip on the Flaming Ring of Fire as described below, and picture your favorite clown . . . or trapeze artist . . . or a large tiger attacking its flamboyant trainer to the horror of his nearby boyfriend.

FLAMING RING OF FIRE ▶

1/2	oz rum
1/2	oz whiskey
4–5	drops Tabasco sauce

Pour the rum and whiskey into a shot glass and top it off with the hot sauce. Hold onto your top hat!

For millions of Americans, the phrase "black gold, Texas tea" immediately evokes a mental picture of Jed, Granny, Jethro, and Ellie Mae, the Clampetts from the '6os sitcom *The Beverly Hillbillies*. You see, one day Jed was shooting at a rabbit, or some other such varmint, and missed. Missed in the sense that the target escaped, but struck in the sense that oil started bubbling up through the ground. The Clampetts "hit it big," becoming rich off of the oil they discovered. They moved to Beverly Hills and swam in their ce-ment pond. Likewise, on this date in 1901, oil was struck in Beaumont, Texas, marking what historians call the start of the modern oil industry. We don't know how many Beaumontians eventually moved to Beverly Hills, but we're certain that drinking a shot of Black Gold will make you feel better about your own impoverished state. Enjoy!

BLACK GOLD

3/4 oz Jägermeister
3/4 oz cinnamon Schnapps

Toss both in a shot glass and toss the shot back. Beverly Hillbillies forever!

The view from the rim of the Grand Canyon can only be described as breathtaking. The depth, the width, the history of such a weatherworn place are all seemingly unfathomable. Certainly that's the main reason this wonder of the natural world was made into a national monument by President Theodore Roosevelt in 1908. Be that as it may, today's drink, the Tequila Canyon, is pretty good, too. And you don't have to drive to Flagstaff to see one!

TEQUILA CANYON

1 1/2 oz tequila
1/8 oz Triple Sec
4 oz cranberry juice
1/4 oz pineapple juice
1/4 oz orange juice
1 lime wedge

Pour the tequila, Triple Sec, and cranberry juice into a Collins glass filled with ice. Top with the other juices. Use a lime wedge as a garnish and take in the view.

12

On this date in 1971, *All in the Family* debuted on CBS. It starred Carroll O'Connor as Archie Bunker, perhaps the best-known sitcom character of the decade. He was a curmudgeonly, misogynistic, racist, homophobic anti-Semite, but, God, we loved him! He represented the changes that the white middle class was facing during the tumultuous times of the civil rights movement and the fight over the ERA. His spouse, Edith, a good-hearted Tammy Wynette-esque housewife, was the voice of reason, though that voice was a combination of Screech Monkey and Long Island mother-in-law. She accepted the changes happening around her, so let's drink to her honor! The recipe for an Edith's Fizz follows.

"He that drinks fast, pays slow."

–BENJAMIN FRANKLIN

EDITH'S FIZZ

1 ½ oz white wine
½ oz maraschino liqueur
4 oz orange juice
2 oz soda water

Combine it all in a Collins glass and serve. Oh, Archie!

13

Thanks, digital! Don't you love hitting the buttons on your radio and finding the exact digits you need to access that Top 40 station you so love! Okay, so you don't remember anything prior to buttons? Well, once upon a time there were dials; you had to turn the dial to find the station you were looking for. It took forever and, most frequently, involved a lot of static. We've come a long way since 1910, when the first radio broadcast aired. It starred Enrico Caruso at the Metropolitan Opera, but we don't really know about radio broadcasts either, do we? So let's just make a toast in honor of things we don't have to deal with anymore, and enjoy the Seven Dials Cocktail (seven, what the heck would we need seven for?).

SEVEN DIALS COCKTAIL

- 1 oz cognac
- 1 oz dark crème de cacao
- 1 tsp Grand Marnier
- 1 oz double cream
- 1 egg yolk

Shake well, strain into an old-fashioned glass half-filled with broken ice, and serve.

"Always do sober what you said you'd do when you were drunk. That will teach you to keep your mouth shut!"

—CHARLES SCRIBNER, JR.

14

American history is rife with stories of scrappy immigrants, arriving with nothing more than a few pennies in their pockets, working hard and making something of themselves, and leading to a life of riches. This is not one of those stories. But, it's darn close! You see, one such immigrant, Carlos Ponzi, arrived in the United States on this date in 1896. After trying but failing to earn an honest buck, he developed a scheme to make money: Investors turned over their money to him, and they would receive the initial investment and a 50 percent profit in three months' time. As people heard of this too-good-to-be-true story, they flocked to Ponzi to invest. His original investors were paid on time, fueling the intrigue and interest. As it turns out, Ponzi was paying the original investors with the money coming from the newer investors while holding on to some of the cash himself. The plan, dubbed the Ponzi scam, or "pyramid" scheme, works as long as there are fresh investors and no one asks too many questions. People did ask questions, however, as Ponzi's fame spread; they were especially intrigued by his lavish lifestyle, including owning one of the largest homes in the Boston area and being driven to and fro by his chauffeur. He was eventually caught and deported to Italy. At least he had a little slice of that immigrant's rags-to-riches life before returning home. Let's hope we never suffer such a fate as we try the shot below!

BOSTON BURNOUT

- 1 shot root beer Schnapps
- 1 shot amaretto
- 1 shot butterscotch Schnapps
- 1 shot Bacardi 151 dark rum
- 4 shots Bailey's Irish Cream
- 4–6 drops Tabasco sauce

In a LARGE shot glass (or small juice glass), add root beer Schnapps, amaretto, butterscotch Schnapps, and Bacardi 151 dark rum. Top off with Bailey's Irish Cream. Add 4 to 6 drops (or more, for the daring) of Tabasco on top. Slam, do not sip!

15

Thomas Nast was probably the most famous cartoonist of his time, mostly for the editorial illustrations he produced for *Harper's Weekly*. He took advantage of social and political issues, and his artistic talent was matched by his wit. On this date in 1870, Nast depicted the Democratic party as a "jackass" kicking a lion, who represented Abraham Lincoln's Secretary of War, Edwin M. Stanton. From whence did Nast obtain the donkey? Well, it was a reference borrowed from Andrew Jackson, whose critics frequently called him a jackass while he was running for president many years prior. Nast appreciated the stubborn trait of the donkey, and the political symbol was born. The irony is that the animal has never been officially adopted by the Democrats! Why, we wonder? As you try to reason out an answer, try the "ass" below.

ASS

  1 oz vodka
  1 splash apple Schnapps

Pour the vodka into a shot glass almost to the top. Add the splash of Schnapps and toss it back like you're Teddy Kennedy.

"Whenever someone asks me if I want water with my Scotch, I say I'm thirsty, not dirty."

−JOE E. LEWIS

16

The first disco in the United States, the Whiskey-A-Go-Go, opened on this date in 1963, on Sunset Boulevard in Hollywood. Slightly ahead of the arrival of the music of the era, the Whiskey was ready to take on the disco mantle as John Travolta's dancing and the spillover from salsa took the nation by storm in the early 1970s. The Whiskey, however, is more than a disco-era dance arena. It's much, much more! Many groups have gotten their start at the Whiskey, and many bands and stars, including the Police, Tom Petty, Janis Joplin, The Jimi Hendrix Experience, No Doubt, and Linkin Park have played there. A Disco Ball indeed! Try the drink below and pay homage to this cultural institution.

DISCO BALL

  1 oz melon liqueur
  1 oz cinnamon Schnapps

Mix both over ice and strain into an old-fashioned glass.

17

Talk about a dubious claim to fame! Poor Gary Gilmore! On this date in 1977, Gary became the first person to be executed in the United States since the Supreme Court reinstated the death penalty. Yet, it's actually hard to feel sorry for him. A lifelong criminal, he was convicted of murdering two people in a quest to obtain fast money, despite the fact that they were unarmed and followed his orders. Gary's last words? "Let's do it." One other claim to fame for Gary: Norman Mailer wrote the novel *Executioner's Song* based on his life. To think, you feel guilty for stealing office supplies! Have a shot as you think about Gary's life. The recipe for the Death Sentence follows.

DEATH SENTENCE ▶

  $1/3$ oz bourbon
  $1/3$ oz Jägermeister
  $1/3$ oz dark rum

Ready: Pour it all into a shot glass!
Aim: Throw it down your gullet!
Fire: Feel the warmth in your stomach!

"Now is the
time for
drinking, now
is the time
to make the
earth shake
with dancing."

–HORACE

Why is it that
country-and-western
singers get all the fun?

Well, at least they get away with
saying whatever they want in
their songs and still have it be
considered entertaining. Take
Johnny Paycheck, for example.
On this date in 1978, his song
"Take This Job and Shove It"
reached number one on the
Billboard charts. The irony, of
course, is how would he expect
to earn a paycheck if he were to
shove his job somewhere? Try
the After-Work Special below,
but please remember not to
drunk-dial your boss after too
many of them!

AFTER-WORK SPECIAL

3	oz	amaretto
2	oz	coconut rum
I	oz	white rum
3–6	oz	orange juice
3–6	oz	pineapple juice

Pour the first three liquors into a
hurricane glass with some ice. Add the
orange and pineapple juices to taste
and serve. Do not, repeat, do not start
putting together your new resume
until January 19.

19

Charles Wilkes—now there's a name that will live forever, right? Okay, we had no idea who he was either. It seems that this captain in the U.S. Navy laid claim to a part of Antarctica for the United States on this date in 1840. Thank goodness we have that little slice of heaven right here on earth! Where else would we want the setting for a scary Kurt Russell movie to be (remember *The Thing*, 1982)? Now, if only we could fix the ozone layer before it melts all that ice . . .

SOUTHERN FROST

1 1/2 oz peach liqueur
2 oz cranberry juice
2 oz ginger ale
ice lots and lots of ice

Mix it all together in a highball glass and await the deep freeze.

"Give strong drink unto him that is ready to perish, and wine unto those that be of heavy hearts. Let him drink, and forget his poverty, and remember his misery no more."

—PROVERBS 31:6–7

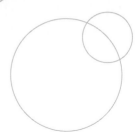

Exploiting the opium trade to fund your government could earn you a big chunk of land in a foreign country. You see, Great Britain found that trading in opium was very profitable in the early 1800s. But British merchants weren't satisfied with the supply from India, so, they started buying from the Chinese. The Chinese government, however, had begun outlawing the sale of opium. It intervened, and British warships were called in, leading to the First Opium War. The British easily overwhelmed the Chinese, ransacked the local countryside, and forced the Chinese government to pay $15 million to the British government. Lastly, on this date in 1840, Hong Kong was ceded to the British. That will show you for not wanting to sell drugs! Of course, we all know who had the last laugh: The British returned Hong Kong to China in 1997. All good things come to an end! Mull that as you try the Hong Kong Fizz, described here.

HONG KONG FIZZ ◗

$^1/_2$ oz vodka
$^1/_2$ oz gin
$^1/_2$ Benedictine herbal liqueur
$^1/_2$ oz Yellow Chartreuse
$^1/_2$ oz Green Chartreuse
$^1/_2$ oz lemon juice
$^1/_2$ tsp powdered sugar
4 oz soda water

Place everything except the soda water in a shaker; shake until the sugar dissolves. Add the soda water and serve in a highball glass.

21

Do you ever have trouble making a decision? You ask your friends if you should date that new guy/gal in accounting, what to eat at the new restaurant around the corner, and whether you should wear that new burka to the Fourth of July parade. These things are okay, because you are not the leader of a country, and the advice given to you probably won't cost you your life. (Let's hope your friends said "no" to the burka.) Back in the mid-eighteenth century, the king of France, Louis XVI, was not so lucky; he had a knack for asking the wrong people for advice. Instead of listening to "the people" or court ministers, who had at least an inkling of what the common folk needed, Louis relied on his wife. Marie Antoinette urged Louis to forget the agreements he had made with the revolutionaries who proposed modernizing the French government, including decreasing the power of the monarchy. Revolutionaries, apparently, don't like to be toyed with. They arrested Louis, tried him, and executed him on this date in 1793. They eventually realized that his bride should bear some responsibility, and Marie Antoinette followed Louis to the guillotine the next year. Poor Louis! Try the King's Ruin below as you contemplate what tough decisions you have, um, er, a-head of you.

KING'S RUIN

    12 oz Champagne
 1 ¹/₂ oz cognac
     1 lemon twist

Pour both liquids into a Collins glass; garnish with a lemon twist. Eat a piece of cake if you have no bread.

22

Unlike the monarch listed on January 21, Queen Victoria died of natural causes on this date in 1901. She was Britain's longest-reigning monarch, and ruled during a time when England's preeminence—on the seas and in global politics—was never doubted. Another interesting fact about Vicky, however, is that she married her first cousin, Albert. At first she sought other potential suitors, but found none suitable. Albert, who was German, seemed the most appropriate spouse because he was highly educated. He ended up being indispensable in dispensing advice (unlike Marie Antoinette), and acted as Victoria's chief advisor and confidante. Try the Queen's Cousin, below.

QUEEN'S COUSIN

- 1 oz vodka
- 1/2 oz orange liqueur
- 1/2 oz lime juice
- 2 dashes bitters
- 1 tsp Cointreau
- 3 oz sparkling white wine

Pour everything except the wine into a shaker with ice; shake well. Strain into a wine glass and stir in the wine.

"The three-martini lunch is the epitome of American efficiency. Where else can you get an earful, a bellyful, and a snootful at the same time?" –GERALD R. FORD

23

"Candy is dandy, but liquor is quicker."

–OGDEN NASH

Finally, in the new millennium, women are treated as equals! Equal access to jobs, equal pay for the same jobs, and all-around respect is earned by men and women equally. Have you stopped laughing yet? Indeed. Well, it's important to note that, while the ladies aren't all the way there yet, they have crossed many milestones. One of those milestones was reached on this date in 1849, when Elizabeth Blackwell became the first woman in the United States to be granted a medical degree. Congrats, ladies! Have a drink, to the Doctor, to celebrate.

DOCTOR

- 1 part fruit punch
- 1 part gin
- 1 part lemon juice

Mix all the ingredients gently and pour into a cocktail glass. In the morning, take two pills. (Don't call.)

24

Who doesn't want to strike it rich in the easiest way possible? Dot.com bubble, anyone? In similar fashion, people rushed to Sacramento, California, on this date in 1848, when gold was discovered by James Marshall while he was working in a sawmill owned by John Sutter. As with most stories about easily found wealth, this did not end happily for either man. They both ended life without the riches that were reaped by the other gold-seekers who followed them. Remember, friends, all that glitters is not gold. Or, even if it is gold, someone else will probably end up with it! That's why we drink! Try the California Gold Rush below to drown your gold-diggin' sorrows.

"I have taken more out of alcohol than alcohol has taken out of me."

–WINSTON CHURCHILL

CALIFORNIA GOLD RUSH

12 oz 7-Up
2 oz vodka
1 $\frac{1}{2}$ oz cinnamon Schnapps

Pour the 7-Up into a Collins glass and add the vodka and Schnapps; stir. The bubbles from the soft drink will move the gold flakes around as you sip.

What we have learned so far while writing this book: 1. Drinks taste good and make us feel good, and 2. the "easy way out" frequently is the illegal way out! On this date in 1960, the National Association of Broadcasters (NAB) finally began to deal with the payola scandal. What the Elvis-Presley-gyrating-hips is that, you ask? It seems, back in the day, that radio disc jockeys were taking money, a.k.a. bribes, to play records (those black round discs that came before CDs and cassettes—we know, they're hard to imagine, but try to keep up). The public, in turn, would buy the albums (the other word for record—again, try to keep up) and make the record companies rich. Apparently, some people found this unethical; the NAB instituted fines to stop the practice. A few DJs, Alan Freed the most famous of them, were financially ruined as they were banished from the industry. Thankfully, you've never taken a gift from a client or patron to "help them out." Have a DJ Shooter, described here, and play your favorite song.

◖ DJ SHOOTER

    3 oz peach Schnapps
 1 ½ oz gin
 1 ½ oz coconut rum
 1 ½ oz vodka
   ⅓ oz pineapple juice
   ⅓ oz orange juice
   ⅓ oz cranberry juice

Mix all the ingredients in a pitcher filled with ice and strain into shot glasses.

26

Some of the best drinks happen by accident. Take, for example, the gin and tonic. The subcontinent known as India had been ruled by the British since the beginning of the seventeenth century. Leaving a humid, rainy island for a more humid part of the earth had it problems for the British, beyond profuse sweating and a language barrier. The Brits also had to deal with malaria. To protect themselves, the English ingested quinine, which was found in tonic water; gin was added for taste and to actually lure the Brits into drinking the malaria-fighter. Perhaps all this gin-and-tonic drinking led the British to be a bit more relaxed: On this date in 1950, the Republic of India became a sovereign nation. Have a gin and tonic to celebrate your own independence!

GIN AND TONIC

  2 oz gin
  5 oz tonic water
  1 lime wedge

Mix the ingredients over ice in a high-ball glass; garnish with a lime wedge.

27

While growing up, we considered the TV our third parent, except that the TV couldn't make us do homework or smack our little behinds when we were fresh! On this date in 1926, the first demonstration of TV took place. This, contrary to popular (American) belief, took place in London. A Scotsman by the name of John Logie Baird shared his new invention with the Royal Institution of Great Britain. Surprisingly, Baird's fellow scientists were said to be very impressed, despite the fact that the telly only had one show—no *Seinfeld*, no *Real World* marathon, no Skin-emax. Ah, the evolution of our favorite pastime! Have a TV Cocktail and give thanks.

TV COCKTAIL

  3 oz iced tea
  1 oz. vodka

Mix the iced tea and vodka over ice in a Collins glass. Now you'll have something to do during commercials!

28

The passion of young love! The faster pulse, the communication through the eyes, the engorged body parts! Charles Starkweather and Caril Ann Fugate had all of these and more! They were teenage lovers, you see, and, after Charles got into an argument with Caril's parents on this date in 1958, while waiting for her at her home, he shot them. With a shotgun. Caril arrived home to witness the acts of violence, which were followed by his strangling Caril's two-year-old sister to death. Eventually caught, Charles met his demise on the electric chair while Caril spent the rest of her days behind bars. Ten victims in all were killed by the two lovebirds. Have a drink, the First Love, and think about how happy you are with your significant other.

"Drink to me."

–PABLO PICASSO'S LAST WORDS

FIRST LOVE

- $2/3$ oz Champagne
- $1/3$ oz gin
- 1 tsp sugar
- 2 dashes Cherry Heering

Shake the ingredients with ice; strain into a cocktail glass.

"I drink no more than a sponge."

—FRANÇOIS RABELAIS

Few poems are as well known as "The Raven" by Edgar Allan Poe, which was first published on this date in 1845. The poem was even used on a *Simpsons* episode, with the part of the raven played by Bart. Our friend Edgar apparently had his issues—with depression, with drug use, and even, gulp, with the drink. Tortured artist, anyone? Despite his issues, his writing—both nonfiction and poetry—did garner him some wealth and international recognition. "The Raven" especially won him national acclaim—not a dreary event for Poe, we're betting! Eventually, his "issues" won out; he was found delirious in a Baltimore gutter, and died at the age of 40. Drink the Black Bird Cider, below, and then try to recite this famous work by Poe.

BLACK BIRD CIDER ▶

1 shot blackberry Schnapps
1 pint cider

Add the schnapps to the cider in a pint glass. Drink until you can't say "Nevermore."

"I don't drink. I don't like it. It makes me feel good."

—OSCAR LEVANT

Ah, the Irish. Nothing comes easy to them, nothing is earned without sacrifice, and drama abounds at every turn of their history. On this date in 1972, one of the saddest events occurred in Ireland. The Irish were protesting the internment of their fellow nationals without trials. British paratroopers dispersed the march and actually fired on unarmed civilians. Fourteen men and boys were killed. The IRA (Irish Republican Army) had, until that point, wavering support from the Catholic Irish, but, after the shootings that came to be known as Bloody Sunday, the terrorist organization flourished. But, hey, we have booze to help us forget! Try the Irish Bloody Mary, described below.

IRISH BLOODY MARY

	celery salt
1 1/2 oz	Bailey's Irish Cream
6 oz	Bloody Mary mix
1	pickle spear

Use celery salt to rim a coffee mug. Pour the Bailey's over ice in the mug and fill with the Bloody Mary mix. Garnish with a pickle spear.

31

We both wonder why we were never asked to dress in a loin-cloth to be swung over audiences who pay to see us! Hey, if it can happen for Sandy Duncan, it should happen for us! On this date in 1982, Sandy gave her last performance as Peter Pan, after a run of 956 shows. Can you imagine? First, she was a she . . . as if Peter didn't have enough issues, what with hanging around with Tinkerbell and playing with pirates! And what with all that flying around, how did she manage to brandish a sword against the aforementioned pirates without impaling a lost boy or two? The marvels of modern theater! Let's lift a glass—full of the Peter Pan Cocktail—in her honor. By the way, it should be noted that she "flew" approximately 260 miles while performing in her role. (Now we wonder whether they counted toward her United Airlines frequent flier account?)

PETER PAN COCKTAIL

$^3/_4$ oz gin
$^3/_4$ oz dry vermouth
$^3/_4$ oz orange juice
2 dashes bitters

Mix all the ingredients with ice and strain into a cocktail glass. Soon you'll be flying!

FEBRUARY

1

Since the very first Super Bowl, the halftime show has held a special place in our hearts. It's a time when Mom can forget her disdain for football and the children can take a break from their homework and join Dad on the sofa for a rousing but wholesome variety show reminiscent of the vaudeville stage shows of times gone by . . . or the vaudeville stage show performed every night at the Moulin Rouge during Paris's Golden Age, as Janet Jackson proved on this day in 2004 when her breast was exposed to the entire country at the end of her live halftime-show performance. Quelle horreur! Fines were imposed, apologies made, but nothing could shield the horrible truth: Our anatomies are dirty and shameful, and we should pretend that they simply don't exist. Right?

GOLDEN NIPPLE

¹/₂ oz cinnamon Schnapps
¹/₂ oz butterscotch Schnapps
Bailey's Irish Cream

Combine the cinnamon and butterscotch Schnapps in a large shot glass. Finish with Irish Cream and serve.

2

Name changing is not just a privilege of rock stars and members of the Witness Protection Program. Oh no. As a matter of fact, many of the world's greatest cities once held monikers that they managed to lose for one reason or another. As that hip 1980s rock band They Might Be Giants proclaimed, "It's Istanbul, not Constantinople . . . even Old New York was once New Amsterdam." It was on this day in 1653 that New Amsterdam took the first step in shaking its Dutch namesake for a newer, shorter British one, and New York City was incorporated.

BIG APPLE ▶

2 oz vodka
4 oz apple juice
1 tsp green crème de menthe

Pour the vodka into a Collins glass half-filled with ice, and fill with apple juice. Add the crème de menthe, stir, and serve.

3 It was a sad day in 1959 when a plane crash near Clear Lake, Iowa, claimed the lives of rock 'n' roll stars Buddy Holly, Ritchie Valens, and J.P. "The Big Bopper" Richardson. In the midst of the "Winter Dance Party Tour," Holly, tired of riding in a cold tour bus, decided to charter a small plane to get himself and two others to the next stop. Country superstar Waylon Jennings gave his seat up to Richardson, who was running a fever and had trouble fitting his stocky frame comfortably into the bus seats. To this day, many get teary when listening to Don McLean's touching tribute, "American Pie," while others get downright hysterical when listening to Madonna's questionable rendition.

GOLDEN OLDIE

    3/4   oz dark rum
    1/2   oz crème de banane
    4   oz pineapple juice

Combine all the ingredients in a highball glass filled with ice. Stir well and serve.

4 Let's face it: Rich kids suck. They get everything they want, treat others like crap, and still go through that awkward rebellious stage where they try and get chummy and pretend they're just like the rest of us. Nobody did it better than newspaper heiress Patricia Hearst, who was kidnapped on this day in 1974 in Berkeley, California, by the Symbionese Liberation Army. According to Hearst, she was locked in a closet for weeks and forced under duress to do despicable things. According to security tapes, she robbed a bank at gunpoint, denounced her capitalist roots, changed her name to Tania, and extorted $6 million from her family. She is just Patty from the block!

STOCKHOLM SYNDROME

    1 1/2   oz aquavit
    2   tsp superfine sugar
    1 1/2   oz lemon juice
    4   oz chilled Champagne
    1   twist orange peel

In a shaker half-filled with ice, combine the aquavit, sugar, and lemon juice. Shake well. Pour into a cocktail glass. Top with Champagne and garnish with an orange twist.

5

On this day in 1948, a modern King of Comedy was born. Christopher Guest is a British actor, writer, director, composer, and musician. He also happens to be Fifth Baron Haden-Guest, of Saling in the County of Essex . . . no, really, he is. He's best known for his portrayal of Nigel Tufnel in the mockumentary movie *This Is Spinal Tap* and for his portrayal of Corky St. Clair in the 1996 mockumentary movie *Waiting for Guffman*. He wrote and directed both movies, making him single-handedly responsible for introducing the phrase "ass face" into the American vernacular. Thanks, Christopher!

SPINAL TAP

1	oz vodka
1/2	oz peach Schnapps
1/2	oz white crème de cacao

Combine the ingredients in a shaker with ice. Shake well and strain into a shot glass.

"I drink when I have occasion, and sometimes when I have no occasion."

–MIGUEL DE CERVANTES SAAVEDRA

6

Many of us love the blustery, white winter months when we have the opportunity to frolic in snow dunes, build snowmen, and go skiing—or, even better, ice fishing. We, your authors, don't really relate. In our view, the sane among us are counting down the days until we can shimmy into a pair of shorts and sandals and banish the jackets to the closets for several months. Good news for folks like us, because as of today we've reached the halfway mark! February 6 is observed annually as the point at which winter is exactly half over.

◀ **WINTER BREAK**

> $^1/3$ oz Southern Comfort
> $^1/3$ oz peach Schnapps
> $^1/3$ oz banana Liqueur

Layer the ingredients in a shot glass.

7

Ma! Pa! Alonzo! Pull out the candles and bake up a cake in the wood-burning stove, it's Laura Ingalls Wilder's birthday. The prairie-dwelling Ingalls Wilder was born on this date in 1867 in a little log house in the Big Woods of Wisconsin. Laura's childhood was spent traveling West by covered wagon to Kansas Indian Territory, to Grasshopper Country in Minnesota, and then to the Dakota Territory. Today she would take a Greyhound. In searching for a drink to commemorate this special day, we found a concoction truly reminiscent of the Old West. Don't wrinkle your noses, you cackling gaggle of Nellie Olesons, just drink it!

PRAIRIE CHICKEN

> l   egg
> l   oz gin
>   salt and pepper

Open an egg without breaking the yolk and pour it into a red wine glass. Pour the gin on top, add salt and pepper to taste (as if!), and serve.

8

On this day in 1910, The Boy Scouts of America was incorporated.

THE BOY SCOUT OATH
On my honor I will do my best:
To do my duty to God and my country
and to obey the Scout Law
To help other people at all times
To keep myself physically strong,
mentally awake, and
morally straight

THE AUTHORS' OATH
On our barstools we will do our best:
To do our duty and make sure
everybody has a drink
To help other people finish their
drinks at all times
To keep ourselves physically upright,
legally awake, and straight
until we've had three drinks and
then it's anybody's game

BOY SCOUT

1/2	oz peppermint Schnapps
1/2	oz dark crème de cacao
1/2	oz Tennessee whiskey
1	tsp green crème de menthe
1	maraschino cherry

To make this drink and earn your badge, combine all the ingredients in an ice-filled shaker, shake well, and strain into an old-fashioned glass. Garnish with a cherry.

9

On this day in 1964, Paul McCartney, age 21, Ringo Starr, 23, John Lennon, 23, and George Harrison, 20, a.k.a. The Beatles, made their first appearance on *The Ed Sullivan Show*, a popular television variety show (think SNL in black and white with fewer expletives). An estimated 73 million U.S. television viewers, or about 40 percent of the population, tuned in to watch. Of course, they weren't competing with reality TV, a cliffhanger on a popular nighttime soap opera, or the season premiere of *The West Wing*, but a studio full of underwear-slinging teenage girls (18+ of course) is enough to write home about: Dear Mum and Dad, America's far-out, won't be needing the job serving chips and ale at the pub. The girls are nice; more on that later. Peace, John.

RINGO COCKTAIL

6	oz cola
2	oz sloe gin
2	oz coconut rum
1	oz brandy
1	splash grenadine

Layer the ingredients in a hurricane glass half-filled with ice.

10

On this day in 1962, the Soviet Union exchanged captured American U-2 pilot Francis Gary Powers for Rudolph Ivanovich Abel, a Soviet spy held by the United States. Although we're guessing there was intrigue out the wazoo, scrambled messages, deals made in dark Russian basements and deep inside the walls of the CIA, all we can think is: Moscow in February? Ivanovich Abel was the one making the true sacrifice by going back. Warm yourself with a nice cocktail, and think about poor, shivering Rudy. Home is home no matter how cold it gets.

SPYMASTER

- 1 1/2 oz vodka
- 1/2 oz crème de banane
- 1/2 oz lemon juice
- 1 egg white

Pour the vodka, banana liqueur, lemon juice, and egg white into a cocktail shaker half-filled with ice. Shake, strain into an old-fashioned glass with ice, and serve. Don't tell anybody where you got this recipe or you will be eliminated.

"Gimme a whiskey—ginger ale on the side. And don't be stingy, baby."

—GRETA GARBO, *ANNA CHRISTIE*

11

> "Of all the gin joints in all the towns in all the world, she walks into mine."

–HUMPHREY BOGART, *CASABLANCA*

What to say about Thomas Edison, who was born on this day in 1847? Besides completing only three months of formal education, he was, apparently, what's the scientific term for it? Oh, yes: a total freaking genius. Not only did the Father of Invention invent the lightbulb, but he also was responsible for creating the first economically viable model for generating and distributing electric light and power worldwide. That said, take this opportunity to revel in the moment when you thought you had invented a patentable lint remover by wrapping a roll of scotch tape backwards around your hand. While you do that, try this drink . . . that we did not invent.

COMBUSTIBLE EDISON

- 1 oz Campari bitters
- 1 oz fresh lemon juice
- 2 oz brandy

Combine the Campari and lemon juice in an ice-filled shaker. Shake and strain into a chilled cocktail glass. Heat the brandy in a chafing dish. When warm, ignite the brandy and pour it in a flaming stream into the cocktail glass. Eureka! You've burned your lips off!

12

Nary a one of us can hear the opening movement of George Gershwin's "Rhapsody in Blue," which premiered in New York City on this day in 1924, without totally and completely feeling "in the zone." Oh yes, we are all cosmopolitan classical music aficionados, hanging out at SoHo hotspots, sipping cocktails with Woody Allen, and wearing all black. So break out the shaker and the blue curaçao and throw on the Gershwin CD your mom gave you for you last birthday. You are in heaven . . .

"I often sit back and think, "I wish I'd done that," and find out later that I already have."

−RICHARD HARRIS

BLUE HEAVEN

2 oz amaretto
2 oz rum
   pineapple juice
4 oz blue curaçao
1 slice pineapple

Combine the amaretto, rum, and pineapple juice in an ice-filled shaker. Shake and pour into a Collins glass. Add the blue curaçao and stir. Garnish with the pineapple slice.

13

February

On this day in 2000, the Doctor was "In" for the last time, as Charles Schulz's final "Peanuts" strip ran in newspapers the day after the cartoonist died at age 77. The passing of the man who created the ever-unlucky Charlie Brown, his daredevil but imaginative dog Snoopy, and the brother-sister team Linus and Lucy, among others, sent a shockwave through the Sunday comics pages. The anguish of a nation in mourning can best be summed up in the words of Charlie Brown's teacher: "Wha, wa, wa, wa, wa, wa, wa, waaaah." Powerful words indeed.

PEPPERMINT PATTY

- 1 shot peppermint Schnapps
- 1 squirt chocolate syrup

Keep a shot of peppermint Schnapps in your mouth, and squirt chocolate syrup in. Shake head vigorously and swallow.

"You'd be surprised how much fun you can have sober. When you get the hang of it."

—JACK LEMMON,
DAYS OF WINE AND ROSES

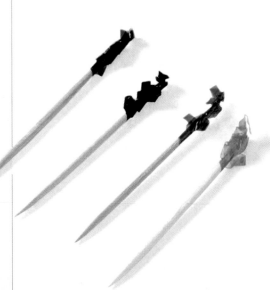

14

Happy Valentine's Day, lovebirds! Today is the day to celebrate your googly-eyed happiness with the one who makes your heart go zing. There are drinks aplenty in your day, so off with you and begin your celebratory boozing. But what about the rest of you? The lost and lovelorn, who cringed at the first sound of the morning alarm and will wince your way through this miserable day ducking floral deliveries and stealing chocolate off of coworkers' desks. You suffer through this day year after year, and by the end of each one you are, frankly, ready for murder a la infamous crime boss Al Capone. On this day in 1929, Capone was the alleged mastermind behind the gunning down of seven members of a rival crime syndicate at a Chicago garage. To help you get through this day sans a semiautomatic rifle, we humbly (and delicately) present:

◀ ST. VALENTINE'S DAY MASSACRE

1 1/2	oz vodka
1	oz Campari bitters
1/2	oz lime juice
1	tsp superfine sugar
1	oz cranberry juice
1	lemon twist

Fill a shaker three-quarters full of ice. Add all the ingredients except the lemon twist, and shake violently (as you might your younger, cuter, more successful best friend, who's on a date this very moment with the chiseled, six-figure-a-year bachelor who's just looking to "settle down"). Strain into a cocktail glass, rub the lemon into your aching, bleeding heart until it burns, then drop it into the glass and drop the contents down your throat.

15

D'oh! February 15 marks the birthday of cartoonist Matt Groening. Perhaps the most influential cartoonist of our time, Groening created the hapless but hilarious Simpson family, the central characters for television's longest-running animated prime-time show. But *The Simpsons* isn't only about Homer, Marge, Bart, Lisa, and Maggie. It also features the odd but lovable characters of Springfield. Bartender Moe Sizlack is one of the show's principle townspeople. In honor of Groening and Springfield's down-on-his-luck barkeep, stir up a Flaming Moe today. It's a drink that is simply animated!

FLAMING MOE COCKTAIL

    1   part tequila
    1   part Schnapps
    1   part crème de menthe
        and the "secret" ingredient:
        Krusty's Non Narkotik Kough
        Syrup for Kids (we suggest you
        substitute with 1 part
        Jägermeister)

Combine all the ingredients in a shot glass, and light the surface on fire. Drink!

16

Emergency! Emergency! On this day in 1968, the nation's first 911 emergency telephone system was inaugurated in Haleyville, Alabama. While we can imagine that there's an emergency on almost every square mile of Alabama on a daily basis (don't worry, Southern friends, on a per capita basis, NYC has you beat hands down . . . promise), we're clueless as to why it all started here in lil' ol' Haleyville. We were going to do some research to find out why, but we were drunk. Somebody dial 9-1-1.

CHAOS CALMER

    1 1/2   oz gin
      1/4   oz Triple Sec
    1 1/2   oz orange juice
      3/4   oz lime juice
        1   tsp grenadine

Shake all the ingredients with a glassful of broken ice and pour unstrained into a red wine glass. Garnish with fruit and serve.

17

It was on this day in 1962 that the totally unknown Beach Boys brought an instant thaw to the February chill when their first hit, "Surfin'," hit the charts. The song marked the beginning of a whole new era in pop music, launching the Beach Boys into uber-cool status and paving the way for themselves and other bands to create an entire style of music, which spawned a subculture of hippie beatniks whose lives centered around surfing, drag racing, and girls. Can you dig it? Groovy . . .

SEX ON THE BEACH

    1   oz vodka
    3/4 oz Chambord
    3/4 oz peach Schnapps
        Splashes of pineapple,
        orange, and cranberry
        juices

Combine all the ingredients and shake with ice. Serve in a Collins or decorative glass. Be sure to use a protective rubber coaster, and remember: sand chafes.

"A man can take a little bourbon without getting drunk, but if you hold his mouth open and pour in a quart, he's going to get sick on it. "

–LYNDON B. JOHNSON

59

18

On this day in 1930, the most amazing thing was discovered hovering just beyond Uranus. The planet Pluto was spotted by a scientist pointing his telescope into the stars looking for . . . who the hell knows, what do they look for? Anyway, looking for it or not, he found Pluto, the smallest and least-inhabitable of all planets.

SUNRISE ON PLUTO

- 1 oz vodka
- 1 oz tequila
- 1/2 oz blue curaçao
- lemonade
- dash grenadine

Layer the vodka, tequila, and blue curaçao in a highball glass. Fill almost to the top with lemonade. Then add a dash of grenadine to glass and take it to the outer limits.

19

February 19 marked a very, very dark day in history for drinkers across the land. It was on this day in 1881 that Kansas became the first state to prohibit all alcoholic beverages. Riddle me this, drinking buddies: What could possibly be worse than living on the prairie in 1881 without booze? We think so, too . . . Isn't Laura Ingalls Wilder around here somewhere?

PROHIBITION COCKTAIL

- 2 oz gin
- 2 oz white wine
- 1/2 tsp apricot brandy
- 1 tsp orange juice
- 1 lemon twist

Combine the gin, wine, brandy, and orange juice in a shaker with ice, shake, and strain into a cocktail glass. Squeeze in a twist of lemon, discard, and thank God for the 21st Amendment!

> "Soul, thou hast much goods laid up for many years; take thine ease, eat, drink, and be merry."
>
> —LUKE 12:19

20

Today in 1725, a group of American colonists attacked a Native American encampment in New Hampshire, killing ten Indians (a.k.a. Native Americans), for which the British government paid £100 each. The colonists, led by Captain John Lovewell, had been authorized to conduct the revenge attacks for raids by the Indians. Payback is, indeed, a bitch. The dead were scalped, and in early March, Lovewell marched into Boston, wearing a wig constructed from several scalps. Later, he was overheard complaining that he'd given his number to several young, single colonists, but nobody had called. Wonder why . . .

RAGING INDIAN

1/4   shot grain alcohol
1/4   shot coffee liqueur
1/4   shot orange juice
1/4   shot mango juice

Mix all the ingredients in a shaker. Strain into a shot glass, and serve.

21

It was on this day in 1842 that John J. Greenough of Washington, DC made the sacrifice of a single pair of unmentionables—not such a tragic loss—by patenting the sewing machine. Although Greenough's patent was granted in 1842, he did absolutely nothing about it until 1850, when, with just one year before its expiration, he sold it to the Singer Company for $500 . . . Yes, that's right, $500. Apparently, Greenough could figure out how to stitch together two pieces of fabric, but he couldn't seem to put together a clue. Today, the Singers are billionaires, and the Greenoughs are not.

FANCY PANTIES

- 2 oz vodka
- 2 oz pink lemonade
- 4 oz Champagne

Combine the vodka and lemonade in an ice-filled Collins glass and stir. Add the Champagne until full, and serve.

"Drink today, and drown all sorrow, you shall perhaps not do it tomorrow. Best, while you have it, use your breath; There is no drinking after death."

—JOHN FLETCHER

In 1732, George Washington, the first president of the United States, was born on his parents' plantation in the Virginia Colony. In addition to eventually becoming the father of the nation, he once reportedly uttered a very famous line to his own father upon the questioning of the demise of a certain beloved cherry tree of dear old dad's: "I cannot tell a lie, Father, you know I cannot tell a lie! I did cut it with my little hatchet." Faced with similar challenges throughout history, subsequent presidents have not been quite so forthright. Today, have a drink in honor of our first—and possibly last—honest president.

◀ CHERRY TREE CLIMBER

   1 oz cherry brandy
   1 oz white crème de cacao
   1/2 oz peppermint Schnapps
   1 tbsp vanilla ice cream

Combine all the ingredients in a blender with ice. Blend and pour into a double-cocktail glass.

"If you drink, don't drive. Don't even putt." –DEAN MARTIN

> "Man, being reasonable, must get drunk; The best of life is but intoxication."
>
> –LORD BYRON

On this day in 1836, the siege of the Alamo began in San Antonio, Texas, when the cranky Mexican General Santa Anna became determined to retake this key location and at the same time impress upon the Texans the futility of further resistance to Mexican rule. The odds were stacked against the Texans, who numbered a total of 189, versus the Mexicans, who swelled to over 2,000. So it was no real surprise to anybody when the Mexicans won by killing all of the Texans and reclaiming the Alamo. Today, the Alamo and the territory it sits in are 100 percent American, which just goes to show, you can win a battle, but you can't mess with Texas.

ALAMO COCKTAIL

    1 1/2   oz bourbon whiskey
    1 1/2   oz tequila
    1 1/2   oz 151 proof rum
      1/2   oz hot sauce
      1   dash black pepper

Layer the ingredients in a Collins glass, and serve.

24 Hallelujah, this is a historic day for all of us out there who have drunk ourselves into bed . . . somebody else's bed, that is. It was today in 1997 that the Food and Drug Administration named six brands of birth control as safe and effective "morning-after" pills for preventing pregnancy. Women rejoiced at the notion of making whoopee without taking months of birth control beforehand. Men tingled at the thought of going fully "commando" during lovemaking. But alas, on closer inspection of the fine print, it turned out the "morning after pill" had more restrictions attached to it than a free airline ticket to paradise. Oh well, nothing's ever really free, is it?

MORNING AFTER COCKTAIL

- 2 oz whiskey
- 2 oz cinnamon Schnapps
- 4 oz spiced rum
- 8 oz lime soda

Combine the whiskey, Schnapps, and rum in a Collins glass. Finish with lime soda, and serve.

"The cocktail party . . . is a device either for getting rid of social obligations hurriedly en masse or for making overtures toward more serious social relationships, as in the etiquette of whoring."

—BROOKS ATKINSON

"I can resist everything except temptation."

–OSCAR WILDE

On this day in 1836, inventor Samuel Colt made history by patenting his five-shot revolver. The son of a factory owner, Colt was born in Hartford, Connecticut, in 1814. He was always fascinated by machinery, and spent much of his spare time during his youth disassembling and reassembling his father's rifles, because apparently back in those days, it was okay to let children play with guns. Other hobbies of Colt's included running with scissors, playing with poisonous spiders, and sticking forks into power outlets. No, wait—power outlets didn't come along for another couple of years. In honor of Colt's crowning patent, pull out the shaker and stare down the barrel of this gun.

25

GUN BARREL

1 1/2 oz currant vodka
1/2 oz Triple Sec
1 splash cranberry juice

Combine the vodka, Triple Sec, and cranberry juice in an ice-filled shaker. Shake well, aim, and serve in a cocktail glass.

One of our favorite campfire stories is that of the most powerful woman in the media, who succeeded in besting a whole heap of hopping mad cowboys in the Lone Star State. It was on this day in 1998 that a jury in Amarillo, Texas, rejected an $11 million lawsuit brought by Texas cattlemen who blamed Oprah Winfrey's talk show for a price fall after a segment on mad-cow disease. It seems Ms. Winfrey, whose word is undeniably gospel, decided to exercise her First Amendment right one day and stretched her mouth deep into the heart of Texas. After a lot of hootin' and hollerin', Oprah's brand on the hide of the Texas Cattleman's Association left a nasty sting and was clear to all who gazed upon it: My mad cow can beat up your cash cow any day.

"Abstainer. A weak person who yields to the temptation of denying himself a pleasure."

—AMBROSE BIERCE

MAD COW

- 1 part coffee liqueur
- 1 part cream
- 1 part 151 proof rum

Combine all the ingredients in an ice-filled shaker. Shake well, and serve in a shot glass.

27

It wasn't such a beautiful day in the neighborhood on this day in 2003, when Fred Rogers, the host of TV's *Mr. Rogers' Neighborhood,* died at age 74. Most of us grew up with Mr. Rogers on PBS every afternoon before dinner, changing sweaters and shoes with him and traveling by trolley to the Land of Make-Believe, where we hobnobbed with King Friday, Daniel Tiger, and Lady Elaine Fairchilde. It was a simpler time, when it never would have occurred to us or our parents that King Friday was a bumbling megalomaniac and Daniel was clearly an abandoned child. Let's all pretend we still live in that time and mix up one of these happy concoctions.

MAKE-BELIEVE COCKTAIL

    1   oz cherry liqueur
    1/2 oz light rum
    1/4 oz framboise liqueur
    1/4 oz pineapple juice
    1   mint leaf

Combine all the ingredients except the mint leaf in a shaker with ice. Shake well, garnish with the mint leaf, and serve in a cocktail glass. Oh no, it's the freight train that will be roaring through your head in the morning.

28

On this date in 1901, Linus Pauling, the American Nobel Prize–winning chemist and political activist, was born. Pauling is single-handedly responsible for the widespread myth that high doses of vitamin C are effective against the common cold. Somebody cover Mom's ears because at least 16 well-designed, double-blind studies have shown that vitamin C does not prevent colds, and at best may only slightly reduce the symptoms of a nasty case of the wheezies. Come on, doesn't a vitamin C–heavy Mimosa make us all feel better when we have the sniffles?

MIMOSA ▶

    2   oz orange juice
    5 oz Champagne

Pour the orange juice into a Collins glass half-filled with ice. Finish with the chilled Champagne, stir, turn your head when you sneeze, and serve.

29

Since your birthday comes only once every four years you're probably too young to drink anyway.

MARCH

1

Be thankful you're not a witch. Or, at least be thankful you weren't a witch living in Salem, Massachusetts, in the early days. On this date in 1692, the Witch Hunt began, more or less because television hadn't been invented yet. Two young girls, Elizabeth Parris and Abigail Williams, were bored. For entertainment, they would listen to scary stories told by Tituba, a servant who worked in their home. They began acting out, in crazy fashion, twitching their arms and legs erratically and saying inappropriate things. Their malady spread to some of their girlfriends. The adults who encountered them blamed witchcraft. The girls were encouraged to inform the adults as to who was responsible. The girls named Tituba. She was apprehended, and she in turn was encouraged to name fellow witches to escape execution. Witch-hunting fever broke out, as neighbors started accusing one another. In all, 150 were named, many were jailed,

and 19 were executed. Eighteen were hanged, and one man, Giles Corey, was crushed to death by rocks. Ouch! Eventually the special court that had been set up to hear the cases was disbanded and the names of those accused were cleared. Try the Salem Witch below and think how lucky we are to have Nicole Kidman ride around on her broom twitching her nose instead. Bewitched indeed!

SALEM WITCH

- ¹/₂ oz vodka
- ¹/₂ oz raspberry Schnapps
- ¹/₂ oz Midori
- I splash lime juice
     sour mix
     soda water
- I splash grenadine

Pour the vodka, Midori, and raspberry Schnapps over ice into a Collins glass; add the splash of lime juice. Add the sour mix and top off the "brew" with soda water (or seltzer). Stir and then add a splash of grenadine.

2

Did you know that Texas was its own little country for 12 years? The Texans, who really were Americans living in northern Mexico, disagreed with some of the policies handed down by the Mexican government. Did they try to negotiate and compromise? No way—apparently they were saying "Don't mess with Texas" even then. Instead, they proclaimed their independence on this date in 1836. (By the way, we can't help but share with you this coincidence: Sam Houston, the first president of Texas, was born on this date in 1793.) Have a shot of Texas Lightning to celebrate our Lone Star State friends!

"Moderation is a fatal thing. Nothing succeeds like excess."

—OSCAR WILDE

TEXAS LIGHTNING

¹/₂   oz vodka
¹/₂   oz thawed lemon juice
       concentrate

Pour both into a shot glass and toss it back!

3

One man's fun is another man's trip to the cell block! Take, for example, sending pornography or other obscene material through the mail. On this date in 1873, Congress decided this act was a no-no. (But, we were just reading the articles!) It wasn't until the Supreme Court decided that anything with literary value was exempt from the law that the standards were finally relaxed. Enjoy the Special Delivery as you thank your postal carrier for delivering only the "clean" mail.

SPECIAL DELIVERY

- ¹/₂ oz Southern Comfort Peach Liqueur
- ¹/₂ oz peach Schnapps
- 2 ¹/₂ oz sour mix
- 2 ¹/₂ oz lemon-lime soda

Combine the liqueur and Schnapps in a Collins glass filled with ice. Add the sour mix and soda. Stir, and you are ready to serve.

4

Some of you more literary-minded readers (see March 3 for rules about appropriate literary value) know that Ernest Hemingway was referred to as Papa. On this date in 1952, Papa finished writing *The Old Man and the Sea*, considered by many to be one of the best novels of the twentieth century. We of course don't like to disagree with the literati, but jeez-Louise, how many pages of "man fishes, man fishes, man catches a fish, man's fish is eaten by a mako shark" can one person be expected to read? Enjoy the Hemingway as you think about your next seafood dinner.

HEMINGWAY

- ³/₄ oz licorice liqueur
- 4 oz Champagne

Pour the liqueur into a Champagne flute and fill with the bubbly. And thank your Papa!

5

Propaganda? Here in America?! Check out the first recorded instance: On this date in 1770, the Boston Massacre took place. What actually happened was a group of surly teens and young men were taunting some British soldiers, they began throwing rocks at them, and the soldiers fired into the crowd. Hundreds died and many more were injured. No, not really. Five people died. Pro-independence newspapers, however, dubbed the shooting "a massacre," helping to fuel the flames of war. Have a Boston Cocktail as you think of some propaganda of your own. "I was drinking to complete some research on cocktails" is one we've been using for a while!

BOSTON COCKTAIL

$3/4$ oz gin
$3/4$ oz apricot brandy
$1^1/2$ tsp grenadine
$1/2$ oz lemon juice

Combine the ingredients with ice and strain into a cocktail glass.

6

There aren't too many professions that call for you to be working on your back, are there? We can think of only a few, and the first that comes to mind is . . . being the painter of the Sistine Chapel. Yes, yes, Michelangelo, who was born on this date in 1475, spent four years on his back painting the ceiling of the Sistine Chapel. (He spent another seven years painting the fresco *The Last Judgment*, but that was on the wall behind the altar.) Michelangelo is famous for other paintings, and his sculptures, especially the Pieta and David, were also fame-inducing. Have an Italian Delight as you think about the magnificent masterpieces you've created in your life.

ITALIAN DELIGHT

1 oz amaretto
$1/2$ oz orange juice
$1^1/2$ oz cream
1 maraschino cherry

Mix all of the liquids with ice; strain into a cocktail glass. The cherry is the finishing touch!

Robert Frost is one of the best-known poets in American history. He was awarded the Pulitzer Prize four times. Unfortunately, Frost had a dark side, with some of his best-known poems being named "The Death of the Hired Man" and "Home Burial." He was thought to have suffered from depression, and his poem "Stopping by Woods on a Snowy Evening" was interpreted by many as a kind of suicide note. Does it seem like his last name is very fitting? Jeez, Bob, lighten up! You write poems for Pete's sake, you're not solving the Cuban Missile Crisis! Try a snowflake, the drink listed below, to commemorate his chilly nature and the publication of that poem on this date in 1923.

SNOWFLAKE ▶

1½	oz pear liqueur
3	oz milk
	crushed ice
2-3	oz 7-Up

Mix the pear liqueur, milk, and ice in a blender. Pour the cold, white substance into a cocktail glass, and add 7-Up to taste. Whose woods are these? Who cares? We know whose drink this is!

Matchmaking web sites have become a well-known method for singles to find potential dates and mates in an easy and trustworthy fashion. Back before the Internet, however, singles relied on "lonely hearts club" advertisements to attract significant others. That's where today's story begins! Poor Martha Beck . . . poor overweight and unattractive Martha Beck. She advertised in one of those clubs and received a letter from a potential suitor, Ray Fernandez. Ray apparently was no prize himself; he was injured in World War II, the result being that he was bald. He chose to cover his lack of hair with a cheap toupee. Add to this enticing description the fact that he was a petty criminal, and you can see why Martha fell head over heels! Ray apparently had a scam: He would date women until they trusted him enough to give him access to their bank accounts. His next step, of course, was to rob them blind! He was about to try the same ploy with Martha, but they fell in love. He told her—maybe in a fit of passion?—his prior intention. She was intrigued, and decided to help him to continue his efforts while she posed as his sister. Not satisfied with merely robbing their victims, however, they began to murder these lonely women, and then commit lascivious acts near the bodies. What good, old-fashioned American fun! They were eventually apprehended and the two "Lonely Hearts Killers" were put to death on this date in 1951. Have a Lady Killer, described below, and enjoy some real old-fashioned American fun.

LADY KILLER

- ¹/₂ oz gin
- ¹/₂ oz orange liqueur
- ¹/₂ oz apricot brandy
- 2 oz passion-fruit juice
- 2 oz pineapple juice
- 1 maraschino cherry

Pour everything into a shaker over ice and then strain into a Champagne flute. Add a cherry for that extra touch!

9

You may be aware of the race between the Soviets and Americans in the 1960s to be the first nation to have a man travel in space. You are probably also aware that the Americans, of course, were the first to reach that milestone . . . oh, wait. This just in from our editor: No, no, it was the Russians who were first. Dammit! Anyhoo, on this date in 1934, Yuri Gagarin was born. He was the first man to travel in space, and he was indeed a Russian. The Russians even have a cooler name for a space traveler—a cosmonaut. It has a freakin' drink right in the name! Who's ever drunk an astro? Well, we Americans can't win them all! Have a Cosmonaut and think good space thoughts!

COSMONAUT

2 parts powdered orange drink
1 part vodka
3 crushed ice cubes

Shake this like a Polaroid picture and serve in a cocktail glass.

"Let school-masters puzzle their brain. With grammar, and nonsense, and learning; Good liquor, I stoutly maintain, Gives genius a better discerning."

—OLIVER GOLDSMITH

10

History is rife with famous committers of treason. One such famous scoundrel was convicted on this date in 1949, and said scoundrel was a woman! Gasp! Mildred Gillars was an actress/announcer for Radio Berlin. Her sultry voice was broadcast to American servicemen during World War II as she tried to convince them that their cause was futile. For her efforts, she was dubbed "Axis Sally." Mildred, a.k.a. Sally, was arrested after Berlin was captured by the Allies in 1945. She was extradited to the United States in 1948; her trial apparently caused quite a furor. (Ha! Get it?! We kill us!) Mildred was convicted of only one count of treason, and served 12 years in prison. Enjoy the Sally Fudpucker as you listen to the radio.

SALLY FUDPUCKER

    2   oz tequila
    4   oz pink grapefruit juice
    1/2 oz Galliano

Fill a Collins glass almost to the top with ice cubes and then pour in the tequila and juice. Pour the Galliano slowly over the back of a spoon so that the liqueur "floats" on top.

11

On this date in 1818, *Frankenstein* was published.
Written by Mary Wollstonecraft Shelley, it told the story of a scientist who brings to life a hideous-looking creature made up of body parts obtained from newly interred cemetery inhabitants. The creature was misunderstood, partially because of his unsightly appearance. What have we learned from this famous story? We have learned that life should be taken seriously. Most important, we have learned that a day at the spa, including exfoliation, a little bit of color in the hair, and some whitening of the teeth, can help anyone who's worried about making a bad first impression! Have a Green Monster, described below, and go ahead and make that appointment. Helga and a loofah await!

GREEN MONSTER ▶

    4   ice cubes
    4   oz vodka
    1   small pickled pepper

Place the ice cubes in an old-fashioned glass and pour the vodka over them. Use the pepper to "stir" the drink. Toss back the drink and then eat the pepper.

12

At the end of World War II, the Allies were divided over how to handle the withdrawal of troops from Europe and how to help rebuild governments that had been crushed by the Nazis. The major difficulty was ideological: The United States wanted to promote democracy and capitalism. The Soviet Union sought to spread its Communist ways. The thought of countries turning "red" was apparently frightening to many, including President Truman. On this date in 1947, he spoke before a joint session of Congress—which means both the Senate and the House of Representatives at the same time, not the "joint sessions" you had in college. Truman urged financial and military support for the troubled democracies of Greece and Turkey. Congress agreed, allocating $400 million to help the foreign countries fight "the Commies." Thus began the Cold War, which wasn't really a war but more like a really expensive game between superpowers. But, heck, without it, where would

we have gotten all those James Bond flicks? The Cold War ended with the fall of the Berlin Wall; read the description for November 9 to get even smarter about the nonwar!

RED ALERT

- 1½ oz tequila
- 1 oz banana liqueur
- 1 oz sloe gin
- sour mix

Mix all the ingredients in a Collins glass and you're good to go!

13

Uranus, detected on this date in 1781, was the first planet discovered since antiquity. The discovery was made by William Herschel, a well-known astronomer of the time. With all this discovering of and about Uranus, we have to ask: How did the planet earn such a marvelous moniker? Well, it wasn't Herschel's fault! He had originally named the planet Georgium Sidus, meaning the Georgian planet, in honor of King George III. Finding this name too unwieldy, another astronomer, Johann Elert Bode, opted for Uranus, the name of the Greek god of the Heavens. To the delight of elementary school boys worldwide, Bode's name stuck. Enjoy the Royal Butt below, and think about how close we came to having a royally named planet and losing the fodder for so many jokes.

ROYAL BUTT

1/2 oz whiskey
1/2 oz butterscotch liqueur

Mix the whiskey and liqueur with ice; strain into a shot glass.

"Claret is the liquor for boys; port for men; but he who aspires to be a hero must drink brandy."

—SAMUEL JOHNSON

MARCH

> "The secret to a long life is to stay busy, get plenty of exercise and don't drink too much. Then again, don't drink too little."
>
> —HERMANN SMITH-JOHANNSON

14

These days, it is hard to imagine anyone becoming famous just because he is smart. We have the exception who proves the rule, however: Albert Einstein. He was born on this date in 1879, and in his 76 years on this planet, he: 1. formulated the theory of relativity, 2. furthered the understanding of quantum mechanics and statistical mechanics, and 3. explained the photoelectric effect, for which he won the Nobel Prize for Physics in 1921. Now, we don't know the difference between quantum mechanics and our Audi Quattro mechanic, but we do know you should have a Smarty, described below. The drink might not make you smarter, but it will make you feel better about not being smart!

SMARTY

1	oz amaretto
1	oz peach liqueur
1	oz blackberry brandy
1/2	oz sour mix

Mix everything together with ice, strain, and pour into a shot glass.

If you are anything like us, you are good-looking, well read, and want to know what the hell an "Ides" is. We did some digging: In Roman times, the Ides were the fifteenth of March, May, July, and October. (To be more confusing, the Ides fall on the thirteenth of the other months. What the heck, Romans!?!?) The Romans used the Ides to help tell the date: Dates were told in reference to how far they fell from the Ides. Next question— but this one you probably know the answer to—why did they become famous? It seems that a soothsayer warned Julius Caesar that something bad would befall him on the Ides of March. Here's a hint: If you live with ancient Romans, listen to a soothsayer. On this date in 44 b.c.e., Julius Caesar was assassinated. Et tu, soothsayer? The Bloody Caesar below should be drunk carefully: Keep your back to the wall, and beware if some of your "friends" come knocking.

BLOODY CAESAR

  celery salt
1 oz vodka
1 dash Worcestershire sauce
1 dash Tabasco sauce
6 oz Clamato juice
  salt and pepper
1 celery stalk

This is a Roman take on the Bloody Mary. Rim a Collins glass with celery salt, fill with ice, and add remaining ingredients, fill with Clamato juice. Don't forget the celery stalk!

16

What's the worst thing you've ever done? Okay, maybe we should ask you that after you've had a drink. Well, imagine being caught for what you've done, and then being made to wear a letter to remind everyone. All day. Every day. A character in one of America's most famous novels—*The Scarlet Letter* by Nathaniel Hawthorne—had to endure exactly that. Hester Prynne was married, but she had an affair with the local clergyman. She became pregnant, but refused to divulge the name of her holy lover. She was forced to wear a scarlet letter "A" for adultery. Then millions of Americans were forced to read the book in high school. Thank goodness for Cliffs Notes! As you sip a Scarlet Fever (or two), you'll find it easier to appreciate that *The Scarlet Letter* was published on this date in 1850.

◖SCARLET FEVER

12	oz vodka
12	oz white rum
6	oz dry gin
6	oz cranberry juice
1	lemon slice

Mix all the liquids together and pour into a beer mug. Add a few ice cubes and the slice of lemon.

"O God, that Men should put an enemy in their mouths to steal away their brains! That we should with joy, pleasance, revel, and applause transform ourselves into beasts!"

–WILLIAM SHAKESPEARE

"At the punchbowl's brink, Let the thirsty think, What they say in Japan: First the man takes a drink, Then the drink takes a drink, Then the drink takes the man!"

—EDWARD ROWLAND SILL

17

Interestingly, St. Patrick's Day, the holiday considered the most Irish in America, isn't celebrated with nearly as much vim and vigor in the home country. It seems that St. Patrick's feats, including the removal of snakes from the Emerald Isle, are only commemorated as a time for indulging in green beer, green hats, and green gills (the next day, anyhow) on this side of the Atlantic. The Irish drink the more sophisticated Black and Tan, described below, which is a combination of two of their famous beers, on this, the anniversary of St. Patrick's death in the fifth century, and the date of the religious feast designated in his honor.

BLACK AND TAN

Guinness beer
Bass ale

There are different ways to serve a Black and Tan. In some cases (in the United States, for example), the beers are "layered" on one another, with the Guinness on top. In Ireland, it is typical to pour both beers into a pint glass at the same time. It is also common to serve Harp's lager in place of the Bass, or another light-colored beer, preferably a lager or an ale.

We have always assumed that a martyr is a person who dies in the name of his/her cause. We have been proven wrong, however, with our newfound knowledge of the Tolpuddle Martyrs. (We love to learn, and we hope you do, too! Further, we love to say Tolpuddle, and we hope you do, too!) Six farm laborers, who lived in a village by the name of—you guessed it—Tolpuddle, in Dorset, England, had finally grown frustrated with their thrice-decreased wages. They formed the Friendly Society of Agricultural Labourers, pledging to support one another in their quest to have their wages restored. They swore an oath to do so, and approached the manager of the farm where they worked. At the time of this congenial conversation, unions were legal but—and this is the kicker—swearing oaths to one another was not. The six men were convicted of this heinous crime and, on this date in 1834, the Tolpuddle Martyrs were banished to Australia. The ruling was eventually overturned and the men returned to England, albeit temporarily for most of them, since five of the men moved to Canada. Apparently moving to a country with freezing weather where people say "eh" was more appealing than living in a country with hot surfers who say "Good-ay, mate." Silly martyrs! Have a Down Under as you contemplate that decision.

DOWN UNDER

- ¹/₂ oz vodka
- ¹/₄ oz rum
- ¹/₄ oz tequila
- ¹/₄ oz Triple Sec
- ¹/₄ oz blue curaçao
- 1 ¹/₂ oz soda water

Fill a shaker halfway with ice; pour in all the ingredients. Shake well and strain into a cocktail glass.

19

We just love the thought of this drink, let alone the actual taste of it. It just screams, "I grew up in a trailer but I still want the good things in life!" Anyway, here's the skinny: On this date in 1931, Nevada legalized gambling. Since then, rich and poor alike have been drawn to the purported money-making meccas of Las Vegas and other Nevada towns. Most, however, leave with nothing but lint in their pockets. (Like they say, what happens in Vegas stays in Vegas—especially when it comes to your money.) Please, oh, please, try the Poor Man's Mimosa described below. And don't try to make it fancy-schmancy by using good beer—stick to American beer in a can and OJ from concentrate. A few of these and you'll be heading to the Elvis chapel!

◀ POOR MAN'S MIMOSA

4 oz beer
4 oz orange juice

Pour half a can of beer into a highball glass, then add orange juice to taste. (Taste?!?)

20 Before there were red-state Republicans, before, actually, there were even Republicans, there were Whigs. Oh, why couldn't we still have a political party with such a great name? Wouldn't Letterman and Leno have a field day with Whig jokes? Alas, the Whigs apparently were split down the middle over the issue of slavery, with those from the North opposed to slavery and its encroachment into the Western territories. Northern Whigs, in the very northern state of Wisconsin, gathered to establish a new party. On this date in 1854, the party was formed, taking the name "Republicans." In 1860, only six years later, their popularity had grown so fast that their candidate, Abraham Lincoln, won the White House. Have a Party Starter to celebrate the birth of the Republican Party.

PARTY STARTER

1 1/2	oz orange liqueur
3	oz lemon juice
3	oz lime juice
5	drops bitters

Shake all the ingredients with ice in a shaker and strain into a Collins glass over ice cubes.

"Only one marriage I regret. I remember after I got that marriage license I went across from the license bureau to a bar for a drink. The bartender said, 'What will you have, sir?' And I said, 'A glass of hemlock.' "

—ERNEST HEMINGWAY

> "Drinking when we are not thirsty and making love at any time, madam, is all that distinguishes us from the other animals."
>
> –PIERRE DE BEAUMARCHAIS

21

Okay, we have to admit, we have trouble locating our car keys every once in a while. We are amazed, therefore, that a man took it upon himself to find another man, on, of all places, the second-largest continent on the planet. But that's exactly what Henry M. Stanley set out to do on this date in 1871. He was commissioned by the *New York Herald* to locate David Livingstone, a missing Scottish missionary who had sought the source of the Nile. Stanley found the ailing man in November of 1871, uttering the famous words, "Dr. Livingstone, I presume?" We wonder: If Stanley were alive today, could he help us find our keys? Have a Stanley Cocktail as you decide yea or nay.

STANLEY COCKTAIL

- 1/4 oz light rum
- 3/4 oz gin
- 1 splash lemon juice
- 1 tsp grenadine

Pour all the ingredients into a shaker with ice cubes, move to the groove, and strain into a cocktail glass. Fun cocktail, I presume?

GLASS: Cocktail

22

On this date in 1972, the Equal Rights Amendment was passed by Congress. Great, huh? Well, except for the fact that for an amendment to be written into the Constitution it's required that at least 38 states pass the amendment and, in most cases, the states have to approve the amendment within seven years. Well, that happened, right? No, you jackaninny. Indiana was the 35th state to ratify the amendment, and that occurred in 1977. The ladies still don't have all the rights and privileges bestowed on the gents. There may still be hope for the womenfolk, though, because it turns out the seven-year limit may be illegal. Have a Go Girl! and be supportive of all the ladies in your life.

GO GIRL!

- 1   shot Chambord
- 1   shot vodka
- 1/2 cup club soda
- 2   tbsp sour mix

Mix it all up with some ice in a Champagne saucer and drink up. You go, girl!

"My rule of life prescribed as an absolutely sacred rite smoking cigars and also the drinking of alcohol before, after and if need be during all meals and in the intervals between them."

—WINSTON CHURCHILL

23

You may be aware that not all colonists desired separation from Great Britain at the time of the American Revolution. Many took some convincing, such as a bunch of legislators in the House of Burgesses—the state's legislative house—in colonial Virginia. On this date in 1775, Patrick Henry delivered his famous "Give Me Liberty or Give Me Death!" speech, and he was able to convince enough of the burgesses to support sending troops to fight the British. Wow! The most successful we've ever been is convincing the bartender we deserve another drink . . . and another . . . and another . . . you get the idea. Have a Henry's Special to celebrate Patrick Henry delivering his famous speech. Give us drinks or give us death!

◀ **HENRY'S SPECIAL**

1/3	oz brandy
1	tsp honey
1	oz grapefruit juice
1	tsp lemon juice
3	oz Champagne

Mix the brandy, honey, and grapefruit and lemon juices over ice. Add the Champagne and serve in a cocktail glass.

24

Mendacity means "to lie"; in the noun form, it means "a lie." Tennessee Williams frequently included them in the plots of his plays. Mendacity, of course, is a central theme in his most famous play, *Cat on a Hot Tin Roof*, which opened on this date in 1955. The main character is the younger of two brothers, who has an "unnatural" relationship with his college friend whom he idolized. His wife beds the friend in order to prove to her husband that the "best friend" relationship was unworthy. The friend kills himself, and the husband drinks himself into oblivion. Why does alcohol always have to be a bad thing in these dramas? We think that's a case of mendacity! Think back over some of the lies you've told as you try the Hot Pussy, below.

HOT PUSSY

1/2	oz cinnamon Schnapps
2	drops Tabasco sauce
1	oz La Grande Passion liqueur

Combine the ingredients in a shaker with ice. Shake well, strain into a Collins glass, and serve.

25

Thank God for glamour, prestige, and conspicuous consumption! And, thank God for Mercedes, which made its debut on this date in 1901. How did this event come to fruition? One Emil Jellinek, a wealthy, successful businessman of the late nineteenth century, had toyed with the emerging vehicle market during the 1890s. He traveled to Germany to visit the Daimler factory and ordered a car. The model did not prove fast enough, however, so he urged the company to focus on engineering to produce speedier cars. Daimler was indeed successful; Jellinek began racing the improved version near his residence in Nice, France. The vehicle, named the Mercedes, out-performed all others. The "modern" car was born.

You're still wondering, "Why the name Mercedes?" That was the name of Jellinek's daughter, who was born in 1889. The name is of Spanish origin, and, befittingly, means "grace." We of course don't want you, dear reader, to think us pretentious, so we are just as happy to know that you're driving the latest Hyundai Sonata. Seriously. No, not seriously, but you did believe us for a moment, didn't you? Have a Money Shot and start saving your pennies. No one gets laid in a Hyundai Sonata.

MONEY SHOT

- 1/2 oz vodka
- 1/2 oz Irish Cream
- 1/4 oz coffee liqueur
  splash of cream

Mix the ingredients in a shaker with ice and strain into a shot glass.

"A woman should never be seen eating and Champagne, the only true feminine

26

When we come across real-life events that sound like even the *National Enquirer* wouldn't include them in their highly respected newspaper, we are giddy with delight. Sometimes you can't make this stuff up! On this date in 1997, thirty-nine members of the Heaven's Gate cult were found dead. The founder of the cult, Marshall Applewhite, had convinced his followers that they were aliens. The "aliens" would have to leave their earthly bodies to hitch a ride on a spacecraft that was approaching the planet, but was hidden by the comet Hale-Bopp. Yes, they committed mass suicide by drinking an applesauce/vodka concoction laced with phenobarbital. What a waste . . . of vodka! As if this isn't wacky enough, the cult members were found with bags packed next to their beds as if they thought they'd be taking a cab to the airport and catching the next flight to Hale-Bopp on United Airlines. The hopeful aliens were all wearing similar outfits, garbed in black T-shirts and jeans and new, black Nike sneakers. (We assume they weren't the impetus behind the "Just do it" advertising campaign!) Have a Death from Above, the drink described below, and marvel at your superior intelligence.

DEATH FROM ABOVE

- 1 oz Bacardi 151 rum
- 1 oz gin
- 3 oz cola

This takes some setup time! Put some old-fashioned glasses in your freezer and wait. When they are freezing to the touch, pour in the rum and gin. Light the mixture on fire for a few seconds, then add the cola. Serve, and drink up!

or drinking, unless it be lobster salad
nd becoming viands."   –LORD BYRON

27

On this date in 1958, Nikita Khrushchev became the Soviet premier, the first Russian ruler since Stalin to hold that position and the title of Soviet First Secretary at the same time. What does that mean? Well, he was absolute leader of the USSR, taking charge of the national government and the Communist Party. To his benefit, he promulgated dramatic changes to social and fiscal policy, frequently reversing Stalin's iron-fisted dictatorial methods. The Russian economy improved, and gulags decreased in number. Khrushchev had trouble shaking a somewhat boorish reputation, however; he interrupted several speeches at the U.N. by banging his fist—or even his shoe—on a table. He approved the nuclear missile program in Cuba, which led to the crisis JFK faced. One of his most famous lines was "We will bury you," implying that Soviet military technology was superior to that of the United States. Eventually, even the Soviets couldn't put up with his outbursts, and they unseated him. He spent the last seven years of his life under house arrest. Poor Khrushchev! We know that absolute power begets absolute tyranny. We also know that Absolut vodka begets absolutely great drinks! Try a Red Vodkatini or we will bury you!

◀ RED VODKATINI

- 2 oz vodka (Absolut or not—you decide!)
- 1 oz vermouth
- 1 dash crème de cassis
- 1 slice orange

Mix the liquids together and pour over crushed ice in a cocktail glass. Add a slice of orange as a garnish. These will crush you!

28

Nuclear accidents can be such fun! Just ask the residents around Three Mile Island in Middletown, Pennsylvania. On this date in 1979, the Three Mile Island "incident" occurred, known since then as the worst accident in U.S. nuclear power history. Apparently, mechanical failure caused an increase in pressure in one of the reactors. A valve was opened to alleviate the pressure. The valve remained open, and coolant leaked out of the reactor. This caused the core to overheat. A portion of the reactor suffered a meltdown. On-site personnel misread the gauges and other measuring whoozi-whatzits and exacerbated the problem. Frying pan, fire, any-one? The problem worsened: Gases were released into the environment, eventually necessitating that pregnant women and children under the age of five be evacuated from the area. Those lucky enough to be six years old and older got to stay home! The accident was not as bad as some had expected,

though it significantly and perhaps permanently undermined the faith of the American public in nuclear energy. Why not try the Nuclear Iced Tea before you fill up the gas tank on your SUV?!

NUCLEAR ICED TEA

- $1/2$ oz vodka
- $1/2$ oz gin
- $1/2$ oz rum
- $1/2$ oz Triple Sec
- 1 oz melon liqueur
  sour mix
  7-Up

Mix the first five ingredients in a Collins glass filled with ice. Fill (almost) to the top of the glass with the sour mix, and top off with 7-Up.

29

Okay, half of you reading this probably don't even know who M.C. Hammer is. Hammer, born Stanley Kirk Burrell (makes M.C. Hammer sound appealing, doesn't it?) sold millions of hip-hop albums. His first album sold three million copies and his second album sold ten million. Unfortunately, as we know, fame is fleeting and silk parachute pants are expensive. Hammer ended up blowing a lot of his cash on a $10 million mansion with accoutrements so cheesy that, when he tried to sell it later on, the crib went for only $5 million. What a travesty! Lift your glass, filled with the Hammer Horror concoction described below, and help M.C. celebrate his birthday; he was born on this date in 1963.

HAMMER HORROR

- 1 oz vodka
- 1 oz Kahlúa
- 4 tbsp vanilla ice cream
    grated chocolate

Mix the vodka, Kahlúa, and ice cream in a Collins glass; sprinkle with grated chocolate. Serve with a straw while wearing your favorite parachute pants.

"A torchlight procession marching down your throat."

–JOHN LOUIS O'SULLIVAN

30

On this date in 1981, President Ronald Reagan was shot by John Hinckley, Jr. in what appeared to be a straightforward assassination attempt, right? Nope. Hinckley was a certifiable wackadoo. A bit of a recluse to boot, Hinckley spent one whole summer watching the Robert De Niro–Jody Foster classic *Taxi Driver*. Discontented with the depravity in New York City, Travis Bickle, De Niro's character, decides he's had enough and violently lashes out—partly to protect a 12-year-old prostitute (played by Foster). His first move is to plan the assassination of a presidential candidate. What does the plot have to do with Hinckley? First, you may have noticed Hinckley and Bickle shared "loner" status. Apparently, Hinckley noticed that, too. So, he moved to New Haven, Connecticut, to get closer to Foster, a Yale student at the time. He slipped notes and poems under her door and the two even spoke once or twice. To really impress her, though, he tried to assassinate Reagan. (What says "I love you" to a woman more than murder?) Hinckley was found not guilty by reason of insanity (big surprise!) and is serving time in a mental hospital. Reagan served two terms in office. In his honor, we present: The Gipper.

THE GIPPER

2 oz whiskey
2 oz vodka
$1/2$ oz Coca-Cola

Mix all the ingredients over ice in a Collins glass. Drink until you feel like you, too, can win one.

"I do not live in the world of sobriety." —OLIVER REED

31

Ah, l'amour! We love to be in love! The tingly feeling in the fingers and toes, the heart skipping a beat, the red, flustered look on the face! Oh, wait . . . we just realized we described ourselves after a few drinks! Well, we do love the drinks, too! If you are in love, impress your significant other with a trip to Paris, the City of Love, and include a trip to the top of the Eiffel Tower to take in the grand views of the city, for, on this date in 1889, the Eiffel Tower opened to the public. How could you and your lover not be impressed by this huge erection in the middle of the city? Designed by Gustav Eiffel, the tower took two years to build; it is made of more than 7,000 tons of steel and 2.5 million rivets. More than 200 million visitors have paid homage to the Tower. To celebrate, let's have the Parisian Cocktail.

PARISIAN COCKTAIL

    1   oz dry vermouth
    1   oz gin
    1/4 oz crème de cassis

Mix all the ingredients with ice and strain into a cocktail glass. Bon appetit!

"It takes that *je ne sais quoi* which we call sophistication for a woman to be magnificent in a drawing room when her faculties have departed but she herself has not yet gone home."

–JAMES THURBER

APRIL

1 Stop reading now, because they've just reinstated Prohibition! Okay, not really, that's not even funny . . . better have a drink to get over that one! Today is April Fool's Day, which, believe it or not, was once New Year's Day. This was back before the flawed Julian calendar (which made the start of the new year somewhere around January 1) and the corrective Gregorian calendar (which set the date in stone). Many countries resisted the change and kept New Year's on April 1 for centuries (Scotland until 1660; Germany, Denmark, and Norway until 1700; and England until 1752). When France switched over in 1582, many people refused to recognize the new date. People began to make fun of these traditionalists, sending them on "fool's errands" or trying to trick them into believing something false. Humiliation proved to be a popular sport, and when England finally converted, ruffling feathers with the traditionalists on the British Isles, they began to celebrate April Fool's Day, too. The American colonies adopted it shortly thereafter. No joke!

FONDLING FOOL

1 1/2 oz brandy
1 oz Madeira
1/2 oz Triple Sec

Pour the brandy, Madeira, and Triple Sec into a mixing glass half-filled with ice. Stir well. Strain into a cocktail glass and serve.

2

It was on this day in 1513 that the legendary Spanish explorer Ponce de León discovered Florida, landing in what is now the town of St. Augustine. He was searching for the island of Bimini and its supposed Fountain of Youth. What he found instead were miles of absolutely nothing, which today is miles of oceanfront condos populated by retirees playing bingo and shuffleboard, watching *Wheel of Fortune*, and rushing out at 5:30 to get to the early bird buffet on time. Fountain of Youth? Better keep sailing, Ponce...

FLORIDA COCKTAIL

$^1/_2$ oz gin
1$^1/_2$ tsp cherry brandy
1$^1/_2$ tsp Triple Sec
1 oz orange juice
1 tsp lemon juice

Shake all the ingredients with ice, strain into a cocktail glass, and serve.

3

Rushing to the mailbox to grab the day's mail ceased to be the rousing good time it once was when Ted Kaczynski started sending packages around the country. For seventeen years, Kaczynski, aka the Unabomber, who was arrested on this day in 1996, terrorized folks by sending them homemade bombs, often through the mail. The bombs, which were rudimentary at first, became deadlier over time, maiming many and killing three. His rambling manifesto, which was eventually published by several major American newspapers, finally tipped his brother David off that the bombs might be coming from inside the family. David went to the FBI, and Ted was finally caught. Needless to say, David hasn't opened a Christmas gift or letter from the prison since.

◄ **UNABOMBER**

¹/₄ shot gin
¹/₄ shot vodka
¹/₄ shot Triple Sec
¹/₄ shot lime juice

Mix all the ingredients; place in shot glass. Introduce to mouth.

4

The American civil rights movement suffered a heart-wrenching and crippling blow on this day in 1968 when Dr. Martin Luther King Jr., the spiritual leader of America's African-American community, was shot and killed by a man named James Earl Ray on a hotel balcony in Memphis, Tennessee. King was preparing to lead a local march in support of the heavily black Memphis sanitation workers' union, which was on strike at the time. The assassination led to a wave of riots in more than a hundred cities across the country. Four days later, President Lyndon Johnson declared a national day of mourning. A crowd of 300,000 attended King's funeral.

FALLEN ANGEL

1 ¹/₂ oz gin
¹/₂ tsp white crème de menthe
juice of ¹/₂ lemon
1 dash bitters
1 maraschino cherry

Shake all the ingredients (except the cherry) with ice and strain into a cocktail glass. Top with the cherry and serve.

"Drunkenness is nothing but voluntary madness." –SENECA

5

A bunch of animals breathed a huge sigh of relief on this day in 2348 b.c.e., when the cruise ship they were on (also known as Noah's Ark) finally landed on Mt. Ararat after a 40-day cruise where it rained the whole time. According to the daily news (also known as the Bible), Noah was 600 years old when God told him to build the Ark, collect his family and two of every animal, and ride out the coming storm. We thought, that's some job for a 600-year-old man and wondered how we'd fare with a similar task. We decided to put ourselves to the test. Our combined age is 71, the toy boat we made out of Popsicle sticks sank the minute we put it into the tub, and the cat ate the chinchilla. So instead we're sticking to what we do best: drinking!

NOAH COCKTAIL

   2 oz amaretto
      orange juice
      lemon-lime soda

Pour the amaretto into an ice-filled Collins glass. Fill with equal parts orange juice and lemon-lime soda, and set sail.

6

The gay playwright, poet, and short-story writer Oscar Wilde was arrested in London for gross indecency on this day in 1895. "Gross indecency" was a euphemism used to describe any sexual act between men. Homosexuality was illegal at the time, but that didn't stop Wilde from engaging in several trysts. During the trial, Wilde gave an impassioned speech on "the love that dare not speak its name," in which he said: "It is beautiful, it is fine, it is the noblest form of affection . . . That it should be so, the world does not understand." So raise your glass to Wilde today and do something a little gay!

OSCAR COCKTAIL

1	oz gin
1	oz vodka
3/4	oz cherry brandy
1	dash grenadine
1	oz pineapple juice
1	oz orange soda
1	orange wedge
1	maraschino cherry

Add the liquid ingredients to a brandy snifter filled with ice. Garnish with an orange wedge and a stemmed cherry.

"'Tis not the drinking that is to be blamed, but the excess."

– JOHN SELDEN

7

Everybody loves the circus: the elephants, the cotton candy, the bearded lady. But the father of the circus, P.T. Barnum, was shot from the cannon for the last time when he passed away on this day in 1891. In Brooklyn, New York, in 1871, he established "The Greatest Show on Earth," a traveling amalgamation of circus, menagerie, and museum of "freaks." In 1881, he merged his show with James Bailey's to create the Barnum & Bailey Circus, which toured around the world. Although we're sure that Barnum's funeral was a somber one, we can't help but imagine that everybody showed up at the gravesite in a single Volkswagen Bug, filing out one at a time.

◀ **CIRCUS PEANUT MARGARITA**

3   oz tequila
2   oz Pisang Ambon liqueur
1   oz sweetened lime juice
    sugar
1   candy "peanut"

In a blender, mix the tequila, liqueur, and lime juice with ice and serve in a margarita glass rimmed with sugar. Garnish with a Day-Glo orange circus peanut.

"It provokes the desire but it takes away the performance. Therefore much drink may be said to be an equivocator with lechery: it makes him and it mars him; it sets him on and it takes him off."

—WILLIAM SHAKESPEARE

8

Today is a special day: the birthday of the namesake of that institution where you might be heading if you've made it this far in the book. On April 8, 1918, former first lady Betty Ford was born. After her years in the White House, poor Betty was often left alone as hubby and ex-prez Gerry Ford pursued his interests—politics, lectures, and golf (mostly golf). Betty kept herself busy with her new friends: Jack Daniels, Moet & Chandon, and Jose Cuervo. In 1978, family and friends staged an intervention. Her experiences led her to create the Betty Ford Treatment Center in Rancho Mirage, California. Let this be a lesson to you if you're still with us: hide your drinking from the family! It will make things easier in the long run.

BETTY FORD COCKTAIL

$1/2$ oz grenadine
$1^1/2$ oz citrus-flavored vodka
10 oz Sprite

Add the grenadine (based on desired sweetness) into a Collins glass, followed by the vodka. Add ice and then Sprite (this is how Betty liked it).

GLASS: Collins

9

It was on April 9, 1926, that the man whom most red-blooded American men consider the luckiest person alive was born. Hugh Hefner started his magazine, *Playboy*, in 1953. *Playboy* flaunted sexuality at a time when most Americans blushed to talk about such things. Issue number one included a now-famous photo of Marilyn Monroe, and quickly sold out. Playboy became a smashing success, and Hef became a celebrity. Hef's cadre of scantily clad women, known as Playboy Bunnies, has caused the biggest stir and most speculation over the years. We mixed up today's concoction in Hef's honor.

DRUNKEN BUNNY

1 oz orange rum
1 oz blue curaçao
1 oz melon liqueur
$1/2$ oz whipped cream

Blend the first three ingredients together in a cocktail glass. The drink should turn bright turquoise. Top with whipped cream, and serve.

10

On this day in 1970, Yoko Ono became Public Enemy #1 when the Beatles, believed by many to be the greatest band of all time, broke up. Yes, it's been widely debated, and though many don't believe that meek little tree-hugging Ono could do such a hideously evil thing, most do believe that the onus is completely on the second wife of lead singer John Lennon. The rumors and the accusations will continue to fly, and we may never know why the Beatles really called it splits, but one thing we know for sure: if you say "Yoko Ono" over and over again, it's really funny. And Paul McCartney is still alive . . . or is he?

"Water is the only drink for a wise man."

–HENRY DAVID THOREAU

BITCH-ON-WHEELS

- 2 oz gin
- 1/2 oz dry vermouth
- 1/2 oz white crème de menthe
- 1 tsp licorice liqueur

In a mixing glass half-filled with ice cubes, combine all of the ingredients. Stir well. Strain into a cocktail glass.

"I told you, sir, they were red-hot with drinking; So full of valour that they smote the air, For breathing in their faces, beat the ground For kissing of their feet."

11

The American space program's first brush with disaster was with the Apollo 13 mission, which was launched on April 11, 1970. The mission was planned as a lunar landing mission, but it was aborted en route after about 56 hours of flight due to loss of service module cryogenic oxygen and the consequent loss of capability to generate electrical power. There were explosions, loss of air and water, and external damage to the ship. In short, they were in trouble. MacGyver-like, however, the astronauts patched things up, hightailed it home, and splashed down in the ocean as planned.

ROCKET FUEL ⟩

- 1   shot vodka
- 1   shot tequila
- 1   shot light rum

Combine the ingredients in an old fashioned glass, and serve.

12

On April 12, 1861, Captain George S. James fired the first shot of the Civil War from a Confederate artillery battery. The shot was fired, along with plenty more, and the war between the North and the South had begun. The bloody war resulted in Patrick Swayze's strong but misguided Southern soldier dying on a swing set in a deserted park, a death that was ultimately avenged by Demi Moore and Whoopi Goldberg. Wait a minute . . . I think we're getting our Patrick Swayze death scenes mixed up! On April 15, President Lincoln issued a proclamation calling for 75,000 men to serve to put down "a combination too powerful to be suppressed" by the ordinary mechanism of government. We suggest you try the combination below: we found it much too powerful to be suppressed, and had to have several.

ARTILLERY COCKTAIL

1 1/2	tsp sweet vermouth
1 1/2	oz gin
2	dashes bitters

Stir all the ingredients with ice, strain into a cocktail glass, and serve.

13

Thomas Jefferson, author of the Declaration of Independence and the third president of the United States, was born on April 13, 1743. In addition to his aforementioned accomplishments, Jefferson was also the father of presidential sex scandals. Although not so scandalous in his time, his affair and siring of at least one child with his slave/mistress has raised quite a few eyebrows with presidential watchers through the years. Stir yourself up a Presidente, described below, light a cigar, and ponder a few of the more recent sex scandals coming from within the White House.

PRESIDENTE

2	oz white rum
1	oz Rosso vermouth
1/3	oz dry vermouth
1	tsp grenadine
1	slice orange
1	maraschino cherry

Stir together the rum, both vermouths, and grenadine and strain into an old-fashioned glass filled with crushed ice. Garnish with an orange slice and a cherry.

14

Other than that, Mrs. Lincoln, how was the show? On this date in 1865, one of the most famous assassinations in the history of American politics took place. While watching a performance of *Our American Cousin* with his wife at the Ford Theater, President Abraham Lincoln was shot in the back of the head at near point-blank range by a disgruntled Confederate actor named John Wilkes Booth. Of course, living in this day and age, we've come to realize the horrible truth that acting leads to murder. Looking back at Hollywood over the past thirty or forty years, we've seen actors turn to murder time and again . . . allegedly, people, allegedly!

"There are two things that will be believed of any man whatsoever, and one of them is that he has taken to drink."

–BOOTH TARKINGTON

ASSASSIN

- ⅓ oz Tennessee whiskey
- ⅓ oz tequila
- ⅓ oz peppermint Schnapps
- 3 oz chilled cola

Pour the whiskey, tequila, and peppermint Schnapps into a cocktail shaker half-filled with ice cubes. Shake well. Strain into a cocktail glass, fill with chilled cola, and serve.

117

15

At 2:20 a.m. on April 15, 1912, the Titanic, a British ocean liner made oh-so-famous by the tragedy of its maiden voyage, sank in the North Atlantic. The cruise liner, which carried 2,200 passengers and crew, had struck an iceberg two and half hours before. Due to a shortage of lifeboats and unsatisfactory emergency procedures, more than 1,500 people went down in the sinking ship or froze to death in the icy waters. Compounding the tragedy of that fateful night is that it is now synonymous to most of the world with images of Leo DiCaprio and Kate Winslet's naughty antics in the back seat of a Model T and that annoying ballad by Celine Dion. Tsk, tsk. Where's that iceberg when you need it? Oh, here it is:

◀ **ICEBERG COCKTAIL**
    1 oz white crème de menthe
    ¹/₂ oz peppermint Schnapps
    ¹/₂ oz cinnamon Schnapps
        Milk, to fill
    1 cinnamon stick and
        chocolate shavings

Combine the liquid ingredients over ice in a blender. Blend and serve in a frozen cocktail glass. Garnish with a cinnamon stick and chocolate shavings. Drink enough to make the music stop.

"It's a great advantage not to drink among hard-drinking people. You can hold your tongue and, moreover, you can time any little irregularity of your own so that everybody else is so blind that they don't see or care."

–F. SCOTT FITZGERALD,
THE GREAT GATSBY

119

16

Far out dude, far freaking ooooouuuuuutttttttt. April 16, 1943, witnessed the discovery that has singlehandedly catapulted the sightings of little green men and rainbows to record highs. No, it's not St. Patrick's Day—that was last month—but instead it's the day the hallucinogenic properties of LSD were discovered. However would a discovery such as this be made, you might ask? We have no idea, but suggest you stop asking stupid questions and pay attention to the herd of miniature purple-and-orange antelopes marching toward the liquor cabinet. Enjoy the following and make sure you drink lots of water with it.

SURFER ON ACID

1 1/4 oz Malibu rum
1 1/4 oz Jägermeister
       splash of pineapple juice

Pour the ingredientsinto a stainless steel shaker over ice and shake until completely cold. Strain into a large shot glass or an old-fashioned glass and shoot. Yowza!

17

The car that has men's knees knocking and their lips quivering to this day was introduced on April 17, 1964, when the first Ford Mustang rolled off the assembly line and was put on display at the World's Fair. Sleek and sexy, small and stylish, the Mustang offered men the metaphorical penis extension they'd been seeking for years, while women liked the way it highlighted their feminine figures and rock-star sunglasses. Packed with power and never-ending sex appeal, it's no surprise that the Mustang is still one of the most sought-after American cars on the market.

FIERY BLUE MUSTANG

1/2 oz banana liqueur
1/2 oz blue curaçao
1/2 oz Everclear alcohol

Mix the ingredients, pour into a shot glass, and light on fire. Blow out the flame, saddle up, and enjoy the ride!

18

The great San Francisco earthquake of 1906 was considered at the time to be the most devastating natural disaster to hit the United States. At 5:12 a.m. on April 18 the quake hit, lasting for less than a minute but unleashing a fury on the city that resulted in the burning of four square miles and the deaths of what is estimated today to be almost three thousand San Franciscans. A committee of professors and scientists painstakingly studied the quake and released a report two years later. To this day, the Lawson report remains a highly regarded document used to investigate the effects of earthquakes in the U.S. Substantially less research went into the Earthquake described below, but we're sure you're going to love it.

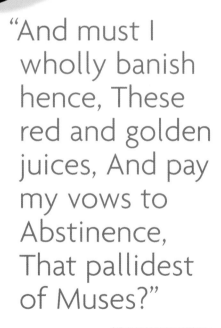

EARTHQUAKE

1	oz gin
1	oz bourbon whiskey
3/4	oz anise liqueur

Combine the ingredients, shake, shake, shake with ice, and strain into a Collins glass.

"And must I wholly banish hence, These red and golden juices, And pay my vows to Abstinence, That pallidest of Muses?"

—SIR WILLIAM WATSON

> "The best audience is intelligent, well-educated, and a little drunk."
>
> —ALBEN W. BARKLEY

19

A shot was heard around the world . . . No, not that kind of shot, you alkie, this one had historical significance, so pay attention! The Battle of Lexington and Concord on April 19, 1775, was the first battle of the American Revolutionary War, and was described as "the shot heard round the world." We won't bore you with the details of this battle, nor the war that ensued, but the short of it is that the Americans won, thereby ensuring that our bars stay open later, we get to eat soggy, over-processed cereal in the morning instead of the traditional English breakfast, and we can drive on the right side of the road. Cheerio, mate!

GUNFIRE ❯

- 1 cup strong black tea
- 1 shot dark rum

Pour the strong black tea into an Irish coffee cup, add the rum, and stir.

"The decline of the aperitif may well be one of the most depressing phenomena of our time."

—LUIS BUÑUEL

20

On the short list of birth dates that changed the world, you're sure to find April 20 near the top. It was on this day, in 1889, that Adolf Hitler, the son of Alois and Klara Hitler, was born in the small Austrian town of Braunau. If we need to go over the horrendous details of Hitler's rise and fall or the effect he had on the twentieth century, then you probably should have picked up a history book while you were at the bookstore. To describe him as anything other than Just Plain Evil would be a disservice. What luck! We came up with a drink of the same name, described below.

JUST PLAIN EVIL

    1   oz Jägermeister
    1   oz cinnamon Schnapps

Combine the Jägermeister and Schnapps in a shot glass.

21

We're torn by the tragic story of Rosie Ruiz, the Boston Marathon runner who, on this day in 1980, won the marathon by jogging right into a nearby subway station, depositing a token, and riding a good chunk of the way to the winner's circle. We understand how tiring it must be to run 26 miles; we're winded jogging back and forth to the bar for drink refills, and every time we return with a fresh round, we feel like we deserve a medal. But cheating your way to winning the Boston Marathon? That's low. Doing it by riding public transportation? That is rock bottom! Rosie, this drink is for you . . .

CHEATERITA

> 2   oz tequila
> 6   oz limeade
> 1   slice lime

Combine the tequila, limeade, and ice in a Collins glass. Squeeze the juice from the lime slice into the mixture, and then drop the rind into the glass as well. Stir and serve.

"One drink is too many for me and a thousand not enough."

—BRENDAN BEHAN

22

Vladimir Ilyich Lenin was born on this day in 1870. Lenin was a Russian revolutionary, the leader of the Bolshevik party, the first premier of the Soviet Union, and the main theorist of Leninism, which he described as an adaptation of Marxism to "the age of imperialism." Leninism eventually became Communism, which the Soviet people lived under until the fall of the Iron Curtain in 1989. One person who was not living under it for long, however, was Lenin himself, who died in 1924, was pumped full of preservatives, and put on permanent display in the Lenin Mausoleum in Moscow. Creepy, huh? We think so, too. Preserve yourself with a White Russian instead!

WHITE RUSSIAN

2 oz vodka
1 oz coffee liqueur
  light cream

Pour the vodka and coffee liqueur over ice cubes in an old-fashioned glass. Fill with light cream and serve.

23

'Tis a joyous event, the birth of a bard, e'er say we. Today is uber-famous playwright William Shakespeare's birthday. Shakespeare was born on April 23, 1564 (and incidentally also died on April 23 of 1616—we're just full of creepy this week, aren't we?). An English poet and playwright, The Bard has the reputation of being the greatest of all writers in the English language, as well as one of the world's preeminent dramatists. Today we get our drama on reality TV, thank you major networks! Shirley Temple was also born on this day. For obvious reasons, we're skipping over this.

MACBETH'S DREAM ▶

2 oz Scotch whisky
1 tsp orange curaçao
1 tsp amaretto
2 dashes orange bitters
$1/2$ oz lemon juice
$1/2$ tsp superfine sugar

Combine the ingredients in a shaker half-filled with ice cubes. Shake well and strain into a cocktail glass.

"Alcohol is
like love.
The first kiss
is magic,
the second
is intimate,
the third
is routine.
After that
you take
the girl's
clothes off."

–RAYMOND CHANDLER

24

The Irish Easter Uprising, also called the Easter Rebellion, began on this day in 1916 in Dublin, Ireland. Leaders of the Irish Republican Brotherhood and the nationalist Irish Volunteers planned the insurrection against British rule. Claiming the post office and other high-profile locations within the city, the insurrectionists read aloud a proclamation announcing the birth of the Irish Republic. Although the uprising was suppressed, Britain's execution of the insurrection leadeers became powerful propaganda for Ireland. The event is viewed as an important stepping stone in Ireland's struggle for independence.

IRISH PRIDE

3 oz green crème de menthe
3 oz amaretto
2 oz lemon juice

Layer the ingredients in a highball glass and mix.

25

Who doesn't love a brand new toy? Whether it's children with a new set of building blocks or world leaders with a new killin' machine, everybody can appreciate the excitement of getting it home, cracking the seal on the packaging, and taking it out for a spin. So you can imagine the excitement on this day in 1792, when the French government was finally ready to try out their shiny new toy, the guillotine. Nicholas-Jacques Pelletier, a violent robber, has the distinction of being the first to die under the blade, but unfortunately for thousands of French men and women, he wasn't the last. This toy didn't lose its luster and get tossed to the back of the closet until the mid-1970s, when the pressure from their European neighbors finally caused the French to abolish capital punishment. The guillotine being considered a humane, albeit grisly, form of execution, the French were dismayed by the rest of Europe's disdain. President Pompidou was reportedly overheard grumbling, "I don't see what everybody is losing their heads about!"

GUILLOTINE

1 3/4 oz butterscotch Schnapps
1/4 oz Bailey's Irish Cream
1/4 oz cinnamon Schnapps

Fill a shot glass about four-fifths of the way full with butterscotch Schnapps. Float a layer of Bailey's Irish Cream on the Schnapps, and then a layer of cinnamon Schnapps on the Bailey's.

26

As I'm sure you are well aware, strippers come in all shapes and sizes, but former vaudeville child wonder turned burlesque star Gypsy Rose Lee was one of a kind. Her performances were a blend of her own unique brand of striptease, humor, and intelligent commentary. She was a Jane of all Trades who just happened to take off her clothes in public. She became very popular and went on from stripping to write several books, star on both the large and the small screens, and lead one wild life. She was the inspiration for the musical Gypsy and hosted her own talk show late in life. She died on this day 1970 of lung cancer.

STRIP AND YELL

1¼	oz bourbon whiskey
¾	oz peach Schnapps
¼	oz Strega herbal liqueur
4½	oz bitter lemon soda
1	lemon spiral

Pour the liquid ingredients into an ice-filled Collins glass, add a spiral of lemon, and serve.

27

You know it's a slow day in history when the only thing we could find to write about today was that it was the day that wrestler Freddie Blassie coined the term "Pencil-Neck Geek" in 1953. We have researched, and researched, and drunkenly researched, and the closest thing we can come up with surrounding an event when these words actually came out of his mouth for the first time involved witnessing a long-necked man biting the heads off of snakes and chickens at a carnival freak show. (Ozzy Osbourne, take note!) Blassie reportedly turned to a friend and uttered the words, "That man is nothing but a pencil-neck geek."

PENCIL NECK GEEK

1	oz Midori melon liqueur
1	oz blue curaçao liqueur
	lemonade

Pour the Midori and blue curaçao into a Collins glass with a few ice cubes. Fill with lemonade.

28

The *HMS Bounty* sailed on this day in 1787 from Spithead, England (we think it's funny, too), bound for Tahiti. Their mission was to collect breadfruit plants to be transplanted to the West Indies as cheap food for the slaves. After collecting the plants and spending six long months in paradise, the *Bounty* sailed for home. On the morning of April 28, 1789, part of the crew mutinied, took over the ship, and set the captain and eighteen members of the crew adrift in the ship's 23-foot launch. Everybody survived the mutiny, and the launch made it back to civilization. Leave it to our polite British friends to have a full-scale mutiny without losing a single life. How civilized!

"Most Americans are born drunk, and really require a little wine or beer to sober them."

–GILBERT K. CHESTERTON

MUTINY

- 1 ½ oz dark rum
- ½ oz Dubonnet Rouge vermouth
- 2 dashes bitters
- 1 maraschino cherry

Combine the rum, vermouth, and bitters in a mixing glass half-filled with ice cubes. Stir well, strain into a cocktail glass, and garnish with a maraschino cherry.

29

"What you want (hooo) baby
  I got it
What you need (hooo) you know
  I got it
(Hooo) all I'm asking (hooo) is for a
  little respect
Sock it to me, sock it to me,
  sock it to me!"

It was on this day in 1967 that Aretha Franklin released the song that has become the Declaration of Women's Right to a Little R-E-S-P-E-C-T. "Respect" came out of the gates strong, rocketing to number one on the Billboard charts in just a little over a month. We're not too proud to admit that, from time to time, even we find ourselves holding that hairbrush, pursing our lips, and screeching along at the tops of our high-pitched little girly voices.

SHOT OF RESPECT

    1   part tequila
    1   part 151 proof rum
    1   dash Tabasco sauce

Combine the tequila and 151 proof rum in a shot glass, then pour in the Tabasco.

30

On this day in 1997, comedienne and television star Ellen DeGeneres proved that indeed sisters are doing it for themselves . . . and with themselves . . . when her character on her self-titled sitcom *Ellen* came out of the closet. Ellen herself had come out on the cover of *Time* magazine only a few weeks earlier with the headline: "Yep, I'm gay." To which most of us responded: "Yep, we figured." Once everything was said and done, and both Ellen and *Ellen* were finally out of the closet, we all suffered a monster pop-culture hangover, leading us each to ask ourselves: "But really, now . . . what's the big deal?"

GIRLS' NIGHT OUT ▶

    3   oz medium red wine
    1   tsp amaretto
    1   tsp Kirschwasser
        cherry brandy
    3   oz lemonade
    1   maraschino cherry
    1   slice orange

Pour the liquid ingredients into an ice-filled red wine glass. Garnish with a cherry and an orange slice, and serve with straws.

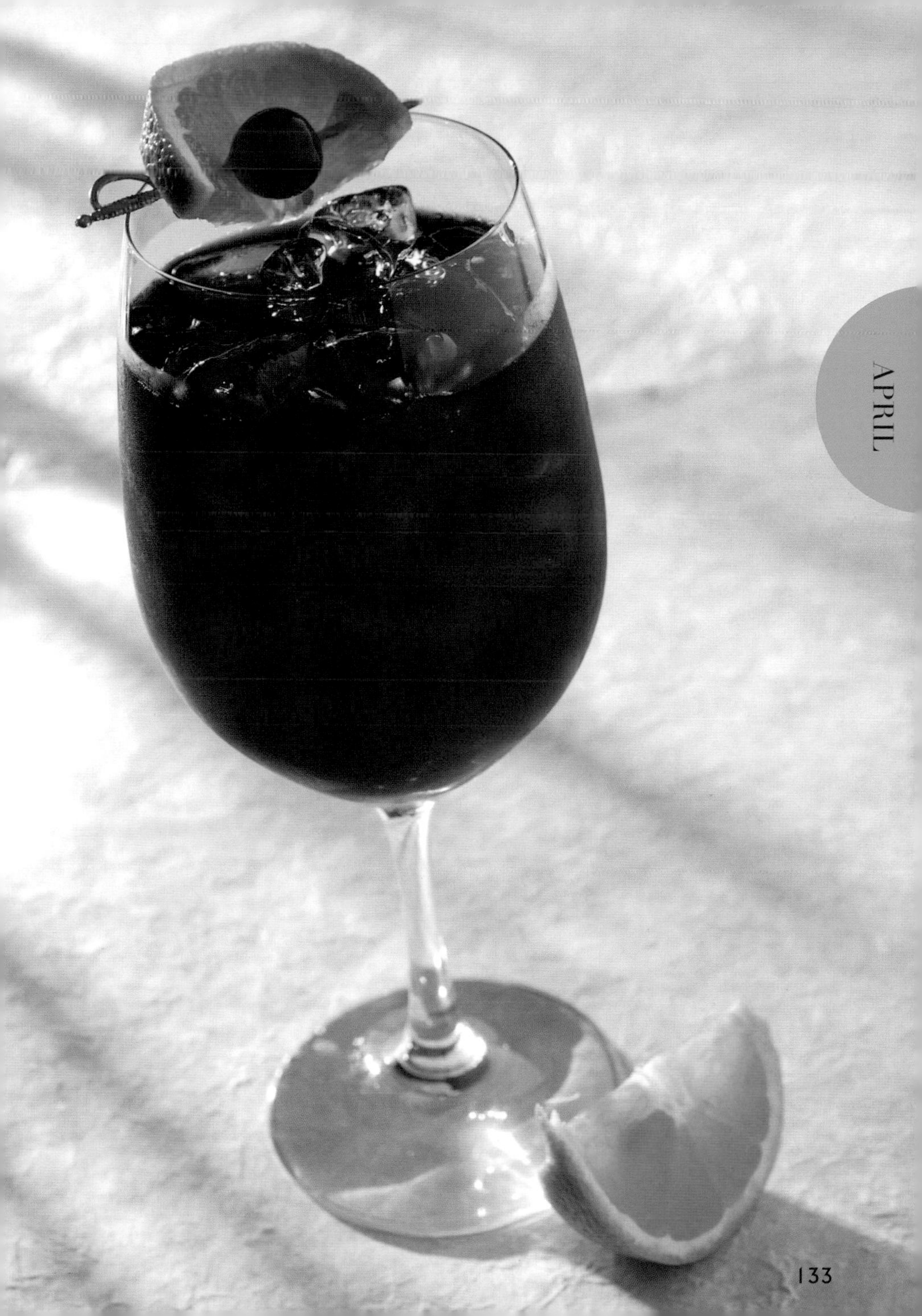

"Some men are like musical glasses; to produce their finest tones, you must keep them wet."

—SAMUEL TAYLOR COLERIDGE

Calamity Jane was born on this day in 1852 in Missouri, as Martha Jane Cannary. Calamity Jane was the Mother of all Tomboys (these days we have another word for that, see April 30), and was well known for dressing in men's clothing and for her shooting and riding skills. Her foul mouth and drunkenness caused many a problem for her, and she adopted the moniker "Calamity," as that's what she threatened anybody who crossed her with. We're fairly sure that if Jane were around today, she'd be married to Bobby Brown.

WILD, WILD WEST

- 1½ oz whiskey
- 1 oz peach Schnapps
- 2 oz cranberry juice

Combine all the ingredients in a Collins glass and mix well. Yee-haw!

2

Although accounts of an aquatic beast living in Scotland's Loch Ness date back thousands of years, the modern legend of the Loch Ness Monster began when a sighting made the local news on May 2, 1933. The newspaper related an account of a local couple who claimed to have seen "an enormous animal rolling and plunging on the surface." The story of the "monster" became a media sensation. London newspapers descended on the loch and offered a handsome reward for capture of the beast. Sightings have occurred off and on ever since. So far, no one's claimed the reward . . .

LOCH NESS MYSTERY

$3/4$ oz Scotch whisky
$1/4$ oz apricot brandy
1 dash orange curaçao
2 oz grapefruit juice
$1/4$ oz lime juice
1 lime wedge

Shake all the liquid ingredients with ice and strain into a Collins glass filled with crushed ice. Garnish with a lime wedge. Warning: More than two of these, and you will most likely be spotting scary green monsters swimming in the lake.

"A sudden violent jolt of it has been known to stop the victim's watch, snap his suspenders and crack his glass eye right across."

—IRVIN S. COBB

3 Harry Lillis "Bing" Crosby was born on this day in 1903. He was one of the most popular and influential American singers and actors of the twentieth century. His career spanned from 1926, when he debuted with the Whiteman Orchestra, until his death in 1977. So popular was he, he is considered by many to be rivaled only by Elvis Presley and the Beatles. With a reputation like that and such a long, successful career, it causes one to wonder: what was his net worth? Crosby is perhaps best known for his holiday favorite, "White Christmas." Although we know it's only May, enjoy a White Christmas now—and any other time, up through Christmas itself!

WHITE CHRISTMAS

1 part crème de banane
1 part white crème de cacao
1 part Scotch whisky
1 part double cream
grated chocolate

Shake the liquid ingredients together, strain into a cocktail glass, and sprinkle with grated chocolate.

4 It's a double whammy today, as not only was this the day Margaret Thatcher was sworn in as Prime Minister of Great Britain in 1979, but it is also Audrey Hepburn's birthday (she was born in 1929). What's the connection, you might ask, and why should you take precious time away from the cocktail shaker to continue reading about this? Well, we'll tell you: it all comes down to speech. Thatcher had to take speech lessons to overcome a hard-to-understand accent in order to succeed in politics, while Hepburn's character, Eliza, in My Fair Lady also had to take speech lessons in order to transform herself from a Cockney flower girl into a proper lady. We're just full of whacky factoids and coincidences. Isn't it loverly? Now drink.

TONGUE TANGLER ▶

1 oz Bailey's Irish Cream
1/2 oz brandy
3 oz heavy cream

Pour the Bailey's Irish Cream and brandy into an old-fashioned glass. Add the heavy cream. Stir well and serve.

5

It's Cinco de Mayo! What better way to celebrate than with a drinking game! This one's called Mexicali:

What you need:
1	cup
2	dice
2+	players
	A lot of margaritas (see recipe below)

Directions:
1. Everyone at the table has his or her own drink. (Duh!)
2. The object is to shake the dice in the cup, slam it on the table, lift it up and take a peek at the dice (don't let anyone else see them), and then announce what you have.
3. a) If your roll does not match or beat the previous roll, then you must drink.
   b) You may bluff what you rolled in order to avoid drinking. However, the last person to roll before you has the ability to call your bluff. If your bluff is called successfully, you must drink. If someone calls your bluff and loses (i.e., you really did beat the last score), then that person must drink. Play then moves on to the next person
4. Rolls are based on the two-digit number they form when placed side by side (for example, a 3 and a 4 would be 43), or if you throw doubles the value is one die times 100 (for example, a double 2 would count as 200).

Special Rules

There are also some other special rolls that affect the game: 21 (a 2 and a 1) is called a "Mexicali" and beats all other rolls (including double 6, or 600). 31 is a "reverse," and play goes back the other way around the table. 32 is a "social," and everybody drinks.

"Reverse" and "social" both cancel out the previous roll, so you don't have to worry about beating the previous guy's score. If you are caught bluffing a Mexicali, you have to down the whole drink.

MARGARITA

$^1/_2$ oz tequila
$^3/_4$ oz Triple Sec (or Cointreau)
1 splash of sour mix
1 dash lime juice
1 lime wedge

Shake all the liquid ingredients with ice and serve in a salt-rimmed margarita glass on the rocks or strain to serve up straight. Garnish with a lime wedge. For a frozen variation, blend with ice.

"Bring in the bottled lightning, a clean tumbler, and a corkscrew."

—CHARLES DICKENS

"No other human being, no woman, no poem or music, book or painting can replace alcohol in its power to give man the illusion of real creation."

—MARGUERITE DURAS

May 6, 1937, at 6:25 p.m., the German zeppelin Hindenburg caught

6

fire and was totally destroyed in a brilliant blaze in less than one minute while approaching a mooring mast at Lakehurst Naval Air Station in New Jersey. The ship had crossed the Atlantic Ocean from Germany and was only moments away from completing the trip. There were 97 people on board, but only 13 passengers and 22 crew members died. One member of the ground crew was also killed, bringing the death toll to 36. It was the only such disaster involving a zeppelin, but due to the bad publicity, using the ships for transport immediately stopped. Oh, the power of bad PR!

EXPLOSION COCKTAIL

1	oz vodka
1	oz Cointreau
1	splash sweetened lime juice
13	oz pear cider

Pour the vodka, Cointreau, and lime juice into a pint glass. Fill with the cider. Stir and serve.

7

Today is the birthday of Argentina's most powerful first lady of all time. Eva Perón was born on this day in 1919 to a poor family in a village outside of Buenos Aires. She rose to fame through acting, and met Argentina's future president Juan Perón at a fund-raising event in the capital city. Their climb to power was a struggle, but luckily they were able to stop and catalog it through catchy songs along the way. Or at least, that's how it happens in the world of Andrew Lloyd Webber. Evita, as she was called, is perhaps best remembered for her impassioned speeches. Some of our favorite quotes are as follows:

"When the rich think about the poor, they have poor ideas."
"Answer violence with violence. If one of us falls today, five of them must fall tomorrow."

Contemplate that while enjoying an Argentine Julep!

ARGENTINE JULEP

1	oz orange juice
1	oz pineapple juice
1	oz Spanish brandy
1	oz claret
1/4	oz Cointreau
1	slice orange
1	sprig mint

Shake the liquid ingredients with ice and strain into a Collins glass. Garnish with an orange slice and a mint sprig.

"Fill it up.
I take as
large draughts
of liquor as
I did of love.
I hate a
flincher in
either."

–JOHN GAY

8 Speaking of Andrew Lloyd Webber, one of our favorite quotes of his comes from *Sunset Boulevard*, when super-crazy Norma Desmond announces, "I am big, it's the pictures that got small." But on this day in 1914, the pictures were big indeed when Paramount Pictures was formed in Hollywood, California. The studio is responsible for many of the greatest movies of all time, including *Psycho*, *Vertigo*, *Raiders of the Lost Ark*, and *Top Gun*. Today the studio is still churning out hits such as School of *Rock*, *Tomb Raider*, and *The Odd Couple II*. Nothing like a blockbuster, ahem . . .

HOLLYWOOD COCKTAIL ❱

- 1 1/2 oz light rum
- 1/2 egg white
- 1/2 oz grenadine
- 1/2 oz grapefruit juice
  nutmeg

Shake the liquid ingredients with ice and strain into a cocktail glass. Add a sprinkle of nutmeg to the top and apply clever but fashionable sunglass disguise to your face. Fabulous, dahling!

143

9

Before the "morning after pill" was ever even dreamt up, the birth control pill heralded a revolution of its own. On this day in 1960, the Food and Drug Administration approved "the pill," thereby freeing men of any sort of responsibility for protection whatsoever and sentencing women to a daily dosage that does everything from whacking out the hormones to contributing to odd weight-control issues. Good times for everybody! Despite its shortcomings, the pill is still considered one of the most effective forms of birth control around. It certainly beats withdrawal.

BIRTH CONTROL

1 1/2 oz rye whiskey
1 1/2 oz gin

Pour both ingredients into an old-fashioned glass over ice, swish, and serve.

10

It was on this day in 1863 that the Confederate Army lost one of its most revered leaders, General Stonewall Jackson. He earned his nickname "Stonewall" after the battle of Bull Run, where, as he promised, he stood like a stone wall against the enemy. He was by many accounts a very strange man, and often behaved so oddly that his sanity was called into question. He died during the Civil War due to complications from an arm amputation that resulted from a case of mistaken identity leading to friendly fire. His dying words were: "Let us cross the river and rest in the shade of the trees." We're hoping our dying words will be equally poignant, but we're guessing they will be more on par with: "Just one more sip won't kill me . . ."

JACKSON COCKTAIL

1 1/4 oz gin
1 1/4 oz red Dubonnet
2 dashes orange bitters

Combine the ingredients, stir with ice, and strain into a cocktail glass.

11

Salvador Felip Jacint Dalí Domènech, aka Salvador Dalí, was born on this day in 1904. Perhaps the most famous surrealist painter of all time, Dalí's work is noted for its striking combination of bizarre, dreamlike images with excellent draftsmanship and artistic skills clearly influenced by the Renaissance masters. Melting watches, why didn't we think of that? He had an admitted love of doing unusual things to draw attention to himself. Other famous artists who do unusual things to draw attention to themselves include Janet Jackson (see February 1), Pee-Wee Herman, and, of course, George Michael. Oh, Salvador, maybe you should reconsider "unusual things"; just the idea paints you in a bad light. "Paints you," get it?

SURREAL DEAL

- $1/4$ oz lemon juice
- $1/2$ oz Triple Sec
- $1/2$ oz brandy
- 1 oz apple brandy
- 1 tsp powdered sugar

Fill a shaker halfway with ice cubes. Pour all the ingredients into the shaker and shake well. Strain the drink into a cocktail glass and serve.

"I can't say whether we had more wit among us now than usual, but I am certain we had more laughing, which answered the end as well."

—OLIVER GOLDSMITH

MAY

12

On May 12, 1934, "Cocktails for Two" by Duke Ellington hit number one on the charts. Mix up the Duke's a Champ cocktail and sing along:

In some secluded rendezvous
That overlooks the avenue
With someone sharing a
  delightful chat
Of this and that
And cocktails for two

As we enjoy a cigarette
To some exquisite chansonnette
Two hands are sure to slyly
  meet beneath
A serviette
With cocktails for two

My head may go reeling
But my heart will be obedient
With intoxicating kisses
For the principal ingredient

Most any afternoon at five
We'll be so glad we're both alive
Then maybe fortune will complete
  her plan
That all began
With cocktails for two

◖ DUKE'S A CHAMP

1 ½ oz vodka
½ oz blackberry brandy

Pour the vodka and blackberry brandy into a mixing glass half-filled with ice cubes. Stir, strain into a cocktail glass, and serve.

"Drink not the third glass, which thou canst not tame, when once it is within thee."

—GEORGE HERBERT

13

On the afternoon of May 13, 1981, Pope John Paul II was struck by three bullets while being driven in a slow-moving convertible through St. Peter's Square, where 20,000 people had gathered to see the pontiff. Rushed to a hospital, the Pope barely survived a six-hour operation. The would-be assassin, a 23-year-old Turkish man named Mehmet Ali Agca, was immediately apprehended. In his pocket, the police found several notes, one of which read: "I am killing the Pope as a protest against the imperialism of the Soviet Union and the United States and against the genocide that is being carried out in El Salvador and Afghanistan." (We suspect the other two notes said, "Hey, the gays aren't that bad" and "Abstinence may work for you, but come on, give us a break!") The silver cloud behind the assassination attempt was the invention of the PopeMobile, the bulletproof-glass golf cart that the Pope rides around in these days. It alone calls to mind more jokes than we have room to print here.

ANGRY CATHOLIC

1	oz tequila
1 or 2	drops Tabasco sauce
1	splash 151 proof rum

Pour the tequila into a shot glass. Add the Tabasco and let each drop sink to the bottom. Add the 151 and light it on fire. Make sure you blow it out before you drink it!

14

May 14, 1948, marked the official announcement that a new Jewish state, known to you and me as Israel, had been formally established in the British Mandate of Palestine, the land where once the Kingdom of Israel and the Kingdom of Judah had been. Not everybody was so happy about this so-called Jewish state, however, namely the Palestinians, who thought the land belonged to them. Thus began a little skirmish we refer to affectionately as the Middle East Conflict. The details are too far-reaching and confusing for us to figure out completely, plus we'd have to sober up to really wrap our heads around it, and who wants that? Instead, I think we'll have an Israeli Coffee. Care to join us?

ISRAELI COFFEE

    6   oz coffee
    I   oz Sabra liqueur
        whipped cream

Pour the coffee and Sabra liqueur into a coffee cup and garnish with whipped cream.

"When you work hard all day with your head and know you must work again the next day what else can change your ideas and make them run on a different plane like whisky?"

—ERNEST HEMINGWAY

15

In 1602, the English settler Bartholomew Gosnold undertook a small prospecting journey by boat along the coasts of Maine and Massachusetts to explore the northern Virginia coast. What Gosnold hadn't counted on was getting hooked by Cape Cod on his way down. No, we're not talking about the charming beach property and cute little crafts shops of Hyannis and Barnstable, we mean literally "hooked" by the swooping coast, which trapped Gosnold and his ship in the Massachusetts Bay. On May 15, 1602, Gosnold sunk his anchor in the bay and became the first European to set foot on Cape Cod, which got its name for its abundance of codfish. Today, Cape Cod is overrun by people, all trying to discover a patch of beach and the best hotel deal in Paradise.

CAPE COD

```
1 1/2  oz vodka
   4   oz cranberry juice
   I   lime wedge
```

Combine the vodka and cranberry juice in a Collins glass with ice. Garnish with a wedge of lime and serve.

16

Break out the rhinestones and the silver candelabra, it's Liberace's birthday! Born in 1919 in Wisconsin, the entertainer was known for his extravagant costumes, personal charm, and self-deprecating wit. A 1957 article in London's *Daily Mirror* mentioned that Liberace was a "deadly, winking, sniggering, snuggling, chromium-plated, scent-impregnated, luminous, quivering, giggling, fruit-flavored, mincing, ice-covered heap of mother love," a description which did everything it could to imply he was homosexual without saying so. Liberace sued for libel, testified in a London court that he was not a homosexual and had never taken part in homosexual acts, and he won. He died of AIDS at the age of 67.

CHAMPAGNE PUNCH ▶

```
   I   oz orange curaçao
 1/2   tsp sugar
 1/2   oz fresh lemon juice
       Champagne
```

Layer the first three ingredients in a flute. Top off with Champagne.

17 Here's a drink that will put hair on your chest and a slight singsong in your voice. In honor of Norwegian Constitution Day, which was established in 1814, we thought we'd find a drink named after Norway's most famous historical figures. Once you've had a few of these, you'll be ready to sail the North Seas, stopping off at ports to pillage and burn, but not rape, please—it's so un-P.C., you know. Skål!

VIKING

1½ oz Galliano
½ oz aquavit

Combine the ingredients and serve in an old fashioned glass over ice.

18 Imagine you're hanging out at home, minding your own business, when all of a sudden the mountain just up the road blows its top off. We realized we would first change our underwear, and then hightail it out as fast as we could, which is what we believe the residents of the Mt. St. Helen's area did when that volcano erupted on this day in 1980. All in all, 57 people were killed, along with 1,500 elk, 5,000 deer, and an estimated 11 million fish. Just thinking about it makes us need a drink.

VOLCANO COCKTAIL

½ cup grapes
½ apple, sliced
2 slices canned pineapple
6 oz canned pineapple juice
1 cup strawberry sorbet (or ice cream)
2 oz Pisang Ambon liqueur
2 oz banana liqueur

Blend all the ingredients with ice until smooth. Pour into a coconut shell, and garnish with an umbrella and several straws.

19

Thomas Edward Lawrence, also known as Lawrence of Arabia, died on this day in 1935. He became famous for his role as a British liaison officer during the Arab Revolt of 1916 to 1918. Many Arabs consider him a folk hero for promoting their cause for freedom from both Ottoman and European rule; likewise, many Britons count him among one of their country's greatest war heroes. He is credited with dramatically improving relations between the East and the West. We're no experts, but from the cheap seats, it looks to us like we could use another Lawrence of Arabia right about now. Any volunteers?

MAY

BLACK SAND

$1/2$ oz Kahlúa
$1/2$ oz black sambuca
$1/2$ oz amaretto

Layer equal parts of each ingredient into a shot or pony glass.

"When you stop drinking, you have to deal with this marvelous personality that started you drinking in the first place."

–JIMMY BRESLIN

20

Cher (born Cherilyn Sarkisian on May 20, 1946) is one of our favorite entertainers of all time. Not only does she have a questionable past—a variety show with Sonny Bono?—but she's also reinvented herself more times than Madonna. She's sold more than 100 million records worldwide and won an Academy Award. Not surprisingly, she's something of a gay icon because, according to one source, she possesses "style, versatility, a larger-than-life personality, and an unbreakable spirit." All we know is she makes us kind of warm inside. You go, Cher!

◀ **PINK LADY**

   1 1/2 oz gin
   1 1/2 oz apple brandy
    1/2 oz grenadine
    1/2 oz fresh lemon juice
    1 egg white

Combine indgredients over ice, shake and strain into a cocktail glass and serve.

"Sobriety diminishes, discriminates, and says no; drunkenness expands, unites, and says yes."

–WILLIAM JAMES

21

After 33 1/2 hours of flight, it was on this day in 1927 that one of the most fascinating figures in aviation history, Charles Lindbergh, landed in Paris, France, becoming the first person to fly solo across the Atlantic Ocean. We are in awe just thinking about it. Apparently, as he flew solo, there was no in-flight movie, no bathroom breaks, and no cute little glasses of Champagne in first class. Faced with the same challenge, we wouldn't make it across the street. Enjoy the Lindbergh Cocktail as you imagine the trials and tribulations of flying all alone across the ocean.

CHARLIE LINDBERGH COCKTAIL

1 1/4	oz gin
1	oz white wine
1/4	oz apricot brandy
1	dash orange bitters
	sliced apricots

Combine the liquid ingredients and shake with ice. Strain into a cocktail glass and garnish with apricot slices. Note: Not recommended if you have a 33 1/2-hour flight ahead of you.

22

America heard the familiar "Heeeeeeeeeeeeeeeeeeeeeeeere's Johnny!" for the last time on this date in 1992, when Johnny Carson hosted his last *Tonight Show* after nearly 30 years on the job. For all those years, he entered our homes to provide commentary on the day's news, to help determine our next day's conversational agenda, and, of course, to entertain. His sidekick, Ed McMahon, became nearly as famous as Carson himself, and went on to host *Star Search* and give away millions of dollars for Publisher's Clearing House. Gotta run, there's somebody at the door...

JOHNNY ON THE SPOT

1	oz Crown Royal Canadian whisky
1/2	oz amaretto
1/2	oz peach Schnapps
12	oz pineapple juice

Combine all the ingredients in a cocktail shaker with ice. Shake well, strain into a Collins glass, and serve.

23 As much as we love kind, good people, we're not too proud to admit that we love evil bitches even more. I mean, come on, who doesn't? One of our favorites is bad girl Joan Collins, who was born on this day in 1933. Joan played two characters that are especially close to our hearts. The first was in the *Batman* series from the '60s, where she played The Siren, a woman who could put men under her spell by singing a note three octaves above a high C. She would use men for her needs, and then had no problem getting rid of them. She once uttered the words: "I want to become the wickedest woman in Gotham City and thus in the World!" Our second favorite Collins role is, of course, as Alexis Carrington on *Dynasty*, where she made the Wicked Witch of the West look like Shirley Temple. In honor of Miss Joan and one of her all-too-common moves on Dynasty, we've chosen a very special drink.

BITCH SLAP

I oz Smirnoff Blue Label vodka
I splash 7-Up
I oz gin
I oz Everclear alcohol
I oz light rum
   lemonade

Mix the vodka, 7-Up, gin, Everclear, and rum together over ice in a Collins glass. Fill with lemonade, and serve.

MAY

> "There are some sluggish men who are improved by drinking; as there are fruits that are not good until they are rotten."

—SAMUEL JOHNSON

24

Another wildly fascinating day in history, May 24 marks the day the Brooklyn Bridge opened in 1883. Connecting the big borough of Manhattan with Long Island and the town of Brooklyn, the bridge is one of the busiest in the country to this day. At the time of its opening, it was the longest suspension bridge in the world. Today, it has been long surpassed by bigger, more famous bridges. What's so funny about the Brooklyn Bridge, you may ask? Absolutely nothing, so let's shake up a Brooklyn Cocktail and drink it funny!

BROOKLYN COCKTAIL ▶

1 1/2 oz rye or bourbon
1/2 oz dry vermouth
1/4 oz Amer Picon
1/4 oz maraschino liqueur

Combine the liquid ingredients in a shaker with ice. Shake well and serve in a cocktail glass. Garnish with an orange slice.

25

Girls, twist your hair into cinnamon buns, and boys, grab your lightsabers. On this day in 1977, the mother ship of science fiction films was released for the very first time. *Star Wars*, which was panned by critics and projected to become the biggest money loser of all time, opened in theaters around the country, breaking box office records. The movie gave birth to a whole new crowd of sci-fi geeks, who championed paraphernalia such as T-shirts that read "My dad can beat your dad in a lightsaber duel" and bumper stickers that proclaimed "My other car is the Millennium Falcon." Do you think we can use The Force to banish them all to the Death Star?

STAR WARS

- 1 part amaretto
- 1 part Triple Sec
- 1 part Southern Comfort
- 1 part grenadine

Shake all the ingredients over ice. Strain into a chilled cocktail, pony, or shot glass.

26

Saddle up, pardner. The grandfather of the cinematic Western, John Wayne, was born on this day in 1907. Although he made non-Westerns, it was in the action roles that he excelled, exuding a warm and imposing manliness onscreen to which both men and women could respond. Although he went by the screen name John Wayne and the nickname "The Duke," his birth name was Marion. We're just saying.

DUKE COCKTAIL

- 1 tsp orange juice
- 2 tsp lemon juice
- $1/2$ oz Triple Sec
- 1 whole egg
- $1/2$ tsp maraschino cherry juice
  chilled Champagne

Shake all the ingredients except the Champagne with ice, and strain into a Champagne flute. Fill with chilled Champagne, stir, and serve.

27

We all know the story of the three little pigs (which debuted on this day in 1933). Pig builds house, wolf blows it down, pig runs to second, slightly sturdier house, wolf blows that one down too, both pigs run to third house of bricks, wolf has no luck and eventually ends up in a pot of boiling water. Bummer for the wolf, but we can't help but ask ourselves, who did the building inspections on the first pigs' houses, and whoever thought it was a good idea to build houses of straw and sticks? I mean, with that kind of terrorist threat lurking around every corner, you can't be too careful! In honor of the large-lunged but apparently dopey wolf, we've found a drink that will take your breath away. Can you just have a sip of ours, you ask? Not by the hair of our chinny chin chins!

WOLF'S BREATH

    2   oz bourbon
    6   oz orange juice

Huff and puff and fill a Collins glass with ice, pour in quality bourbon, and top off with orange juice.

"Even though a number of people have tried, no one has yet found a way to drink for a living."

–JEAN KERR

28

With so many people trying to get out of Communist Russia near the end of the Cold War, we can't help but marvel at the German Mathias Rust, who flew into Russia from Helsinki and landed his Cessna in Red Square on this day in 1987. What was he thinking? His stunt cost him 18 months in a Russian prison, and causes us to question his sanity. So we did some more research. Following his time in prison, he returned to Germany and got a job in a hospital, where he fell in love with a nurse who rejected him and so he stabbed her. Back to prison. In 1994, he went back to Russia and disappeared, again resurfacing two years later as a shoe salesman in Moscow. He returned to Germany, converted to Hinduism, and ended up in court again in 2001 for stealing a cashmere sweater. We fear there may be still more to come!

◄ RED SQUARE

I	part Russian vodka
I	part white sambuca
I to 3	drops Tabasco sauce

Mix the vodka, sambuca, and a few drops of Tabasco sauce to taste in a shot glass.

29

It was on this day in 1953 that New Zealander Edmund Hillary and Nepalese Sherpa Tenzing Norgay became the first people to reach the summit of Mount Everest, the tallest mountain in the world. They reached the top of the world at 11:30 a.m., after a grueling climb up the southern face, but were only able to stay for 15 minutes due to low oxygen supplies. Turns out there's no air at the top of the world. So inspired were we by their accomplishment (and that of nearly 1,500 people since then) that we thought for a minute we'd try and climb Everest too, but then we remembered we don't even like to climb the stairs, so we made a drink instead.

MOUNTAIN ALTITUDE PUNCH

6	oz amaretto
6	oz brandy
3	qt red wine
6	oz cherry brandy
I	qt ginger ale

Combine the amaretto, brandy, wine, and cherry brandy in large punch bowl over ice. Refrigerate until you're ready to serve, then add the ginger ale just before serving.

"When the liquor's out, why clink the cannikin?"

–ROBERT BROWNING

30

Joan of Arc is one of our favorite women in history. When Joan was about 12 years old, she began hearing the voices of St. Michael, St. Catherine, and St. Margaret, who told her to cut her hair, dress in a man's uniform, and take up arms to defend France against England. She fought valiantly, and was successful for some time, but was finally captured by the English. She continued to dress as a man. It was seen as defiance, and she was burned at the stake on this day in 1431, which is a bummer, because we think that if she could have held out for several hundred years more, she and Calamity Jane (see May 1) could have hung out.

FLAMING COURAGE

- ¹/₃ oz After Shock
- ¹/₃ oz peppermint Schnapps
- ¹/₃ oz Midori
  Bacardi 151 proof rum

Layer the After Shock, Schnapps, and Midori in a shot glass and float the rum on top. Ignite and—after the flames go out!—drink.

31

Today is the day the historic Trans Alaska Pipeline System was completed in 1977. The pipeline was built to transport oil the 800 miles from a frozen oil field up north to the town of Valdez, where tankers would transport the crude oil to refineries. Environmental groups fought the construction of the pipeline in the early days but eventually lost. The pipeline was built, and the oil flows freely. We don't know this for a fact, but we believe the locals wouldn't be nearly as cranky if the pipeline transported something other than oil, say, for example, big batches of the drink below.

PIPELINE

1½ oz light rum
½ tsp powdered sugar
¼ oz apricot brandy
¾ oz lemon juice

Shake the ingredients well with ice, strain into a chilled cocktail glass, and serve.

"Drink, and dance and laugh and lie, Love the reeling midnight through, For tomorrow we shall die! (But, alas, we never do.)"

–DOROTHY PARKER

JUNE 1

"And a one, and a two . . . " Too young to remember Lawrence Welk and his famous song starter? Here's a brief flashback: Before VH1, before MTV, *The Lawrence Welk Show* was a staple of TV viewing for musical entertainment. Mr. Welk and his orchestra appeared on television beginning in 1955 and remained on the air for 27 years. He and the many singers who fronted the band, considered members of the "Welk Family," filled wholesome pastime hours. The music was described by Welk as "Champagne music," and frequently bubbles would float through the air as performers crooned, accompanied by the orchestra. To help us celebrate June 1, the date in 1949 when Lawrence Welk and his orchestra first gained national recognition on the radio show *High Life Review*, please try a Champagne cocktail. Then flip to MTV to watch the bumping and grinding to which we've grown accustomed. We say, thank God for the decline of TV virtue!

CHAMPAGNE COCKTAIL ▶

- 1 sugar cube
- 3 dashes bitters
- 1/2 ounce brandy
  Champagne

Start with the sugar cube in the bottom of your most festive Champagne flute. Pour in the bitters and let soak into the sugar cube, and then pour in the brandy. Fill the rest of the glass with Champagne. Enjoy the bubbles!

"Inebriate of air am I,
And debauchee of dew,
Reeling, through endless summer days, From inns of molten blue."

–EMILY DICKINSON

2

The coronation of Queen Elizabeth II took place on this date in 1953. It was the first coronation to be televised; this was done at the request of the Queen, and was indicative of the great sea of changes the Queen would encounter during her more than fifty years (so far) of ruling the British Commonwealth. Some of these changes were noteworthy, such as the Beatles ushering in the era of Rock 'n' Roll, peace in Northern Ireland, and the building of the Chunnel. Unfortunately, Lizzie has also had to endure the scandal of the Heir Apparent's divorce from Princess Di and his marriage to Mrs. Camilla Parker-Bowles. Did you note the Mrs.? Oops! Isn't it interesting that Charles' predecessor, Edward VIII, had to abdicate the throne when he chose to marry a divorcee? At least Camilla is British! And at least Camilla isn't a blood relative of Charles'— Elizabeth and her husband, Prince Phillip, are both great-great-grandchildren of Queen Victoria. All we can say is "God Save the Queen," and all you should do is try the Queen Elizabeth.

QUEEN ELIZABETH

2 oz French (white) vermouth
1 oz Bénédictine D.O.M.
1 oz lime juice

Shake all the ingredients well with cracked ice. Strain into a chilled cocktail glass.

3 On this date in 1906, the famous entertainer Josephine Baker was born. She had acting, dancing, and comic talent, but was also well known for her risqué costumes: She once took the stage wearing little more than a skirt made from 16 bananas. She was more than the Madonna of her time, however; she was a fighter against tyranny and bigotry. Because of her mixed-race background, she was too dark-skinned to be accepted by American audiences until late in her life. Instead, she gained fame in Paris, France, which was much more accepting and liberal. She became one of the most photographed women in the world; by 1927, she was the best-paid woman in Europe. Baker worked for the French Underground during WWII, earning the title Chevalier of the Legion of Honor from the French government. After the war, she traveled to America, but refused to perform for segregated audiences. She also adopted 12 children of different races to prove that all humans could be brothers and sisters regardless of

the color of their skin, and referred to her brood as "the Rainbow Tribe." Toward the end of her life, Baker performed in Carnegie Hall, earning a standing ovation before her performance. She died in Paris at the age of 68, and was the first American woman to be buried in France with military honors. In her honor, try the Banana Dream.

BANANA DREAM

- 1 shot vodka
- 1 shot banana liqueur
- 5 oz orange juice
- 1 oz cream

Pour all the ingredients into a Parfait glass and stir well, though it is much better if mixed in a blender!

4

With a billion people and thousands of years of history, it should come as no surprise that the Chinese are responsible for plenty of important discoveries and historically significant events. These include, of course, the Great Wall, really inexpensive T-shirts, and Ming vases. In fact, the Chinese were some of the earliest astronomers. In 780 b.c.e., they put this talent to good use and recorded a solar eclipse for, according to some historians, the very first time. Celebrate this anniversary with a solar event of your own!

◖ BURNING SUNSET

| | oz amaretto
3 | oz orange juice
| tsp grenadine

Pour the amaretto and orange juice into a cocktail glass, then add the grenadine. Serve, and admire the sunset.

5

No one appreciates the sliding scale of social norms like we do! Back in the day, we couldn't have gotten away with half of the stuff we've written in this book! Thankfully, almost anything goes in the new millennium. But back in the '50s, the most shocking thing around was the controversy surrounding Elvis Presley's gyrating hips. On this date in 1956, Elvis introduced his new single, "Hound Dog," on *The Milton Berle Show*. The song wasn't the only thing that was new: his dance moves, including some pelvis-thrusting, shocked television audiences. Enjoy the Velvet Presley as you watch other titillating television moments you've saved on TiVo.

VELVET PRESLEY

3 | oz bourbon whiskey
2 | oz chocolate milk

Pour the bourbon over ice, add chocolate milk until creamy, and serve in a Collins glass.

6

Of America's many loves, the two that have perhaps influenced us most during the twentieth century are the automobile and video entertainment. On this date in 1933, the two loves were combined as the first drive-in movie theater in America opened in Camden, New Jersey. The drive-in was the brainchild of Richard Hollingshead. He experimented in his own driveway by first placing a projector on the hood of his car and showing the picture on a sheet attached to trees. As we contemplated this neat feat in entertainment, we also wondered whether Hollingshead ever gave thought to the activities going on in the cars occupied by horny teenaged couples? While you wonder about it yourself, enjoy the Backseat Boogie, described below.

BACKSEAT BOOGIE

$3/4$ oz vodka
$3/4$ oz gin
3   oz cranberry juice
3   oz ginger ale

Pour the vodka and gin over ice cubes in a Collins glass, followed by the cranberry juice and then the ginger ale.

7

Slapstick comedy and musical performances; martinis and cigar smoking; crooning Italian singers and alleged Mafia connections. Dean Martin helped Americans realize the importance of all of these likely and unlikely pairings. Born Dino Crocetti on this date in 1917, Martin was a natural performer; he earned marks as a singer, actor and comedian. He hosted his own successful television show for 10 years, with guest appearances by famous film stars of the day. The attribute we found most appealing? He achieved most of this with a drink in his hand! We love you, Dino! He died on Christmas morning, 1995. Have a dry martini in his honor.

DRY MARTINI

$1^2/3$ oz gin
$1/3$ oz dry vermouth
1   olive

Stir the gin and vermouth with ice in a mixing glass. Strain into a cocktail glass, add the olive, and serve.

8

In the early days of television, shows were less scripted, and stars had to be ready for anything. Actors and comedians with a quick wit and no fear of the unexpected thrived. Milton Berle fit this description perfectly. He hosted his own show, which premiered on this date in 1948. It was originally dubbed *Texaco Star Theater*, and it was a smash success. Berle became a superstar almost immediately, earning the highest ratings on TV. Americans were drawn to his zany antics; he frequently performed in outrageous costumes—even in drag—and the audience loved the ad-libbed slapstick. Have a Captain with a Skirt, described below, as you think of some of your favorite TV stars who favor the feminine flavor of dress. Ally McBeal doesn't count!

CAPTAIN WITH A SKIRT

2 oz Captain Morgan Original Spiced Rum
2 oz white wine
cola
1 slice lime

Mix the Captain Morgan and white wine in a white wine glass. Add the 2 oz cola and some ice cubes. Garnish with a slice of lime.

"A drink a day keeps the shrink away."

–EDWARD ABBEY

JUNE

9

American thoroughbred racing is steeped in tradition—the seersucker suits, the ladies in wide-brimmed hats, the grandmas betting their entire social security checks on the 50 to 1 long shots. We, of course, focus on the traditional drinks, especially the Mint Julep, considered a staple at the Kentucky Derby. The Kentucky Derby is one-third of the Triple Crown; the Preakness and the Belmont Stakes make up the other two-thirds. Rare is the horse that wins all three legs of the Triple Crown, but on this date in 1973, one famous horse did just that. Secretariat had already won the first two races, setting track records while doing so. Secretariat set a new world record while winning the Belmont Stakes, winning by an astounding 31 lengths. By the time Secretariat retired, he had earned over $1.3 million, a record at the time and a heck of a lot of Purina Horse Chow! To keep yourself from despairing over how much (or how little) you've earned so far in your life, sip a Mint Julep. A little bourbon never hurt anyone!

◀ MINT JULEP

  5 sprigs fresh mint
  1 tsp powdered sugar
  2 tsp water
2½ oz bourbon whiskey

Muddle 4 of the mint leaves, the powdered sugar, and the water in a Collins glass. (To muddle, mash them all around with a spoon.) Fill the glass with shaved or crushed ice and add the bourbon. Top with more ice and garnish with the remaining mint sprig. Serve with a straw.

10

When the going gets tough, the tough . . . We really know what the tough do when the going gets tough, right? We've seen it in movies and read it in books; hell, we've seen it when Daddy loses his job. The tough get soused! We realize that this should not turn into a daily occurrence; one should be careful about how much one indulges in the drink. As we like to say, we hope to manage our alcohol intake so that we can continue to drink for the rest of our lives. Alas, it turns out that others aren't so lucky. They grow dependent on alcohol, either because it helps them forget their troubles or it helps them remember some better times in their lives. On this date in 1935, a bunch of these folks banded together for mutual support as they gave up alcohol forever and founded Alcoholics Anonymous. Gasp! Just thinking of this horrible incident makes us want to have a drink! We feel for those who have to give up the hooch, the guilt, the shame—no wonder it's anonymous! Be thankful you can handle your liquor as you try the Drunksimus Maximus below.

DRUNKSIMUS MAXIMUS

1 1/2 oz blackberry brandy
1 oz Southern Comfort Peach Liqueur

Stir both ingredients together in a large shot glass or old-fashioned glass. Shoot.

11

A world-famous prison swimming distance from San Francisco—fabulous! How could Alcatraz not be rife with history and intrigue? The prison, nicknamed The Rock, was supposedly inescapable, though there had been many attempts. The waters swirling around the island are typically frigid, and swimmers would also have to contend with the heavy boat traffic and occasional shark. Prison life would have to be pretty bad to force someone to swim to the mainland. That's what helps prove the intelligence of three escape artists, Frank Morris and brothers John and Clarence Anglin. They had worked for many months during regular shifts to dig themselves out of their cells by enlarging holes for ventilation and replacing the pieces of the wall each day to ensure they wouldn't be discovered. Likewise, they fashioned fake heads, complete with human hair, to place on their pillows the night of the escape so that prison guards would not notice their disappear-

ance. Lastly, and this is the truly smart part, they fashioned life vests and a raft out of raincoats taken from other prisoners. Pretty smart jailbirds, yes? Except for this part: they were never heard from again. FBI officials sought evidence of their making it to land, to no avail. Did they, or didn't they? We will probably never know, despite the Clint Eastwood movie, *Escape from Alcatraz*, that told the tale. The escape—or multiple suicide, depending on your view—took place on this date in 1962. Have a Jailbreak as you try to decide whether they made it to land.

JAILBREAK

    3   oz Guinness stout
    3   oz cola
    1   oz Kahlua
    1   oz Tennessee whiskey
    1   oz amaretto

Pour the Guinness and cola into a white wine glass. Mix Kahlua, Jack Daniel's, and amaretto, separately, with some crushed ice. Pour over the Guinness and cola. Serve, unstirred.

"The thirsty earth soaks up the rain, And drinks, and gapes for drink again. The plants suck in the earth, and are with constant drinking fresh and fair."

–ABRAHAM COWLEY

When was testosterone invented? Well, we know it's a stupid question—what we really mean is when did we finally see the marketing of testosterone? Perhaps it was on this very day in 1952, when the design of the first American sports car was completed. A year later, the first Corvette went on sale to the American public. At first a failure, the Corvette is now seen as an icon in the sports car world, driven by tattoo-covered enthusiasts and midlife-crisis middle managers alike. Like driving the car, the drink below might not make you cooler, but it might make you think are. Have a Corvette and enjoy!

CORVETTE ▶

- 1½ oz Southern Comfort Peach Liqueur
- 1 oz sloe gin
- 1 tsp Campari bitters
- 4 oz chilled lemonade

Combine all the ingredients in an ice-filled Collins glass. Stir well and serve.

13

By the end of the twentieth century, colonialism was in full fervor, with powerful nations dividing up portions of countries and continents. This was the case in Asia as well. Western governments were eager to sell their goods to the burgeoning Chinese market. (Hmm . . . sound familiar?) When government officials refused, the military was called in to help, and by "help" we mean "impose the will of the foreigners." Segments of the Chinese populace, including a society known as the Fists of Righteous Harmony, or Boxers, grew frustrated with Western influence and exploitation. The Boxers began a series of attacks, often bloody and murderous. On this date in 1900, the fighting reached its zenith, and a full-out Boxer Rebellion began. The foreign military were quick to respond, invading port cities and surrounding areas and establishing control for many years. Great Britain was the last to release its claims to portions of China when it returned Hong Kong to Chinese ownership. (See January 20.) We wonder: could this continued foreign exploitation have helped launch the Chinese Revolution? Think this one over as you sip the Chinese Cocktail, described here.

CHINESE COCKTAIL

1 1/2 oz Jamaican dark rum
1 tsp Triple Sec
1 tsp maraschino liqueur
1 tbsp grenadine
1 dash bitters

Pour all the ingredients into a cocktail shaker half-filled with ice cubes. Shake well, strain into a cocktail glass, and serve.

14

If someone threatened your home and loved ones, and if that someone had proven unstoppable in obtaining what he wanted at all costs, would you fight or would you give him access to your valuables? This was the dilemma that faced France on this date in 1940, when, at the beginning of World War II, the Germans marched unimpeded right into Paris. Of course, not all of the French accepted their new landlords or the puppet regime they established, and the Resistance was born. Have a German Wake-up Call as you try to decide what you would have done.

GERMAN WAKE-UP CALL

      3   oz orange juice
      3   oz peach orchard punch juice
1–2   oz Jägermeister herbal liqueur

Stir together the orange juice and peach juice. Add as much Jägermeister as desired, stir again, and serve in a coffee mug.

"If you were to ask me if I'd ever had the bad luck to miss my daily cocktail, I'd have to say that I doubt it; where certain things are concerned, I plan ahead."

—LUIS BUÑUEL

JUNE

15

What's a king to do? More exactly, what's a king to do when surrounded by unhappy, weapon-wielding barons who are sick of paying exorbitant taxes? This was exactly the predicament of King John of England, who ascended to the throne with the passing of his brother, Richard the Lion-hearted. John probably could have been called the Greedy-at-all-costs-hearted, which is how he got himself into his predicament. He had imposed taxes, stolen land, fought the Church—a serious no-no back then—and, in general, gotten the lesser nobles pissed off. They captured him and forced him to sign the Magna Carta, which means "great charter" in Latin, on this date in 1215, on a little island near London called Runnymede. The document restricted the powers of the monarch, reestablished the rights of the Church, and gave the barons a voice in government. Almost as an afterthought, it also established a set of rights for the common man, which proved a resource in the writing of the Declaration of Independence by Thomas Jefferson. (See April 13 for more on Jefferson.) So we Americans have something to thank King John for—and it's not just the Robin Hood movies! Have a Royal Scandal and be thankful!

◀ ROYAL SCANDAL

- 1 part whiskey
- 1 part Southern Comfort Peach Liqueur
- 1 part amaretto
- 1 splash sweet and sour mix
- 1 splash pineapple juice

Combine all the ingredients in a shaker filled with ice. Shake well, strain into a shot glass, and serve.

JUNE

16

If you've been a faithful drinker, um, we mean reader, you will remember that the Soviets launched the first man into space. (See March 9 for information on Gary Gargarin.) Well, the Soviets were apparently a little more forward thinking in equal opportunities for women, too. On this date in 1963, the first female space traveler, Valentina Tereshkova, was launched into orbit aboard Vostok 6. Wow! Pretty cool for a stodgy Communist government, huh? One other cool thing: Tereshkova married another cosmonaut by the name of Andrian Nikolayev. Their daughter Elena was the first child to be born to two parents who had traveled in space. Doctors kept close tabs on her to make sure she didn't grow alien tentacles or develop super-duper "I can control your mind" ESP. She didn't, but it would have been cool! Try the Space Odyssey in Tereshkova's honor, and think of little Elena!

SPACE ODYSSEY

- 1 shot light rum
- 1 shot coconut rum
- 1 shot pineapple juice
  orange juice
- 1 dash grenadine
  maraschino cherries

Fill a cocktail glass with ice and add shots of white and coconut rum. Add a splash of pineapple juice and top with orange juice till almost full. Add grenadine for color and garnish with cherries.

We of the present day have had our share of scandals—the O.J. trial, the Martha Stewart trial, the Michael Jackson trial. We could go on forever! The daddy of all presidential scandals, however, even bigger than that of "My cigar has two uses" Bill Clinton, began to unravel on this date in 1971. Five men were arrested for breaking into the headquarters of the Democratic National Committee in the Watergate Hotel in Washington, DC. Eventually, their efforts to wiretap the office were linked back to Richard Nixon, Republican president. The irony is that he had won the recent election by a landslide and hadn't needed any information from the Dems to help him. In trying to persuade the American public of his innocence, he stated the famous phrase, "I am not a crook." Sounds like "I did not have sex with that woman" to us! Faced with impeachment, Nixon eventually resigned, his Vice President Gerald Ford took over, and then Ford gave Tricky Dick a pardon for his role in the scandal. This is juicier than a *Desperate*

Housewives episode! And it really happened! Consider that as you try a Dirty Dick's Downfall.

DIRTY DICK'S DOWNFALL

  2 oz gin
  $^1/_2$ oz dry vermouth
  $^1/_2$ oz bitters
  I twist lemon peel

In a mixing glass half-filled with ice cubes, combine the gin, vermouth, and bitters. Stir well. Strain into a cocktail glass and garnish with the lemon twist.

JUNE

18

There are those times in your life when everything is going well—you meet with success in all of your ventures. The folly in us all is that we never remember that good things come to an end. And so it was for Napoleon Bonaparte, who rose from nothing to become Napoleon I, Emperor of the French. He was a decisive military commander, winning many battles against seemingly impossible odds. He was overzealous, however, and campaigns meant to be routs of the enemy frequently failed. Such was the case at Waterloo, where Napoleon attempted to defeat the British Army, led by the Duke of Wellington. Plagued by bad weather—this was before Timberland made those comfy, waterproof boots—and the poor decisions of his underlings, Napoleon was defeated on this date in 1815. He was forced into exile for the remainder of his life. So devastating was the defeat that today, a person who endures such a resounding failure in his life is said to "meet his Waterloo." Poor Napoleon! One may question his motives and methods, but he did live according to his mantra, "Glory is fleeting, but obscurity is forever." Obscure he was not! Try the Napoleon as you figure out how you will battle obscurity.

NAPOLEON

2	oz gin
1/2	tsp orange curaçao
1/2	tsp Dubonnet
	French vermouth

Stir all the ingredients with ice, strain into a cocktail glass, and serve.

"Now don't say you can't swear off drinking; it's easy. I've done it a thousand times." –W. C. FIELDS

19

It seems like June is the month of the French—we've shared about them handing Paris to the Germans and the defeat of Napoleon at Waterloo. Now it is time to share some good news, for on this date in 1885, the Statue of Liberty arrived in the United States. It was designed by the famed sculptor Frédéric-Auguste Bartholdi, and was given from the people of France to the people of the United States as a symbol of friendship. The statue weighs 225 tons, and its height from base to the top of the torch is slightly over 151 feet. She's a big girl, isn't she? Lady Liberty was the tallest structure in New York City for over a decade. Also impressive was the way in which the city celebrated the unveiling: 20,000 marched in a parade while over a million watched. Now we can thank the French for delicous cheese and wine, the Statue of Liberty, AND thousands of extra dollars in clean-up costs! Have a Liberty Cocktail and be thankful for your own freedom . . . fries. Okay, we still call them french fries!

LIBERTY COCKTAIL

1	sugar cube
1	lime wedge
$3/4$	oz brandy
$3/4$	oz white rum

Press a sugar cube onto a lime wedge in a small Collins glass. Add the brandy and rum, stir well, and add ice cubes. Stir again, and serve.

JUNE

"Alcohol is good for you. My grandfather proved it irrevocably. He drank two quarts of booze every mature day of his life and lived to the age of 103. I was at the cremation—that fire would not go out."

–DAVE ASTOR

20

On this date in 1963, the United States and the USSR agreed to establish a hotline for instantaneous communication. The Americans and the Soviets were in the throes of the Cold War, having recently survived the Cuban Missile Crisis. The need for the leaders of the two superpowers to be able to speak immediately in the event of impending catastrophe was obvious. Thus, the two sides came together in Geneva to work out the "hotline," a series of phone, teletype, and telegraph wires linked through other major cities worldwide. Can you imagine paying that phone bill? Fortunately, the hotline never had to be used to fend off an atomic attack. Have a Soviet and rethink your own cell phone plan.

SOVIET ▶

1 1/2	oz vodka
1/2	oz dry sherry
1/2	oz dry vermouth
1	twist lemon peel

Shake all the ingredients (except the lemon peel) with ice and strain into an old-fashioned glass over ice cubes. Add the twist of lemon peel and serve.

JUNE

21

On this date in 1788, the U.S. Constitution went into effect after New Hampshire became the ninth state of the original thirteen to ratify it. Aren't we fortunate to have had so many smart Founding Fathers? We suspect we should thank the Founding Mothers more, however, because they were doing all of the work back on the homesteads while the menfolk were arguing over which states get how many votes. "Yeah, I know it's important to discuss a bicameral legislature, George, but these cows aren't milking themselves!" We should recognize the sacrifices the ladies made when we celebrate the founding of our country. Have a Country Time, described here, in their honor.

COUNTRY TIME

1	oz lemon-flavored vodka
1	oz vodka
1/2	oz raspberry Schnapps
2	lemon wedges
1	splash Sprite

Mix the vodkas and Schnapps in a shaker half-filled with ice cubes. Squeeze the lemon wedges into the mix and then shake until very cold. Strain into a large shot glass and top with a splash of Sprite. Serve.

22

Boys growing up in the 1970s sure had their choices of fantasy ladies, including all three (original!) *Charlie's Angels, Wonder Woman,* and our personal favorite, *The Bionic Woman. The Bionic Woman* was a series based on a government agent who had been secretly "bioengineered." She was mostly human, as in blonde hair, blue eyes, and curves, but she had some wicked cool powers. And, she was hot! The star of the show was Lindsay Wagner, who was born on this date in 1949. Try the Bionic Beaver and imagine what you'd be like if some of your body parts were bionic.

BIONIC BEAVER

12	oz lager
2	oz vodka
2	oz peach liqueur
2	oz sloe gin
2	oz gin
2	oz grenadine
	orange juice
	7-Up soda

Put a little crushed ice in the bottom of a pitcher, add the lager, and then add the vodka, peach liqueur, both gins, and grenadine. Top off the pitcher with equal amounts of orange juice and 7-Up. Stir.

23

Ouch. Ouch, ouch, ouch, ouch, ouch. Where does this pain come from? Just ask John Wayne Bobbitt. Why did he feel such pain? If you ask his wife Lorena, she'd say it was his fault. She complained that her husband abused her physically and wouldn't give her an orgasm. So she took justice into her own hands by taking John's johnson into her hands while he slept. She then cut the love muscle in two and drove off. Not reading the "dispose of properly" directions, Lorena tossed her half of John's member out the car window. Police were called to the scene, located the tallywacker, and it was surgically reattached.

Ouch. Ouch, ouch, ouch, ouch, ouch. We know that John must feel great to be whole again. We feel great because this story gets even weirder. To pay for his surgery, Mr. Bobbitt turned to the entertainment industry to earn extra cash—the adult entertainment industry. He starred in two pornographic movies, the titles of which we couldn't love more: *Frankenpenis* and *John Wayne Bobbitt . . . Uncut*. We can't make this stuff up, people! Enjoy the Upper Cut, described here, as you think about ways to protect your important assets.

UPPER CUT

1 1/3   oz Irish whisky
1 1/3   oz espresso
1 1/3   oz coffee
4   tsp brown sugar

Make just like an Irish coffee. Serve in an old-fashioned glass. Wait till it has cooled a bit. Drink all in one gulp.

24

How many artists do you know who can get wealthy by drawing fantastical figures of women with really pointy boobs? Well, we understate the talent of Pablo Picasso. He invented Cubism, the style of painting for which he is probably best known. Of course, what do we find the most appealing aspect of Picasso's life? The fact that he had so many lovers? The fact that his paintings have earned record prices in art auctions (and we mean millions of dollars!)? No, no, we admire him for the way he died: his final words were, apparently, "drink to me." There's a man with his priorities straight! Have a Picasso, the drink described here, as you drink to the artist, for it was on this date in 1901 that the first major exhibit of Picasso's work opened in Paris.

◀ PICASSO

    2   oz cranberry vodka
    1   oz banana syrup
        juice of 1 lime
        tonic water
    1   slice lime
    1   mint stem

Combine the vodka, syrup, and lime juice, in order, in a shaker half-filled with ice cubes and shake well. Strain into a Collins glass filled with ice cubes. Finish with tonic water. Garnish with a slice of lime, a stalk of mint leaves, and a straw.

25

Many of us have the ability to underestimate the negative impact of a bad decision. Fortunately, most of these decisions don't negatively affect hundreds of other people, unlike the bad decision made on this day in 1876. Lt. Col. George Armstrong Custer decided that the small number of Indians his scouts had seen could be defeated without waiting for reinforcements. His scouts apparently had limited math skills. By the time the soldiers realized that they were grossly outnumbered, they were surrounded. Custer and every man with him were killed at the Battle of Little Big Horn. Have a Massacre as you rethink some of your poor decisions, and be thankful you don't have a bunch of Indians chasing you.

MASSACRE

    2   oz tequila
    1/2 oz bitters
    4   oz ginger ale

Combine all the ingredients in a Collins glass with ice. Stir well and serve.

JUNE

26 On this date in 1945, the United Nations Charter was signed by 50 nations in a meeting in San Francisco. Originally, 50 countries participated, but the number eventually blossomed to include 191 countries. Of course, over the past several decades, some countries have come and gone. Some countries choose not to belong. Vatican City, for example, the world's tiniest country, considers itself ruled by a higher power. We think the United Nations is a pretty good thing. Celebrate its existence with an Around the World, described here.

AROUND THE WORLD

3/4	oz	dark rum
1/4	oz	cognac
1 1/4	oz	orange juice
1	oz	sweet and sour mix
1/4	oz	crème de noyaux
8	oz	crushed ice

Pour the rum, cognac, orange juice, sour mix, and crème de noyaux into a blender with the crushed ice. Blend until smooth, pour into a white wine glass, and serve.

27 Okay, when it takes the police in one of the United States' toughest cities several days to calm down a bunch of rioting gays, you know they must have been pissed off! What had been a supposedly typical, let's-raid-a-gay-bar-and-harass-the-boys event backfired. The gays started throwing coins at the policemen—seven plainclothes police and one in uniform—mocking them for the alleged acceptance of payoffs—called "gayola"—that they expected to receive to allow gay bars to stay open. The police retreated into the bar, locking the angry gays outside. After a few days, the crowd disbanded, but not before proving to the world that they just weren't going to take it from The Man anymore. The Summer of '69 was apparently quite a success. Have a Pink Police, described here, as you celebrate your brothers—and sisters—in arms!

PINK POLICE

2	oz	beer
2	oz	frozen pink lemonade
2	oz	vodka

Pour the beer into a pitcher. Add the frozen pink lemonade. Add the vodka (in place of the water), stir, and serve in a Collins glass.

28

Could the murder of an unpopular noble and his wife lead to global conflict? Nah! Impossible! No way! Unfortunately, the real answer is "Holy crap, yes!" for on this date in 1914, Archduke Ferdinand and his wife were assassinated. They had traveled from their home in the Austrian part of the Austro-Hungarian Empire to Sarajevo and were killed by an unhappy Serb. In retaliation for the assassination, Austria and Hungary declared war. It should have ended there, right? Nope. One by one, the countries of Europe were pulled into the conflict, beginning the worldwide conflagration we know as World War I. Fortunately, we have the United Nations now (see June 26), so maybe we won't see the End of the World. Try the drink described here, anyway.

END OF THE WORLD ▶

1/2 oz rum
1/2 oz bourbon
1/2 oz vodka

Serve warm. Straight into the shot glass.

29

Sacre bleu! Another French entry in the month of June. We have a love/hate relationship with the French, don't we? And we suspect the Tahitians have a similar relationship, for, on this date in 1880, France annexed the island. You can't blame France really, considering the gorgeous climate, beautiful view, and scantily clad residents. The island in French Polynesia was seen as a utopia of sorts, and word spread about the supposed paradise. Foreigners flocked to the island, the crew of the *HMS Bounty* among them. (See April 28 for information about that fun voyage!) The French, of course, thought they were bringing civilization to the "noble savages." Instead, they brought disease, alcohol, prostitution, and more disease. At the time of the island's "discovery" in the 1760s, the population was estimated at between 120,000 and 200,000 residents. By 1797, the population had plummeted to 16,000. This would probably constitute the "hate" part of the Tahiti/France relationship. Well, the artist Gauguin loved the Tahitians; he spent a great deal of time in Tahiti, painting the aforementioned scantily clad residents. Have a Tahitian Treat, as we're sure Monsieur Gauguin did many times.

TAHITIAN TREAT

- 1 oz Bacardi Limon rum
- 1 oz amaretto
- 4 oz cranberry juice
  Sprite soda

Fill a Collis glass with ice cubes. Add the rum, amaretto, and juice, and then the Sprite.

"Back in my rummy days, I would tremble and shake for hours upon arising. It was the only exercise I got." —W. C. FIELDS

30

One of our favorite femme fatales of all time has to be Scarlett O'Hara, the protagonist/antagonist of Margaret Mitchell's *Gone with the Wind*. The book was published on this date in 1936. Though reviews were mixed, it won the Pulitzer Prize for fiction the following year. The book was a smash success with the public, selling millions of copies in the first few years, and eventually topping 28 million. The movie, the rights of which earned Ms. Mitchell a cool $50,000, was a blockbuster as well. It earned 10 Academy Awards in a year that also produced *The Wizard of Oz* and *Mr. Smith Goes to Washington*. Not bad, eh? Try the Scarlett O'Hara, and if people complain about your drinking, reply, "Frankly, my dear, I don't give a damn."

SCARLETT O'HARA

- 2 oz Southern Comfort Peach Liqueur
- 6 oz cranberry juice
- 1 lime wedge

Pour the peach liqueur over ice in a Collins glass. Fill with cranberry juice. Squeeze one wedge of lime into your drink. Stir and serve.

"I exercise extreme self-control. I never drink anything stronger than gin before breakfast."

–W. C. FIELDS

JUNE

JULY

1

Oh Canada! It must be good to be free . . . sort of. Canada celebrates the establishment of its federal government on July 1st. Now known as Canada Day, it previously was known as Dominion Day and Confederation Day. The day commemorates the British North America Act of July 1, 1867, which gave Canadians home rule. But seeing as it's still a part of the Commonwealth and under the rule of the Queen, we think that, instead of "independence," it's really more like being left to watch the house while Mom runs out to do her errands. Break free, Canada, and have a cocktail!

CANADA COCKTAIL

1 1/2 oz Canadian whisky
 1/2 oz orange liqueur
 3 drops bitters
 1 sprig mint

Combine all the liquid ingredients over ice in an old-fashioned glass and garnish with a sprig of mint. Easy, eh?

2

The normally soft-spoken and well-behaved Alabama-born and -raised actress Polly Holliday hit it big on '70s TV as the brash, uninhibited, gum-smacking waitress Florence Jean Castleberry (better known as "Flo") on the popular sitcom *Alice*. It's hard to find anybody who grew up in the time of *Alice* who doesn't remember the larger-than-life Flo. Weekly, we were thrilled by the abuse she heaped on her boss, Mel, and sat riveted on the edge of our seats waiting for her signature one-liner that sooner or later always came: "Mel, kiss my grits!" Classic.

KISS MY GRITS ▶

 1/2 oz orange juice
 1/4 oz lemon juice
1 1/2 oz sloe gin
 1 tsp powdered sugar
 1 splash of club soda
 1 lime wedge

Combine all the ingredients except the club soda and lime wedge in a shaker with ice and shake well. Pour into a Collins glass filled with ice and top off with club soda. Stir well. Garnish with the lime and serve with a bowl of grits.

199.

3

It was on this day in 1940 that the legendary comedy team of Bud Abbott and Lou Costello debuted with their network radio show on NBC. It was a summer replacement for *The Fred Allen Show*, but it paved the way for future radio shows, movies, and television appearances for the team. The comedy duo were the highest-paid entertainers during World War II, and are probably best remembered for their baseball skit, "Who's on First?"

WHO'S ON FIRST?

2 shots vodka
  Orange juice
1 jigger whiskey
1 jigger amaretto

Combine all the ingredients in a shaker with ice. Shake well and serve in a Collins glass on the rocks.

4

We love big drinking holidays, and this day certainly rates up there with the best of them. The Fourth of July, American Independence Day, the day when drunken fathers across the country end up in the hospital after trying to light faulty fireworks for their children's amusement. How can we not love it? We stay away from roadside fireworks stands in July, but not away from the hooch. Enjoy the appropriately named cocktail below and remember: our forefathers died so you can drink.

FOURTH OF JULY

$1/2$ oz grenadine
$1/2$ oz blue curaçao
$1/2$ oz cream

Layer the ingredients in a shot glass, starting with the grenadine (red), then the curaçao (blue), and finish with the cream (white). Don't drink too many, though: the dawn's early light will come awfully quickly the next day.

5

It was itsy bitsy and teenie weenie, and in the mid-40s it revolutionized the world of bathing attire as we know it. The modern bikini was invented by engineer Louis Reard in Paris and introduced on this day in 1946. It was named after the Bikini Atoll, the site of nuclear weapons tests in the Marshall Islands, with the belief that the burst of excitement it would cause would be like the atomic bomb. Well, maybe when men got a gander at the skimpy two-piecer, they experienced a private little explosion, but most women were reluctant to go near it. So reluctant were they that in order to introduce it, Reard had to hire a nude dancer to model it. Oh, just wait until the thong is invented!

BIKINI COCKTAIL

    1   oz light rum
    2   oz vodka
    1/2 oz milk
    1   tsp sugar
        Juice of 1/2 lemon
    1   twist lemon peel

Combine all the ingredients except the lemon peel in a shaker with ice. Shake well, garnish with the twist of lemon, and serve in a cocktail glass.

"How well I remember my first encounter with The Devil's Brew. I happened to stumble across a case of bourbon—and went right on stumbling for several days thereafter."

—W. C. FIELDS

6

For the first time in history, women were enrolled into the United States Military Academy at West Point, New York, on this day in 1976. The hardships they endured were numerous and unimaginable, but none were so poignant or heartrending as the daily battle they faced to get the men to learn to put the toilet seat down. On May 28, 1980, 62 of these female cadets graduated and were commissioned as second lieutenants. Today, the Academy has an enrollment of more than 4,000 students of both genders.

FEMALE CADET

- 1 oz vodka
- 1 oz Midori
- 1 dash orange juice
- 1 dash pineapple juice

Shake all the ingredients over ice. Strain into a chilled cocktail, pony, or shot glass.

7

On this day in 1958, the 49th of the current 50 states dropped into place when President Eisenhower signed the Alaska Statehood Act, paving the way for its admission into the Union in early 1959. Oddly located, with no actual land connection to the first 48, Alaska shines and sticks out as the largest state in the Union, wresting the distinction from Texas. Everything may be bigger in the Lone Star State, but Alaska takes the cake for size. See whether everything starts looking bigger to you after a couple of these!

ALASKA COCKTAIL ▶

- 2 oz gin
- 1/2 oz Yellow Chartreuse
- 1 dash orange bitters

Combine all the ingredients in a mixing glass with ice. Stir well, then strain into a cocktail glass.

8

We can't decide whether it's worse to have to sit at the dining room table and tell your parents that you are a high-paid porn star with 13-inch . . . er, talent, or tell them that you've been convicted of receiving stolen property, which is what happened to porn star John Holmes on this day in 1982. Regardless, we're pretty sure that either is better than having to tell them that you're addicted to crack cocaine and being investigated for involvement in a high-profile murder case, which also happened to Holmes. By the time he had to explain that he had lost his edge in the straight porn world and was doing gay porn, we suspect his parents were used to disappointing news from their little boy. Oh well, it's a slippery, slippery slope, we suppose. Have a Slippery Dick and hope you never have to find out!

> "I never drink water. I'm afraid it will become habit-forming."
>
> –W. C. FIELDS

SLIPPERY DICK

1 ½ oz butterscotch Schnapps
2 oz Bailey's Irish Cream
3–4 oz half-and-half

Combine all the ingredients over ice in a 10- to 12-ounce (or perhaps 13, hmmm) rocks/old-fashioned glass.

9

On July 9, 1956, the eternally young Dick Clark made his debut on *American Bandstand*, the television dance show that dominated the airwaves for 50 years (nationally for 30) and had nearly every major rock artist on with the exception of Elvis Presley and the Beatles. Sadly, it wasn't long after MTV hit the cable wires that Americans were simply done with dance shows, and *American Bandstand* slunk into the shadows. Apparently, video went on a killing spree, doing away with not only the radio star but also the dance show star. But don't worry, Dick, New Year's Eve in Times Square is as timeless as you are.

DANCE WITH A DREAM

2 oz brandy
$^1/_2$ oz Triple Sec
1 tsp anisette

Combine all the ingredients in a shaker with ice. Shake well, then strain into a cocktail glass.

"I like to keep a bottle of stimulant handy in case I see a snake, which I also keep handy."

—W. C. FIELDS

"We shall drink to our partnership. Do you like gin? It is my only weakness."

—ERNEST THESIGER, AS DR. PRETORIUS IN *THE BRIDE OF FRANKENSTEIN*

10

Coca-Cola would like to teach the world to sing in perfect harmony (ha, now you have it stuck in your head!). But as many of us remember, it was mayhem, far from harmony, in the early '80s, when the company shook up its formula and introduced "New Coke" to a fickle American market. Nobody liked it. Actually, we think that the popular kids didn't like it and everybody else just hopped on board. Regardless, the trick worked. (What, you don't think this was all a big accident, do you?) This day in 1985 marked the end of Coca-Cola's "New Coke" experiment. The company started restocking the shelves with "Classic Coke" the next day, to the joy of everybody except PepsiCo, which were allegedly responsible for Coke's sly little marketing move in the first place. How do you like that challenge, Pepsi?

GOLDEN COKE ▶

12 oz Coca-Cola
1 oz Goldschlager cinnamon Schnapps

Pour Schnapps into old-fashioned glass over ice. Fill with cola.

11

The date was July 11, 1914. A very young southpaw named George Herman Ruth made his major-league debut for the Boston Red Sox. He was the victor in a 4-3 nipping of the lowly Cleveland Naps. That was how the Babe began as a pitcher, and he just kept getting better. He was sold to the Yankees for $125,000 in 1920, setting into motion what many Bostonians know as the Curse of the Bambino, a curse that kept the Sox from winning a World Series championship for an astonishing 86 years. Yikes, and we thought it was cold in Boston before all this!

SLUGGER'S DELIGHT

12 oz Rock and Rye liqueur
1 shot 151 proof rum

Pour the Rock and Rye into a Collins glass with ice. While the Rock and Rye is still fizzing, quickly add the 151 proof rum. Stir thoroughly before drinking.

12

One of the top-selling children's toys of all time went on sale on this day in 1960, when the first Etch A Sketch hit shelves nationwide. The red-framed square "palette" allowed children and adults to create two-dimensional masterpieces with only two knobs in the bottom two corners. The toy makers didn't realize, however, the volatility of the product they were putting into the hands of the consumer, as families have been ripped apart and friendships destroyed forever with one single act: the upside-down shake, shake, shake that wiped the screen clean. In honor of this magnificent toy, we designed the cover of this book with an Etch A Sketch. Really . . .

ARTIST'S SPECIAL

1 oz Scotch whisky
1 oz sweet sherry
$1/2$ oz grenadine
$1/2$ oz lemon juice

Combine all the ingredients in a shaker with ice. Shake well, then strain into a cocktail glass over ice.

13

Frank Sinatra, considered one of the finest vocalists of all time and renowned for his impeccable phrasing and timing, made his recording debut with the Harry James Band on this day in 1939. Because of a booming music and screen career and his position in the high-profile group of musical bad boys, the Rat Pack, Sinatra had a larger-than-life presence in the public eye and became an American icon, known for his brash, often pompous attitude, as embodied by his signature song "My Way." Below is a classic that hearkens back to Sinatra's heyday. Pull out the shaker and try it "our way."

VODKA MARTINI

1 1/2 oz vodka
   3/4 oz dry vermouth
   1   green olive

Combine the vodka and vermouth in a shaker with ice. Shake well and strain into a cocktail glass, garnish with an olive, and serve.

"I never drink water; that is the stuff that rusts pipes."

—W. C. FIELDS

14

Today is the day we celebrate France's independence. It's Bastille Day! As you mix up the tasty treat below, ponder all of the wonderful things the French have given the world: French Bread, French Nails, French Braids, French Cuffs, French Kissing, French's Mustard, French Stewart, Dawn French, Samuel French, *The French Connection*, *The French Lieutenant's Woman*, French Doors, the French Quarter, French Dressing, the French Maid, *How the French Stole Christmas* . . . Wait a minute—that last one doesn't seem quite right. Oh well, vive la France!

◀ **FRENCH REVOLUTION**

- 2 oz brandy
- 1/2 oz framboise liqueur
- 3 oz chilled Champagne

Pour the brandy and liqueur into a mixing glass over ice. Stir well, and strain into a Champagne flute. Add the Champagne, and serve.

"No government could survive without champagne . . . in the throats of our diplomatic people [it] is like oil in the wheels of an engine."

—JOSEPH DARGENT

15

Desperate housewives' lives got a lot more interesting on this day in 1968, when ABC first presented the soap opera *One Life to Live*. It wasn't the first soap on the air, but it quickly became the most popular. Each day, millions still tune in to find out who's having an affair with whom, whose illegitimate child will show up out of the blue, who's getting murdered, who's doing the murdering, who's checking into rehab, who's breaking out of rehab, who's sleeping with a member of the same sex, and who's sleeping with an alien. So, really, it's just like real life.

SOAP OPERA SPECIAL

1 oz tequila
1 oz gin
1 oz white rum
1 oz vodka
1 oz pineapple juice
1 oz orange juice
1 oz sweet and sour mix

Kick husband out, start affair with the gardener, have illegitimate child who will eventually sue you and run away with an alien, then combine all ingredients over ice in a shaker, shake well, slap your recently surfaced long-lost sibling, strain into an old-fashioned glass, drink, and wake up the next day to discover it was all a bad dream.

16

On July 16, 1945, the United States stretched its wings further than it ever had before with terrifying results when it conducted its first test of the atomic bomb at White Sands Missile Range in south central New Mexico. At 05:29 a.m., the bomb exploded, lighting the New Mexican sky for hundreds of miles in every direction. It left a crater in the desert 3 meters deep and 330 meters wide. As J. Robert Oppenheimer, the father of the atomic bomb, watched the demonstration, he muttered a line from the Hindu scripture the Bhagavad Gita: "I am become Death, the destroyer of worlds." Test director Kenneth Bainbridge was said to have replied, "Now we are all sons of bitches." Poetic, really . . .

BOMB POP

2 oz raspberry vodka
4 oz lemonade
1 splash of blue curacao

Combine the ingredients over ice in a small rocks glass, and serve. Sure to be an explosive hit.

17

One man's dream became a reality on July 17, 1955, when children were able to enter a magical place and leave their problems behind while they enjoyed rides and shows in imaginary places. No, we're not talking about Michael Jackson's Neverland Ranch, we're talking about Disneyland in Anaheim, California. The self-proclaimed "happiest place on Earth" introduced children and adults alike to the worlds of Adventureland and Fantasyland, among others. While the children were thrilled, fathers tittered as they imagined their own "fantasylands." Sorry, Pop, leave that naughtiness at home and get your picture taken with the life-sized mouse.

MAD HATTER

$1/4$ oz vodka
$1/4$ oz peach Schnapps
$1/4$ oz lemonade
$1/4$ oz cola

Combine all the ingredients in a shaker filled with ice. Shake, strain, and serve straight up in a shot glass. Serve at your next tea party.

"Work is the curse of the drinking classes."

—BOB HOPE, AS WILLY CAMPBELL, IN *THE CAT AND THE CANARY*

JULY

18

Hunter S. Thompson was born on July 18, 1937. An American journalist and author, he was known for his flamboyant writing style, most famously demonstrated in his popular Beat-era novel *Fear and Loathing in Las Vegas*, which blurred the distinctions between writer and subject and fiction and nonfiction. The distinction that wasn't blurred, however, was that between sober and high as a freaking kite. It is quite clear straight through that he didn't have a sober moment when writing it. Thompson committed suicide in early 2005, but ever the entertainer, he left instructions that his ashes be shot out of a cannon of his own design as Bob Dylan's "Mr. Tambourine Man" played in the background. No, really, we don't make this stuff up, people.

ACID TRIP

1 1/2 oz melon liqueur
  1/2 oz gin
  1/2 oz vodka
  1/2 oz rum
  1/2 oz tequila

Combine all the ingredients in a shaker filled with ice. Shake well and strain into a cocktail glass. Whoa, groovy, man!

19

On this day in 1993, President Bill Clinton announced what has become famously known as the "Don't Ask, Don't Tell" policy, which allows gays and lesbians to serve in the military, but only if they don't disclose their sexuality or engage in homosexual activity. It also promises that as long as they stay on the straight (so to speak) and narrow, they will not be investigated. We think this policy is idiotic, yep, there, we said it. We're sticking with the "separate but equal is not equal" point of view, and standing behind our gays in the military and their right to be out and proud and shoot their guns.

GAY MARINE ❯

  4 sprigs mint
4–5 lime wedges
  1 tbsp sugar
  1/2 oz Grand Marnier
1 1/2 oz Mount Gay Barbados rum
1–2 oz apple juice

Muddle three of the mint sprigs and the lime wedges with cane sugar and Grand Marnier in a cocktail shaker. Add crushed ice and pour in the Mount Gay Barbados rum. Stir and top up with apple juice. Serve in an old-fashioned glass with the remaining mint sprig as garnish. We promise you, this drink is faaaaaaabulous!

215

"Come on.
Let's get
something
to eat.
I'm thirsty."

—WILLIAM POWELL AS
NICK CHARLES, IN
AFTER THE THIN MAN

"One small step for man, one giant step for mankind" were the words Neil Armstrong broadcast to the world on this day in 1969, when he became the first man to walk on the moon. The world sat riveted in front of their black-and-white televisions and watched as Armstrong stepped out of the lunar module and onto the surface. There's something special about those first few steps: it wasn't long before Armstrong was climbing stairs, running with scissors, and terrorizing all the rest of the astronauts on the playground. All right, Neil, naptime!

HIGH MOON

1 1/2 oz framboise liqueur
1 oz apricot brandy
1/2 oz cognac
1 tsp grenadine
4 1/2 oz sparkling bitter lemon soda
1 maraschino cherry
1 half-slice lemon

Combine all the liquid ingredients in an ice-filled Collins glass and stir well. Garnish with a cherry and a half-slice of lemon and serve.

21

On this day in 1873, the first train robbery in America was pulled off by Jesse James and his gang. The Rock Island Express was rolling through Adair, Iowa, when James and his cronies boarded the train and took $3,000 from its passengers. Today, train robbery has taken on a completely different meaning every time we pay the exorbitant fares to ride Amtrak's express trains along the Eastern seaboard. Our suggestion that counter attendants wear cowboy hats and bandanas has apparently fallen on deaf ears.

FLAMING JESSE

1	oz coconut rum
1/2	oz vodka
1/2	oz Bailey's Irish Cream
4–6	oz orange juice
1	slice orange

Combine all the ingredients except the orange slice in a shaker with ice. Shake, strain into a Collins glass, garnish with the orange slice, and serve.

"I'll admit I may have seen better days . . . but I'm still not to be had for the price of a cocktail, like a salted peanut."

—BETTE DAVIS AS MARGO CHANNING, IN *ALL ABOUT EVE*

JULY

22

On July 22, 1994, O.J. Simpson (no, it doesn't stand for Orange Juice, but we like it better that way) pleaded innocent to the murder of his ex-wife, Nicole, and her friend, Ronald Goldman. Who doesn't remember watching every moment of the whole thing? When we think back on the media circus of the O.J. Simpson affair, our favorite memories are of the car chase through the streets of L.A. We remember grilling burgers, making cocktails, and inventing a drinking game on the spot, where everybody in the room had to drink every time we saw a spectator holding a sign that read: Head for the border, O.J.!

"Drinking spirits cannot cause spiritual damage."

—JOSÉ BERGAMÍN

◄ CUT TO THE CHASE

- 1 part bourbon whiskey
- 1 part orange juice
- 1 part tomato juice
- 1 dash soda water
- 1 slice lime

Pour the liquid ingredients over two crushed ice cubes in an old-fashioned glass. Stir, and garnish with a slice of lime.

Dear *Penthouse*, I never thought I'd be writing one of these letters, but . . . On this day in 1984, Vanessa Williams became the first Miss America to relinquish her title. Why, you ask? What sort of scandal could possibly lead somebody with the weighty and all-important title of Miss America to give up her crown? Well, nudity, of course, you silly. It would seem that what we want as a society is to see our reigning beauty queen mostly naked, but once she reveals the whole enchilada, we're done with her. What an odd people we are! Miss Williams, also the first African-American Miss America, had allowed a photographer to shoot her naked years before, after he promised that the photos were completely confidential and would never go anywhere. Surprise of all surprises, though, once Vanessa became Miss America, the photographer turned right around and sold them to *Penthouse*—can you imagine?! As shocking and humiliating as it must have been for Vanessa in 1984, it launched a career that is still at the top of its game today. Therefore, we suggest that everybody pose nude for top-shelf magazines in order to further your careers. After all, it's the American way.

NAKED TWISTER

- 1 oz melon liqueur
- 1/2 oz vodka
- 1/2 oz citrus liqueur
  pineapple juice
- 1 splash 7-Up
- 1 maraschino cherry

Pour the melon liqueur, vodka, and citrus liqueur into a pint glass. Almost fill with pineapple juice and top off with 7-Up. Garnish with a cherry and serve.

What to do **24**
about Tennessee?
We're guessing that
was the question on the lips of
lawmakers in 1866, when after
much debate, Tennessee became
the first state to be readmitted to
the Union after the Civil War. We
think it must have gone something like this:

IMPORTANT NORTHERN POLITICIAN #1:
Tennessee wants back in, what
should we do?

IMPORTANT NORTHERN POLITICIAN #2:
Do they know the secret pass-
word?

IMPORTANT NORTHERN POLITICIAN #1:
Well, no, but they're offering some
damn good whiskey as a bribe.

IMPORTANT NORTHERN POLITICIAN #2:
Guess we'd better let 'em in, then.
Think they've got any tobacco?

TENNESSEE TEA ▶

  1 part Tennessee whiskey
  1 part Triple Sec
  1 part sweet and sour mix
  2 parts cola

Combine all the ingredients and pour
over ice into a Mason jar.

JULY

21

> "Ale, man, ale's the stuff to drink
> For fellows whom it hurts to think."

—A.E. HOUSMAN

25

Another one of those thrilling days in history, July 25, 1871, was the day Seth Wheeler of Albany, New York, patented perforated toilet paper. This falls into the category of inventions we wish we knew the origins of. I mean, we can only imagine what caused poor Seth, sitting on his throne, to think: "Hey, this would be a hell of a lot easier if it separated smoothly from the roll. I know, I think I'll invent perforated toilet paper!" Thanks to Seth and his active imagination, we all take care of business just a little bit easier, so tear off a square and raise your glasses to Seth in Albany, who just couldn't take the unraveling for one more day.

ON THE SQUARE

1   oz apricot brandy
$^1/_2$ oz gin
$^1/_2$ oz Calvados brandy

Combine the apricot brandy, gin, and Calvados brandy in a mixing glass with ice. Stir well, strain into a cocktail glass, and serve.

26

Sir Michael Philip "Mick" Jagger was born on this day in 1943 in Kent, England. He is obviously most famous for being the lead singer and cofounder of the Rolling Stones. His second claim to fame is having the largest and most animated lips in show business. His juicy love life had him paired with several famous women over the years, but perhaps the most publicized was his nine-year marriage to Texas model Jerry Hall in the '90s. But, apparently, Mick couldn't get no satisfaction, because that marriage came to a screeching halt in 1999. Sorry, Mick, you really can't always get what you want.

JAGGER'S SATISFACTION

    1   oz bourbon whiskey
    ¹/₂ oz Compari bitters
    ¹/₂ oz sweet sherry
    ¹/₂ oz Rum Tree liqueur
    4   oz lemonade

Combine all the ingredients in an ice-filled Collins glass, stir well, and serve.

"Why don't you get out of that wet coat and into a dry martini?"

—ROBERT BENCHLEY AS ALBERT OSBORNE, IN *THE MAJOR AND THE MINOR*

JULY

"Look, sweetheart, I can drink you under any goddamn table you want, so don't worry about me."

27

Home to 85 of the world's 105 ecosystems, Peru is bursting not only with the toughest terrains to traverse on the planet, but is also a veritable explosion of culinary treasures. From beef to fish to fruits and vegetables nobody's ever heard of, it is one rockin' place to get a bite to eat. Of course, we're not so concerned with the eating as we are with the drinking, and so we did a little research to find the Peruvian national drink. So today, in honor of Peruvian Independence Day, whip yourself up a Pisco Sour. Pisco is the Peruvian national spirit, and the drink below gave us tons of spirit . . . Yes, that's what we're calling it now (i.e., I woke up with one hell of a spirit headache this morning, whew!).

PISCO SOUR

  2 oz pisco
  1 oz lime juice
  1/4 oz simple syrup
  1/2 egg white
  1 dash bitters

Shake the pisco, lime juice, simple syrup, and egg white vigorously with ice. Strain into a Champagne flute, and add the bitters as an aromatic garnish.

28

Second only to "The Mouse," Bugs Bunny was the most enduring American cartoon character of the twentieth century. The Warner Brothers' star was a cocky, wisecracking, good-hearted hare who battled Elmer Fudd, Daffy Duck, and other slapstick nemeses in dozens of animated short films. Bugs's screen debut took place on this day in 1940, when he showed up in the animated short *A Wild Hare* and uttered his trademark line, "What's up, Doc?" We love Bugs, but have often wondered about his mental state. I mean, we're concerned with the cross-dressing, sure, but how many wrong turns can you take in Albuquerque? While you consider that, why not pay tribute to the voice of Bugs Bunny, Mel Blanc.

MEL'S SWING

- 1 oz Midori
- 1 oz crème de cassis
- 4 oz grapefruit juice

Shake all the ingredients with ice cubes in a cocktail shaker. Strain into a highball glass and serve. Th-th-th-th-that's all, folks!

LADY ASTOR:

"Winston, if I were your wife I'd put poison in your coffee."

WINSTON:

"Nancy, if I were your husband I'd drink it."

—WINSTON CHURCHILL

"Nothing in Nature's sober found, But an eternal health goes round. Fill up the bowl, then, fill it high, Fill all the glasses there— for why should every creature drink but I? Why, man of morals, tell me why?"

—ABRAHAM COWLEY

It was the wedding of the century, and the entire world either went to bed late or woke up early in order to sit, eyes glazed over, staring at the television as Britain's Prince Charles married Lady Diana Spencer on this day in 1981 in St. Paul's Cathedral in London. The wedding was fairy-tale perfection; the marriage, unfortunately, was not. But it sure made for good television: the affairs, the eating disorders, the lies, the deceit, the staff betrayals, the divorce, and, of course, the makeovers! As far as we're concerned, it was the best drama on TV for 17 years straight!

DIANA COCKTAIL ❯

2 oz white crème de menthe
1/2 oz brandy

Pour the white crème de menthe into a brandy snifter filled with crushed ice. Carefully pour the brandy over the back of a teaspoon to float it on top of the crème de menthe. Serve.

30

On this day in 1975, the former Teamsters Union president Jimmy Hoffa disappeared in suburban Detroit. Although Hoffa was presumed dead, his remains have never been found. There are many guesses as to what happened to him. Among these are that Hoffa was dumped from a boat into Lake St. Clair, Lake Huron, or Lake Erie; or is buried in Northern Michigan, in the yard of either his house in Bloomfield or another Detroit-area house, under the New Jersey Turnpike, in an abandoned shaft of a coal mine near Pittston, Pennsylvania, somewhere in Fresh Kills landfill in Staten Island, New York, under the end zone at Giants Stadium in New Jersey, or at the PJP Landfill in Jersey City underneath the Pulaski Skyway. Others theorize that Hoffa's corpse was actually put in a cement-making machine and turned into cement, dissolved in an acid tank used to rechrome car bumpers, put in a car-crusher at a wrecking yard, or put into a smelter and melted in a local Detroit plant. Options, we definitely like options. In honor of Hoffa, we've chosen a drink that goes along with our favorite theory.

CEMENT MIXER

$^1/_2$ oz tequila
$^1/_2$ oz half-and-half

Combine the tequila and half-and-half in a shot glass and serve. Beware, however: too many of these and you'll want to disappear.

31

Leo, the MGM lion seen at the beginning of every MGM feature film, made his debut on this day in 1928. He roared before the movie *White Shadows in the South Seas*. Of course, the roar was heard via a phonograph record, since it was a silent movie. As it was the silent age, the phonograph record only turned out to be the second-best option. Earlier tests with actually having the lion in the theater turned out horribly, horribly badly. We mean he ate everybody's popcorn and roared through the whole movie, and at one point his cell phone rang and he had a five-minute-long conversation with one of his lion friends back at the zoo. What did you think we meant?

LEO THE LION

2 oz dry vermouth
1/2 oz brandy
1 tsp white crème de menthe

Combine the vermouth, brandy, and crème de menthe in a mixing glass with ice. Stir well, strain into a cocktail glass, and serve.

"When I have one martini, I feel bigger, wiser, taller. When I have the second, I feel superlative. When I have more, there's no holding me."

—WILLIAM FAULKNER

1 AUGUST 2

We've said it before and we'll say it again: we love these newer norms of social mores! This is certainly most noticeable in today's standards for garb: girls in half-shirts, boys with no shirts, both sexes in low-cut jeans. We haven't seen this much flesh since the 1970s! While some may ask, "Who's to blame?" we prefer to say, "Thank you!" And we'd like to thank MTV, yes Music Television, more than anyone. Who can forget their spring break parties, hosted at fabulous college-kid resorts in Miami, Mexico, and several tropical islands? The video clips are sent back to us in our warm, cozy living rooms to satisfy our voyeuristic sides, all for the price of a monthly cable bill. Have a Rolling Rock and Roll and help us celebrate MTV's birthday, for on this date in 1981, the music video cable channel made its debut.

On this date in 1824, Fifth Avenue opened in New York City. At its start, the street was home only to residences—very expensive residences. It wasn't until 1906 that a retail store opened on this famed fashion boulevard. The neighbors were unhappy, of course, despite the fact that the tony shop was built to resemble a Florentine palace. Other shops opened, and they, too, looked more like expensive homes rather than places to buy new duds. When Lord and Taylor opened, with its very commercial look, the neighbors were so upset that they moved farther up the road. More retailers moved in, and Fifth Avenue became known as a place to do your shopping—very expensive shopping. Celebrate this stylish street with a drink—the Fifth Avenue, described here.

ROLLING ROCK AND ROLL

l   pint Rolling Rock lager
l   oz whiskey

Drop a shot glass filled with whiskey into a beer mug filled with Rolling Rock lager and serve.

FIFTH AVENUE ▶

$^1/2$ oz crème de cacao
$^1/2$ oz apricot brandy
l   tbsp light cream

Layer the ingredients into a parfait glass so that each ingredient floats on the preceding one. Serve without mixing.

"Do not allow children to mix drinks. It is unseemly and they use too much vermouth."

—STEVE ALLEN

3

So, you've determined that there must be an easier way to get to faraway ports in the East. You sail for days, then weeks, stretching to a couple of months, and you finally hit land. You greet the darker-skinned inhabitants, convinced that you've arrived in India, your destination. You even call them Indians! You become famous: your name, Christopher Columbus, becomes known the world over and endures through history. One more thing: you are also a major dumb-ass, because you are about 9,000 miles away from where you think you are! Try the Columbus Cocktail, described here, for on this date in 1492, Chris and his crew set off on the *Nina*, the *Pinta*, and the *Santa Maria*.

COLUMBUS COCKTAIL

1 ¹/₂ oz gold rum
³/₄ oz apricot brandy
1 oz lime juice
1 slice lime

Combine the liquid ingredients in a shaker with ice. Shake well, garnish with a lime slice, and serve in a cocktail glass.

4

On this date in 1892, Andrew and Abby Borden met their demise in their home in Fall River, Massachusetts. Lizzie, Andrew's daughter from a previous marriage, was accused of the killings. We can only surmise that it had something to do with the evil stepmother thing, but, come on, an axe? How about a nice slow poisoning or maybe a push down a well? You'll be happy to know that she was later acquitted. Enjoy the Axe Murderer as you contemplate the fates of Andrew, Abby, and Lizzie Borden.

AXE MURDERER

- 1 part rum
- 1 part pineapple juice
- 1 part gin
- 1 part tequila
- 1 part Triple Sec
- 1 part vodka
- 1 part Southern Comfort
- 1 part amaretto
- 1 splash citrus soda
- 1 splash grenadine
- 1 slice lime

Shake all the liquid ingredients with ice. Pour everything, including the ice, into an old fashioned glass. Garnish with a slice of lime.

"One martini is alright, two is too many, three is not enough."

—JAMES THURBER

AUGUST

5

On this date in 1962, Norma Jean Baker was found dead in her Los Angeles home of an apparent overdose. This wouldn't be news, of course, since people O.D. in L.A. like, ohmygawd, on a daily basis. Why are we reporting about this event, then? Well, Norma Jean's screen name was Marilyn Monroe, making the deceased one of the most famous women on the planet. The other reason to report the event: the speculation! Though kept under cover then, rumors abound now about Monroe's purported relationship with two brothers. So what, you say, people can date siblings, right? Yes, they can and they do. However, these two brothers were Kennedys: JFK and RFK, the president and attorney general of the United States at the time. Was the overdose accidental? Did Monroe threaten to go public with her relationships? Did she do a bang-up job singing "Happy Birthday" to the president while wearing her fabulous sequined dress? Only this last question can be answered with an emphatic yes! Mull it all over as you have a Marilyn Monroe, described here.

◀ MARILYN MONROE

    4   oz Champagne
    I   oz apple brandy
    I   tsp grenadine
    2   maraschino cherries

Combine the liquid ingredients in a wine glass and stir. Serve with two cherries on a stick. Play the heart-wrenching song "Candle in the Wind" written by Elton John. But avoid taking too many antidepressants!

AUGUST

6

Okay, we know what happens when you get mixed up with a president in a naughty relationship. Look at poor Norma Jean on yesterday's date. However, did one Miss Monica Lewinsky learn from the mistakes of her predecessors? No-sir-ree! The cheerful, chipper intern was drawn to President William Jefferson Clinton, enamored of his power, his charm, and his enormous . . . um, cigar. According to reports, Bill used a cigar as a phallus during a tryst in the White House. We hope it wasn't lit! Who can keep a secret about a relationship with the Prez? Monica couldn't! She spilled the beans to her confidante Linda Tripp, who then wore a wire during a sting operation. The relationship between Lewinsky and Clinton became known worldwide. A world leader schtupping an intern? What a scandal! Lewinsky was forced to testify before a grand jury on this date in 1998 for 8½ hours. Have a Cigar Lover's Martini, described here, and think about whom you've shared your secrets with.

CIGAR LOVER'S MARTINI

2 ½ oz cognac
½ oz tawny port
1 twist orange peel

Combine the cognac and port with ice in a mixing glass and stir to chill. Strain into a chilled cocktaili glass, garnish with a twist of orange peel, and serve.

7

What would it take to have you walk a tightrope 1,350 feet in the air? How about if you walked the tightrope between two buildings above New York City streets? On this date in 1974, that is exactly what happened. A Frenchman by the name of Philippe Petit tightroped his way between the twin towers of the World Trade Center. This being New York City, we suspect most of the pedestrians were chanting something like, "You're gonna fall, you're gonna fall," but this has yet to be confirmed. Also unconfirmed: Petit was trying to prove how manly he was despite his name. Do you have something to prove, Monsieur Philippe? Have a Daredevil, described here, as you think about the riskiest thing you've ever done. Extra points if it's gotten you on Jerry Springer!

> "I envy people who drink; at least they know what to blame everything on."
>
> —OSCAR LEVANT

DAREDEVIL

- 1 oz Bacardi 151 proof rum
- 1/2 oz dark rum
- 2 oz orange juice
- 1 oz cranberry juice
- 1 oz pineapple juice
- 1 splash 7-Up

Combine the ingredients in a Collins glass filled with ice.

8

If you've been reading and drinking faithfully, you will recall that five men were arrested for breaking into the Democratic National Committee offices in the Watergate Hotel on June 17, 1972. More than two years later, on this date in 1974, President Nixon announced his resignation after he was finally linked to the scandal. Rather than face impeachment, Nixon offered the nation his resignation, live on television. He was the first American president to do so. We've all learned a lesson, haven't we? If you're gonna lie, don't get caught doing it. Especially on recordings that you yourself have sanctioned. Have a Nixon, described here, and be thankful you've never lied. About important matters. While being recorded.

NIXON

1–2   oz spiced rum
6   oz citrus soda

Pour the spiced rum into a Collins glass with ice. Fill with soda, stir, and serve.

9

How many years can a person lead a rock-and-roll lifestyle before it catches up with him? Present-day rockers such as those in the Rolling Stones and Aerosmith make it seem like forever. Alas, one rocker, Jerry Garcia, did not make it that long. He died of a heart attack in San Francisco on this date in 1995. The front man for the Grateful Dead, he championed the cause of the good time. Try the Grateful Dead, described here, in Jerry's honor.

GRATEFUL DEAD ❯

1 part tequila
1 part vodka
1 part light rum
1 part gin
1 part Chambord raspberry liqueur

Combine the ingredients in a shaker with ice. Shake well and serve in a Collins glass.

10

Paving the way for Britney Spears, Christina Aguilera, and Pink, Madonna sang, danced, and sexed her way into rock history on this date in 1985. She became the first female solo artist to sell five million copies of a record, in this case her album "Like a Virgin." Our question is, what does "like a virgin" mean? How are you like a virgin, Madonna? Do you giggle when boys touch you and say things like, "I'm not ready yet?" Do you still get to wear white to your wedding? How about off-white? We bought the album like everyone else in the '80s, so obviously we appreciate the mystique. We also appreciate that Madonna has sold more than 130 million albums since, making her very wealthy. She's married now and has two children. This brings us to our last question: if you have two kids, doesn't this prove you're not a virgin? Consider that as you try the Platinum Blonde, in honor of Madonna's "like-a-blonde" hair.

PLATINUM BLONDE

- 1 oz gold rum
- 1 oz Grand Marnier
- 3/4 oz double cream

Combine the ingredients in a shaker with ice. Shake well, strain, and serve in a brandy snifter.

11

On this date in 1933, the Reverend Jerry Falwell was born. He made his name as a televangelist, bringing people the words of Jesus during weekly broadcasts. Just a run-of-the-mill Christian activist, right? Well, except Falwell took this interesting next step: he targeted the character of a popular kids' show, known as Tinky Winky, for being gay. How would the Rev know Mr. Winky was gay? (We want to know how he even knew Tinky was a Mr.?!?!) Well, the character was purple—the gay color—and had a triangle on his head—the gay symbol. Lastly, Tinky carried a purse. We would just like to say that we support Tinky no matter what his—or her—or its—orientation! Have a Tinky Winky cocktail to show your support, too.

"One can drink too much, but one never drinks enough."

–EDWARD BURKE

TINKY WINKY

1 1/2 oz gin
10 oz Wink grapefruit-lemon soda
1 splash Chambord raspberry liqueur

Combine all the ingredients over ice and serve in an old-fashioned glass.

12

> "If the headache would only precede the intoxication, alcoholism would be a virtue."
>
> –SAMUEL BUTLER

In high school, we all knew who the popular kids were. Maybe we wanted to eat at the cafeteria table with them, or we longed to have their talent on the football field or basketball court. Maybe we wanted to be Prom King or Queen, too, or at least part of the Prom "court" like the other sycophants. If the popular kids were nice, it made the situation even more difficult: "They're being nice to me; maybe they'll invite me to their parties." Deep down inside, we knew it would be better if we could hate the cool kids, openly showing our disdain for them as we went off to band practice or the AV Club meeting. When the popular kids threw their popularity in our faces, it was fair game to hate their guts. So how about this: as the Beatles invaded the United States, kick-starting the rock 'n' roll movement, fans thronged their buses and performances. Girls swooned at the very sight of the four band members. They sold millions of records. After realizing the impact of his band on the American music scene,

John Lennon stated, "The Beatles are more popular than Jesus." Oops! Not a smart thing to say, John! His remark caused an uproar, and eventually, on this date in 1966, Lennon apologized at a news conference in Chicago for being one of the popular kids we hate. Nobody fools with Jesus! Have a Whop Me Down Sweet Jesus, described here, and be thankful no one knows you.

WHOP ME DOWN SWEET JESUS

1	oz vodka
1	oz gin
1	oz light rum
1	oz tequila
1	oz Triple Sec
1 1/2–2	oz blue curaçao
1	splash sweet and sour mix
1	splash citrus soda

Combine all the ingredients in a shaker with ice. Shake well, lift your eyes to heaven, and serve in a mason jar.

13

Viva la revolucion! On this date in 1926, Fidel Castro, the man who brought Communism to Cuba, was born. After several interesting attempts, he overthrew the government of Fulgencio Batista and laid claim to power in 1959. He has served as the country's leader ever since. Early on, he upset American businesses by nationalizing industries. President Eisenhower enacted an economic embargo, and American tourists have been forbidden from traveling to Cuba without special permission since that time. We wonder what Cuba would be like today if Castro had not been so absolute in his absolute dictatorship. Would the island country of beautiful old buildings and a long history still be a tourist destination? Can't you picture Americans taking quick jaunts to Havana to drink mojitos while walking in Hemingway's steps? We do have to grant it to Castro: Cuba has the highest literacy rate in the Western Hemisphere and claims to have zero homelessness, and everyone has access to health care. That leads us to one more question: if everything is so great, why are so many people trying to float on rafts made of tires to leave the country? Hmmm . . . have a mojito as you wonder about Castro's Communist Cuba.

◖ MOJITO

3 sprigs fresh mint
2 tsp sugar
3 tbsp fresh lemon juice
1 1/2 oz light rum
club soda or seltzer
1 slice lemon

In a Parfait glass, crush part of the mint with a fork to coat the inside. Add the sugar and lemon juice and stir thoroughly. Top with ice. Add the rum and mix. Finish with club soda. Add a lemon slice and the remaining mint, and serve.

AUGUST

14

Although the Germans and Italians had surrendered to the Allies at the end of World War II, Japan fought on. It wasn't until the dropping of the atomic bomb—first on Hiroshima and then on Nagasaki—that Japan admitted defeat and surrendered unconditionally. The announcement was made by President Truman on this date in 1945. There was no doubt that the use of atomic weapons—the original WMDs—had caused mass destruction and strife, and the debate about the need for the use of such deadly means still exists. The Allies, primarily through the leadership of the United States, took to helping Japan rebuild after the war. So now we know that the United States was successful on two fronts: the Japanese surrendered, and now half of Americans drive a Honda, Toyota, Nissan, or Mitsubishi. If you can't beat 'em, join 'em! Try the Japanese Fizz, described here, and think about what you're driving.

JAPANESE FIZZ

1 1/2 oz blended whiskey
Juice of 1/2 lemon
1 tsp powdered sugar
1 tbsp port
1 egg white
carbonated water

Shake all the ingredients (except the carbonated water) with ice and strain into a Collins glass over two ice cubes. Fill with carbonated water, stir, and serve.

15

As reported on June 30, the year 1939 saw the premieres of some of the most beloved and respected movies of all time, among them *Gone with the Wind* and *Mr. Smith Goes to Washington*. One of our favorites since childhood, however, tops the list: on this date in 1939, *The Wizard of Oz* premiered at Grauman's Chinese Theater in Hollywood. Dorothy and Toto, the Cowardly Lion, the Tinman, and the Scarecrow have become indelibly etched into memories of generations of children ever since. It wasn't until college and several bong hits later that we truly appreciated the pretty colors—one of the first full-color movies—and the special effects. We joke! It was the characters in the movie who were under the spell of poppies. It seems that Dorothy bought a dime bag off one of the munchkins for some good old-fashioned fun. Again, we joke! It was the Wicked Witch of the West who caused the traveling band to walk through a field of poppies—they didn't know about the effects of the poppies. (Yeah, right! And Bill Clinton didn't inhale!) Whatever you want to believe about the abuse of substances is up to you. Now try the drink, The Dorothy, described here.

THE DOROTHY

2 oz silver rum
1/2 oz fresh orange juice
1/2 oz pineapple juice
1/4 oz apricot brandy
1 twist orange peel

Shake the liquid ingredients with ice and strain into a chilled cocktail glass. Garnish with the orange peel, and serve.

AUGUST

16

Once again, truth is stranger than fiction. Picture this: it's 1987 (the hair, the leg warmers!), and thousands of people around the world join in celebration. No, it's not someone's birthday, it's not a holiday . . . it's a harmonic convergence. If you're like us, you, too, are asking, what the *&^%$ is a harmonic convergence? Apparently, it's an event based on a centuries-old calendar signifying the end of the nine cycles of hell. Some believers base this calendar on the date Cortes met Montezuma. Since no one we know was there, we'll just report on what happened in our lifetimes: on this date, believers in this harmonic convergence celebrated the start of a purer age of humankind. Have a Woo Woo, described here, and seek a convergence of your own. Brain cells, meet alcohol! Now that's a convergence!

◀ **WOO WOO**

1 1/2 oz peach Schnapps
1 1/2 oz vodka
3 1/2 oz cranberry juice

Pour all the ingredients into a Collins glass over ice cubes, stir, and serve.

17

On this date in 1992, Woody Allen admitted to being romantically involved with Soon-Yi Previn. This wouldn't have been a problem except for the fact that Soon-Yi was the adopted daughter of actress Mia Farrow. Well, even this wouldn't have been a problem except for the fact that Farrow was Allen's longtime romantic partner. Speculation swirled through New York social circles. Have a Woody Woodpecker and be thankful your relationships are all on the up-and-up.

WOODY WOODPECKER

1 1/2 oz cachaça (a Brazilian liquor)
6 oz orange juice
1 oz Benedictine herbal liqueur

Shake the cachaça and juice with ice and pour into a Collins glass. Add the liqueur and serve.

18

Maybe Woody Allen had been reading *Lolita* prior to his affair with his former lover's adopted daughter? (See August 17.) The novel was published on this date in 1958. Written by Vladimir Nabokov, the plot centers on a man with the horrible name of Humbert Humbert, who falls for a 12-year-old girl. This is a no-no in most countries! Humbert realizes that any relationship with the lass would be an immoral transgression, but he can't help himself. He falls hopelessly in love. The book ends tragically for all. What do we learn from the novel? You can look, but you can't touch. And, don't even get caught looking! And, maybe, it was all his parents' fault for giving him that appalling name?! Have a Lolita, described here, and act your age!

LOLITA

- 2 oz tequila
- 1 oz lime juice
- 1 tsp honey
- 2 dashes bitters

Shake all the ingredients, strain over one or two ice cubes in a cocktail glass, and serve.

19

Not many ladies of fashion are as well known as Gabrielle Chanel, known the world over as Coco. Born on this date in 1883, she spent her youth in an orphanage after her father left her mother. Her road to fashion began in her hat shop in Paris; she later opened a store on the Rue Cambon, home to the fashion houses of the day. She helped define elegance as simple, well-made clothing. So famous was Little Orphan Coco that she was named to *Time's* list of 100 most influential people of the twentieth century. Way to go, Coco! Celebrate Chanel's achievements with a Cosmopoliton, described here, for she helped many women become a little more cosmopolitan in her day.

COSMOPOLITAN

- 1 oz vodka
- 1/2 oz Triple Sec
- 1/2 oz sweetened lime juice
- 1/2 oz cranberry juice
- 1 lime wedge

Shake the vodka, Triple Sec, lime juice, and cranberry juice vigorously in a shaker with ice. Strain into a martini glass, garnish with a lime wedge on the rim, and serve.

20

Like many spoiled children, Lyle and Eric Menendez were tired of having to ask for the car keys or money to go to the mall. What a hassle! "Just 'cause I'm going out doesn't mean I have to fill the gas tank in the Alfa Romeo all the time!" You understand, don't you? How unreasonable! So what do the brothers do? Sit down and talk to their parents about more realistic expectations? Seek family therapy? Get stoned a lot and go to college to get out of the house? Nope. They kill their parents! On this very date in 1989, the boys murdered their parents, Jose and Kitty. After several months of freedom—and a million-dollar spending spree from some of the inheritance—the police began to suspect the boys were responsible. After confessing to one of their therapists, they were arrested. Overwhelming amounts of evidence were collected, so the defense lawyers tried the "they-were-driven-to-it" tactic. The boys claimed they had been physically, emotionally, and sexually abused, and came up with details to prove it. The most interesting?

Eric claimed that he put cinnamon in his father's food and drink to make the taste of his semen more palatable, a ploy he had heard about in school. The jury didn't buy the performance, despite the lurid details, and the brothers were sent to jail for life without parole. Ah, the trappings and tribulations of wealth! Have a Cinnamon Kiss, described here, and be thankful your spoiled children aren't plotting your death.

CINNAMON KISS

1/2 oz grenadine
1 1/2 oz cinnamon Schnapps

Combine both ingredients and serve in a cocktail glass over ice.

AUGUST

22

Painted by Leonardo da Vinci in the early sixteenth century, the Mona Lisa was purchased by King Francis I of France. It stayed in the monarchy, but eventually found a home at the Louvre. The Mona Lisa seemed happy in France—she had that smile going on, right? On this date in 1911, however, she left the country. The painting was stolen by an Italian employee, Vincenzo Perugia, who had been hired to put the museum's more precious works of art under glass. Mouse, cheese, anyone? Perugia was caught after trying to sell the Mona Lisa to the Uffizi Gallery in Florence, Italy. Perugia claimed he wanted to have the Mona Lisa returned to the country from whence she came. What a nobel national! Try the Mona Lisa, described here, and feel glad to know that she was safely returned to the Louvre and there are now lots of extra security measures in place.

MONA LISA

I part vodka
I part lemon soda

Stir ingredients together and pour into a Collins glass.

On this date in 1902, President Theodore Roosevelt became the first U.S. chief executive to ride in an automobile. He was also the first prez to fly in a plane and travel in a submarine. Want some more firsts for Roosevelt? He was the first to entertain an African American in the White House. He was the first to travel abroad during his presidency. Okay, the "cool" list goes on: he established the U.S. Forest Service, designating millions of acres of national forests and parks. He won a Nobel Prize for negotiating the end of the Russo-Japanese War. Check this one out: he was shot while giving a campaign speech in 1912, but continued speaking, stating, "I will deliver this speech or die." And, if that isn't enough, the teddy bear is named after him! Wow! Celebrate Teddy Roosevelt with the Dinky Car Vrroooom, described here.

DINKY CAR VRROOOOM ▶

I tbsp coconut rum
I oz melon liqueur
I oz crème de menthe

Combine over ice, shake. Pour the ingredients into a cocktail glass in any order. Enjoy, but not before driving!

23

On this date in 2000, more than 50 million viewers watched the finale of the hit reality series *Survivor*. The show had been a big hit for the entire season; Americans were intrigued by the backstabbing shenanigans and alliance-forming politics. The nice guy—or so we thought—Richard Hatch had been friendly with the others and had won immunity enough times to make it to the final round. The contestants had to find their own food supply, and Hatch frequently fished for dinner wearing nothing more than his birthday suit. Thereafter, CBS cornered the market on the little gray blur that is superimposed over people's naughty parts! Try the Island Martini, described here, as you adjust your own little gray blur.

ISLAND MARTINI

3 oz gold rum
$1/2$ oz dry vermouth
$1/2$ oz sweet vermouth
1 twist lemon peel

Shake all the liquid ingredients with cracked ice and strain into a chilled cocktail glass. Garnish with a twist of lemon, and serve.

24

It is hard to remember storms with as much impact as the recent Hurricane Katrina, but we need only look back a little more than a decade to find Hurricane Andrew. On this date in 1992, Andrew blew into Florida, causing damage in the billions and billions of dollars. It was the world's most expensive natural disaster in terms of insurance costs. What do you do when Mother Nature delivers a wake-up call? Well, you turn around and put up new buildings right where the old ones were! We just hope that these newer homes withstand today's more powerful "What-global-warming?" storms. Try the Hurricane, described here, and check out your own windows and roofs.

HURRICANE

1 oz vodka
$1/4$ oz grenadine
1 oz gin
1 oz light rum
$1/2$ oz Bacardi 151 proof rum
1 oz amaretto
1 oz Triple Sec
3 oz grapefruit juice
3 oz pineapple juice

Pour all the ingredients except the juices, in the order listed, into a hurricane glass three-quarters filled with ice. Fill with equal parts grapefruit and pineapple juice, and serve.

25

On May 29, you read about the courageous feat of Sir Edmund Hillary's climb to the top of the world's tallest mountain. You've also read about the first man and woman to travel in space, on March 9 and June 16, respectively. Well, on this date in 1875, mankind achieved another first: Matthew Webb swam across the English Channel. The 21 miles from Dover, England, to Calais, France, took him 22 hours. Considering the fact that wetsuits had yet to be invented, we applaud Webb all the more! What kept him going, you ask? We'll tell you what kept him going: booze! Well, it was actually a combination of coffee, brandy, and beer, but that's mostly booze! Ha! Why don't you try the Roger Swims a Mile as you wonder whether you could even copy Roger's feat, let alone Matthew's.

ROGER SWIMS A MILE

1 1/2 oz Drambuie Scotch whisky liqueur
1/2 oz blended whiskey
1/2 oz dry vermouth
1 twist lemon peel

Mix the liquid ingredients with ice. Strain into a cocktail glass, garnish with a twist of lemon, and serve.

> "Give an Irishman lager for a month and he's a dead man. An Irishman's stomach is lined with copper, and the beer corrodes it. But whiskey polishes the copper and is the saving of him."
>
> –MARK TWAIN

AUGUST

26

Abraham Lincoln, as any student of American history knows, was assassinated by John Wilkes Booth at Ford's Theater in Washington, DC. (See April 14.) A famous actor of the day, Booth had established Southern sympathies during the early days of the Civil War after spending time perfecting his acting skills at the Marshall Theater in Richmond, Virginia. He had spent a great deal of time prior to the assassination planning the kidnapping of the president. Lincoln, however, changed his plans at the last minute; instead of visiting a hospital on March 17, 1865, he spoke at a luncheon at the very hotel where Booth was staying. This, coupled with the surrender of General Lee to General Grant, pushed Booth over the edge. He shot the president while Lincoln was watching *Our American Cousin*. He tried to make his escape by jumping to the stage from the private booth, but he broke his leg (some say he broke it later on). He fled to the home of a friend who set his leg, and then continued on. Booth was finally cornered in a barn in Virginia; the barn was set on fire and he was shot as he made his way from the building. In our age, actors become presidents, they don't shoot presidents. The irony! Why don't you try the Shoot Cocktail today, the birth date of John Wilkes Booth in 1838.

◀ SHOOT COCKTAIL

1	oz dry sherry
1	oz Scotch whisky
1	tsp lemon juice
1	tsp orange juice
1/2	tsp powdered sugar

Mix together all the ingredients, shake with ice, and strain into a Collins glass. Serve over ice.

27

A muscular man, wearing nothing but a loincloth, swings through the jungle, pounds his chest, and wrestles lions and crocodiles? If someone tried to write that today, it would be filed at Barnes and Noble under homoerotica. Back in the day, however, it was called *Tarzan of the Apes*. Yes, on this date in 1912, Tarzan was born, or rather, came to life as Edgar Rice Burroughs' novel was published. Come on, Edgar, you're not fooling anyone! Mrs. Burroughs doesn't have her own bedroom because you snore, does she? Okay, we're kidding... but we do wonder. Don't you? As you contemplate your own swinging lifestyle, try the Tarzan's Juicy Cooler described here.

TARZAN'S JUICY COOLER

    3   oz orange juice
    3   oz pineapple juice
  $^1/_4$ oz grenadine
  $^1/_2$ oz lemon juice
    1   tbsp strawberry yogurt
    2   tsp clear honey
    1   slice orange
    1   maraschino cherry

Briefly blend all the ingredients except the orange slice and cherry with half a glassful of crushed ice and pour into a Collins glass. Garnish with a slice of orange speared with a cherry and serve.

28

Few leaders of the twentieth century had the polished oratorical skills of Martin Luther King, Jr. He also had passion, tremendous leadership skills, and an uncanny ability to relate to people. He used all of these attributes on this date in 1963, when he delivered his "I Have a Dream" speech during a march on Washington. Over a quarter million African-Americans and supporters rallied in the nation's capital to stand up for equal rights for people of all races. King's speech was inspiring, and helped further the cause. President Kennedy invited King and the other organizers of the march to the White House. King became the youngest person to receive the Nobel Peace Prize at the age of 35. Perhaps King's dream will someday be realized? Try the American Dream, described here.

AMERICAN DREAM

  $^1/_4$ oz Kahlúa coffee liqueur
  $^1/_4$ oz amaretto
  $^1/_4$ oz Frangelico hazelnut liqueur
  $^1/_4$ oz dark crème de cacao

Chill all the ingredients with ice and strain into a shot glass.

29

Human beings seem to have a passion for creating toys that can kill. Some of these toys can kill others, while some can kill the user of the toy. Today's celebration is an example of the latter. On this date in 1885, the world's first motorcycle, made by Gottlieb Daimler, was patented. So, you want me to get onto a two-wheeled vehicle without any protection and zoom around at breakneck speeds? Wow! That sounds great! We find it interesting that many bikers prefer not to wear helmets; almost half the states in the United States don't mandate their use, and some states don't require helmets under any circumstances. Considering that a motorcycle rider is 16 times more likely to die in a crash than a car driver is, we wonder about the lack of helmet use. It's not that we don't understand the glory of motorcycles. We appreciate the exhilaration, the rush of blood, the sense of control. We just prefer to get these feelings from a good, stiff drink! Try the Bloody Biker, described here, but not if you are going out on your own motorcycle trip.

BLOODY BIKER

  2 oz vodka
$^1/4$ tsp olive juice
  5 oz spicy tomato juice
$^1/4$ tsp Worcestershire sauce
$^1/4$ tsp habanero pepper sauce
    juice of 1 lime wedge

Combine all the ingredients in a shaker and shake until well blended. Pour over ice in an old-fashioned glass and serve.

30

Shakespeare reveled in writing tragedies. And no tragedy was more ripe for revelation than the double suicide of Antony and Cleopatra. Here's some of the soap-opera-esque story: Cleo had assumed the throne of Egypt after her father and two older sisters died. Mark Antony, one of the rulers of Rome, fell in love with her; they had three children. One of the other rulers was outraged that Anthony had set up shop in a foreign land and was flagrantly committing adultery. He convinced the senate to wage war against Egypt. Antony fled, but, disgusted by his failure, committed suicide by falling on his own sword. How did Cleopatra end it? She angered a poisonous snake—an asp—to the point that it bit her. This took place on this date in 30 B.C.E. Ah, true love; when it's wrapped in tragedy, how can there not be a great story? Try the Snakebite and think about your own great story.

SNAKEBITE

- 2 oz whiskey
- 1 dash lime juice

Pour the whiskey over ice; add the lime juice and serve in an old-fashioned glass.

31

Sadly, it seems that a fairy-tale existence is impossible. This was definitely the case for Diana Spencer, better known as Princess Diana. Both Diana and her husband Prince Charles pursued relationships, and Diana was linked with several celebrities. She was eventually drawn to Dodi Fayed, whose father owned the Ritz Hotel in Paris and famed department store Harrods in London. The paparazzi followed them relentlessly, and, on this date in 1997, Diana, Dodi, and their driver were killed in an automobile accident in Paris while being pursued on motorcycles. This drink commemorates the song Elton John rewrote for Diana after her death.

CANDLE IN THE WIND ▶

- 4 oz peach vodka
- 2 oz pineapple juice
- 2 oz orange juice
- 1 oz fresh lemon juice
- 2 tsp sugar
- 7-Up

Pour the peach vodka, juices, and sugar into a cocktail shaker half-filled with ice cubes. Shake well for 30 seconds. Pour unstrained into a large glass (hurricane or otherwise) and add the 7-Up. Stir briefly and serve.

1

"Eat, drink, and be merry, for tomorrow they may cancel your VISA." –UNKNOWN

World War II, as the name suggests, engulfed much of the globe and is considered the most costly and intense war in human history. The war began on September 1, 1939, as Nazi Germany, under the leadership of Adolf Hitler, invaded Poland. Britain and France joined the war shortly after. The United States entered the fray when the Japanese, the surprise bullies on the playground, attacked Pearl Harbor in Hawaii on December 7, 1941. Big scuffles ensued, but eventually the bad guys either politely waved their white flags or committed suicide in an underground Berlin bunker.

WAR CLOUD

$1/2$ oz vodka
$1/2$ oz brandy
$1/2$ oz Kahlúa
$1/2$ oz Bailey's Irish Cream

Shake the ingredients together, strain into a cordial or liqueur glass, and serve.

2

On September 2, 1985, it was announced that a deep-sea expedition had located the wreckage of the *Titanic* about 560 miles off the coast of Newfoundland. A joint American-French expedition, led by Dr. Robert Ballard, of the Woods Hole Oceanographic Institution, and French scientist Jean-Louis Michel located the wreckage using finely tuned, highly sophisticated instruments. It was found at a depth of 2 miles, about 13 miles from where it was originally thought to rest. So impressed by Ballard's skills are we, that we've called his office several times with the proposition that he lead a highly trained team and go in search of the better part of last Saturday night. Those calls have yet to be returned, but we have hope.

"I am thankful for the mess to clean after a party because it means I have been sur- rounded by friends."

–NANCIE J. CARMODY

DEEP-SEA MARTINI

    3   oz gin
    1   oz dry vermouth
  $^1/_2$ tsp licorice liqueur
    1   dash orange bitters

Stir all the ingredients together in a mixing glass half-filled with cracked ice. Strain into a chilled cocktail glass and serve.

3

On September 3, 1976, the unmanned U.S. spacecraft Viking 2 landed on Mars to take the first close-up color photographs of the planet's surface. By scientific standards, the photos beamed back to Earth were amazing, miles and miles of red dirt and rock. We mean miles here, people, of red dirt and rock. The project cost millions. NASA has rejected our offer to travel to Arizona and take hundreds of pictures of red dirt and rock and e-mail them back. All we asked for was first-class airfare, two suites at the Four Seasons, and unlimited use of the minibar. It seems they'd rather spend millions to send robots to Mars.

GIRL FROM MARS ▶

1 $^1/_2$ oz peach Schnapps
$^1/_2$ oz vodka
2 oz strawberry puree
1–2 oz half-and-half
$^1/_2$ oz grenadine

Place the peach Schnapps, vodka, and strawberry puree in a Collins glass and shake well. Add several cubes of ice, and then add the half-and-half until near the top. Slowly pour the grenadine syrup around the edge of the glass (it should produce some odd red rings on the glass, hence the name); serve.

"Drinking makes such fools of people, and people are such fools to begin with, that it's compounding a felony."

–ROBERT BENCHLEY

4

Oh, Reality TV, one of our favorite guilty pleasures . . . next to the obvious, of course. In the summer of 2002, singer Kelly Clarkson battled it out with a dozen other contestants in a bid to be voted the first "American Idol" on the Fox TV series, which swept the nation by storm. After weeks of putting up with Simon Cowell's nasty remarks and Paula Abdul's lukewarm compliments, Clarkson emerged victorious on September 4. We want to make fun of her and point out that Reality TV really is only good for 15 minutes of fame, but the girl's a superstar to this day and we love her. You go, Kelly!

J-POP IDOL

    1 oz Alize Bleu liqueur
    2 oz sake
    2 oz orange juice

Pour the Alize Bleu liqueur down the side of an old-fashioned glass filled with ice cubes. Allow it to sit before adding the sake. Add the orange juice, stir, and serve.

5

The handbook of the Beat Generation was published on this day in 1957. *On the Road* by Jack Kerouac is a largely autobiographical work, written in a stream-of-consciousness style and based on the spontaneous road trips Kerouac and his Beat Generation friends, William S. Burroughs and Allen Ginsberg, took across mid-century America. Upon publication, the book became an overnight success. As the story goes, it was written by Kerouac in only three weeks in a burst of artistic fury, hammered out on one long scroll of teletype paper. Our editors wish we had been so speedy while writing this book, but hey, we were drinking! Oh wait, so was Kerouac—he died at age 47 after a life of heavy drinking. We don't like to think about that, though, so make a drink, grab a good book, and forget about it.

ASPHALT ROAD

    1 shot sweetened lime juice
    1 shot Bailey's Irish Cream
    1 shot vodka

Combine all the ingredients in a shaker with ice. Shake well and serve in a cocktail glass, or pour into a flask and take it on the road.

6

On this day in 1959, the first Barbie Doll was sold by Mattel Toy Corporation. We know: Stop, breathe, count backward from ten . . . okay, calm now? The original Barbie, along with her pals, Ken and Skipper, are now obviously collectors' items, although new versions are continually being produced. A quick search on eBay to find an original turned up nothing, but it did turn up one of her original 1959 outfits—the Roman holiday gear, which at last look was going for $289.00. We're thinking if we can raid our parents' closets and get 300 smackers for some smocks from the '50s, we can take a Roman holiday of our own!

MALIBU BARBIE

   2   oz coconut rum
   8   oz pineapple juice

Stir the ingredients together with ice cubes in a Collins glass and serve.

"The problem with some people is that when they aren't drunk, they're sober."

—WILLIAM BUTLER YEATS

7

The modern beauty pageant can trace its origins to the Miss America pageant, which was first held in Atlantic City on this day in 1921. The money shot, as it were, for this and almost every other beauty pageant is the swimsuit competition, in which women are paraded in front of the audience in the skimpiest and sexiest suits they can find. Now don't get us wrong, we like ogling semi-clad people as much as anybody, but somehow beauty pageants just feel wrong in this day and age. We're sticking with our feminist sisters, who say do away with them! Besides, who can't drink somebody into a beauty queen anyway. I feel pretty, oh so pretty . . .

◀ BEAUTY ON THE BEACH

- 1 oz white rum
- 1 oz Southern Comfort Peach Liqueur
- 1 tbsp Grand Marnier
- 1 tsp lemon juice
- 2 dashes orange bitters

Pour the white rum, Southern Comfort, Grand Marnier, lemon juice, and orange bitters into a cocktail shaker half-filled with ice cubes. Shake well. Strain into a cocktail glass and serve.

"We drink and we die and continue to drink."

–DENNIS LEARY

SEPTEMBER

8

NBC-TV headed into "Space: The Final Frontier" on this day in 1966. The first episode of *Star Trek*, titled, "The Man Trap," was seen on the network. The first episode was appropriately named, as the show became a pop-culture phenomenon, trapping millions of fans for years and years, leading to movie after movie, television series after television series, and our favorite, the Star Trek Convention, where lonely single Trekkies can dress up as Mr. Spock or Lt. Uhuru and snag other lonely singles dressed up as Tribbles. Man trap indeed! Beam me up a drink, Scotty!

GREEN ALIEN

  3   oz Midori
  1   oz lemon juice
  1   oz sweetened lime juice
      lemon/lime soda
      Soda water
  1   lime wedge

Shake the Midori, lemon juice, and lime juice with ice, and pour into a highball glass filled with ice. Fill up with Sprite and soda to taste. Garnish with a lime wedge and add a straw.

9

On September 9, 1850, California became the 31st state of the Union. Having been seized from Mexico, along with several bottles of tequila, and a few of those itchy but warm blankets, California now belonged to the United States. And what better honor than to name it the Golden State? A slice of promised land along the great Pacific Ocean, we had high hopes for California. Would it be the state to stand as a beacon of hope for entrepreneurial foreigners from distant lands? Apparently so, as these days we've left it in the hands of everybody's favorite Austrian bodybuilder cum actor cum politician: Arnold Schwarzenegger, or, as we like to call him, the Governator.

HOTEL CALIFORNIA

  1   oz gold tequila
  2   oz mandarin juice
  2   oz pineapple juice
  4   oz Champagne

Shake the tequila and juices together and strain into an ice-filled piña colada glass. Add the Champagne, straws, and serve.

10

Rod Stewart recorded his first tune, titled "Good Morning Little Schoolgirl" on this day in 1964. It was not one of his more successful recordings; as a matter of fact, nobody seems to remember that it even exists. Luckily for Rod, however, this was not a harbinger of things to come, as he went on to record several major hits, including "Maggie May," "Do Ya Think I'm Sexy," and "Young Turks." He has sold more than 100 million records worldwide. Our favorite Rod tidbit: when asked about his wife, Rachel Hunter, he was quoted as saying that he'd rather have his penis cut off than cheat on her. He was later sued for divorce on the grounds of adultery. Somebody get the garden shears.

ROD ON THE ROCKS

1/4 cup peach Schnapps
1/2 cup apple cider

Pour the peach Schnapps over ice in an old-fashioned whiskey sour glass. Fill with apple cider, stir lightly, and serve.

"When I read about the evils of drinking, I gave up reading."

–HENNY YOUNGMAN

11

This date is still too close to our hearts, and the hearts of all Americans, for us to say more than this: if any event of recent times showed the courage, generosity, and unity of the American people, it was the reaction to the destruction of the World Trade Center in New York, the attack on the Pentagon in Washington, DC., and the hijacking of four American passenger planes by al-Qaeda on this date in 2001. Today, drink an American Glory cocktail and glory in the spirit of this great country.

AMERICAN GLORY

3 oz Champagne
2 oz orange juice
2 oz lemonade

Pour the ingredients into a frosted ice-filled Collins glass.

12

Timmy's in the well, who's going to save him? On this day in 1954, *Lassie* was seen on TV for the first time. The super-intelligent dog found herself rescuing her hapless master from any number of entanglements on a weekly basis, and the show quickly became a household favorite across the country. Often referred to as "the most famous dog in the world," Lassie is one of only three dogs to have been given a star on the Hollywood Walk of Fame. But the True Hollywood Story always ruins the fun, doesn't it? Despite being called "girl" by Timmy, his mom, and millions of fans over the years, Lassie was in fact a male dog. Once the tabloids got hold of this information and paid top dollar for the scandalous pictures to prove it, Lassie's career was ruined. She was last spotted working as a cocktail waitress at a rundown bar on Sunset Boulevard.

DOGGYSTYLE ▶

1 oz coconut rum
1 oz raspberry vodka
6 oz Sprite soda

Pour all the ingredients into a Collins glass filled with crushed ice. Stir well, and serve.

13

Remember the days when Michael Jackson only pretended to be a weirdo from another planet? On this day in 1986, Captain EO, a 17-minute, three-dimensional, science-fiction musical flick starring Michael Jackson, made its gala premiere at Disneyland in Anaheim, California, and at Disney's Epcot Center in Orlando, Florida. Such a big deal was this "premiere" that the marketing gurus (or geniuses, as we like to call them) at Disney hopped in bed with Network TV and aired the hubbub surrounding the event, complete with celebrity "red carpet" action, live for the country to see . . . without actually showing us the movie. Attendance at the parks rose dramatically in the following months, thanks to Captain EO, and Michael Jackson reigned as the King of Disney thanks to his 17-minute freak show.

FREAKSHOW

1 oz sambuca
1 pint Guinness stout

Pour the sambuca into a beer mug. Slowly add the Guinness to float it on top. Serve.

14

Nano, nano! On this day in 1978, the first episode of *Mork & Mindy*, starring the irrepressible Robin Williams as Mork and Pam Dawber as Mindy, aired on ABC-TV. *Mork & Mindy* was a spin-off from an episode of *Happy Days*, in which an alien from the planet Ork landed on Earth and attempted to kidnap Richie. So popular was the nutty alien that it spawned its own show. And on the show, Mork spawned a 225-pound baby, played by Jonathan Winters, who was hatched from an egg. This is apparently where Robin Williams learned that it was okay for grown men to play children.

MARTIAN MARTINI

1 oz Midori
2 oz gin

Combine the Midori and gin in a cocktail shaker with ice. Shake and strain into a cocktail glass.

15

The mother of mystery, novelist Agatha Christie, was born on this day in 1890. The author of such famous books as *Murder on the Orient Express*, *Death on the Nile*, and *And Then There Were None*, Dame Agatha was arguably one of the most prolific and successful authors of the twentieth century, with book sales estimated at over $2 billion. A quick countdown on our fingers and a glance through the bookshelves back home leads us to believe that our mothers and grandmothers are responsible for roughly $1 billion of those sales. How these women were able to read so many of these books and still not figure out how to kill their spouses, which (to hear them tell it) they wanted to do every single day, is a mystery to us.

BALTIC MURDER MYSTERY

1	oz crème de cassis
1	oz vodka
	7-Up or soda water
1	slice lemon

Pour the crème de cassis and vodka over ice into a cocktail glass and fill with 7-Up. If it is too sweet, try soda water instead. A slice of lemon complements the drink quite nicely.

"I'd rather have a free bottle in front of me than a prefrontal lobotomy."

—TOM WAITS

16

On September 16, 1956, David Copperfield was born. Copperfield is a famous magician and illusionist best known for his combination of spectacular illusions with storytelling. His most famous feats include making the Statue of Liberty disappear, levitating over the Grand Canyon, and walking through the Great Wall of China. But in our opinion, his most impressive trick is building a career that made him the tenth-highest-paid entertainer in 2003, taking in a whopping $57 million. We're thinking we'd better put down the hooch and start pulling bunnies out of hats . . . nah . . .

MAGIC TRICK

1 oz amaretto
1 oz vodka
1 oz brandy
1 oz Bailey's Irish Cream
1 oz coffee liqueur
3 oz milk

Pour all the ingredients into a pint glass filled with ice cubes. Stir well, and serve.

17

Inspired by the 1970 film of the same name, M*A*S*H (for Mobile Army Surgical Hospital) was an American television series about a team of medical professionals and support staff stationed at MASH 4077th in Korea during the Korean War. The series originally aired from September 17, 1972, to February 28, 1983, but it can still be seen in syndication. The series lasted longer than the war that served as its setting. The zany cast of characters included the cross-dressing Klinger; "Hawkeye" Pierce, who quickly became the central character; and the hot-headed Margaret "Hot Lips" Houlihan. This drink is for her.

HOT LIPS ▶

2 oz pineapple juice
1 1/2 oz cream
1/2 oz cinnamon Schnapps
1/4 oz raspberry syrup
1 chunk pineapple
1 amarelle cherry

Shake all the liquid ingredients well over ice cubes in a shaker. Strain into a large Collins glass over crushed ice, add a pineapple chunk and an amarelle cherry, and serve.

277

18

On the morning of September 18, 1970, rock legend Jimi Hendrix was found dead in the basement apartment of the Samarkand Hotel at 22 Lansdowne Crescent in London. He had spent the night with a girlfriend and died in bed after taking a reported nine sleeping pills and choking on his own vomit. Sleeping pills weren't Hendrix's only drug of choice, however; he was widely known to be a big fan of all sorts of mind-altering substances, such as PCP and LSD . . . and now, thanks to his love of drugs, he's D.E.A.D. Have a Purple Haze and experience a mind-altering substance of your own.

PURPLE HAZE

    ½ oz sambuca
    ½ oz Chambord raspberry liqueur

Pour the sambucca into a shot glass, then very slowly pour in the Chambord. Serve.

"I was raped by orderlies, gnawed on by rats, and poisoned by tainted food. I was chained in padded cells, strapped into straitjackets, and half-drowned in ice baths." Just another happy day at the sanitarium for actress Frances Farmer, who was born on this day in 1914. The starlet was diagnosed with manic-depressive psychosis. Her story is fascinating and horrific, with treatment ranging from shock therapy to hydrotherapy (icy baths—for eight hours at a time) to a lobotomy . . . with an ice pick! (Allegedly, of course, which is good enough for us.) Put your ice pick to more reasonable use and chunk up some cubes for our Crazy Cocktail. We certainly need one!

CRAZY COCKTAIL

    2 oz coconut rum
  1–1½ oz raspberry Schnapps
  1–1½ oz melon liqueur
    2 oz lime soda
   4–6 oz pineapple juice

Combine all the ingredients in a Collins glass filled with ice cubes. Stir well and serve.

20

Folksinger Jim Croce, perhaps best known for his song "Time in a Bottle," was killed in a plane crash near Natchitoches, Louisiana, on this day in 1973. The plane went down after the pilot apparently suffered a midair heart attack, causing the aircraft to plummet to Earth. Luckily these days we're not only in the able hands of pilots, but auto-pilots as well—you know, machines programmed to fly the plane in case the pilot should have a midair heart attack. Er . . . yeah, cocktail please.

TIME IN A BOTTLE

1	oz Midori
1	oz light rum
1/2	oz amaretto
2	oz pineapple juice

Shake all the ingredients together, strain into a cocktail glass, and serve.

"I drink because she nags, she said I nag because he drinks. But if the truth be known to you, He's a lush and she's a shrew."

–OGDEN NASH

21

On this day in 1949, the People's Republic of China was proclaimed by its Communist leaders. Although the impression of Communist China in the West is often one of barbaric living conditions and masses of unhappy people, the country is actually stunningly beautiful, home to some of the world's most cosmopolitan cities, and a veritable superpower in its own right. Sure the Tiananmen Square "incident" cast a doubtful light on the Chinese leadership, but what government doesn't have embarrassing lapses of judgment it'd rather have the world forget? Kent State anybody?

ASIA TOO ▶

1 ¹/2 oz cranberry vodka
1 ¹/2 oz Passoa liqueur
1 ¹/2 oz bianco vermouth
   3 oz grapefruit juice
1 ¹/2 oz pineapple juice
   1 oz lime juice
   1 splash sweet and sour mix
   1 dash grenadine

Pour all the ingredients except the grenadine into a cocktail shaker half-filled with ice cubes. Shake well and strain into a hurricane glass filled with ice cubes. Add the grenadine, and serve.

"Actually, it only takes one drink to get me loaded. Trouble is, I can't remember if it's the thirteenth or fourteenth."

–GEORGE BURNS

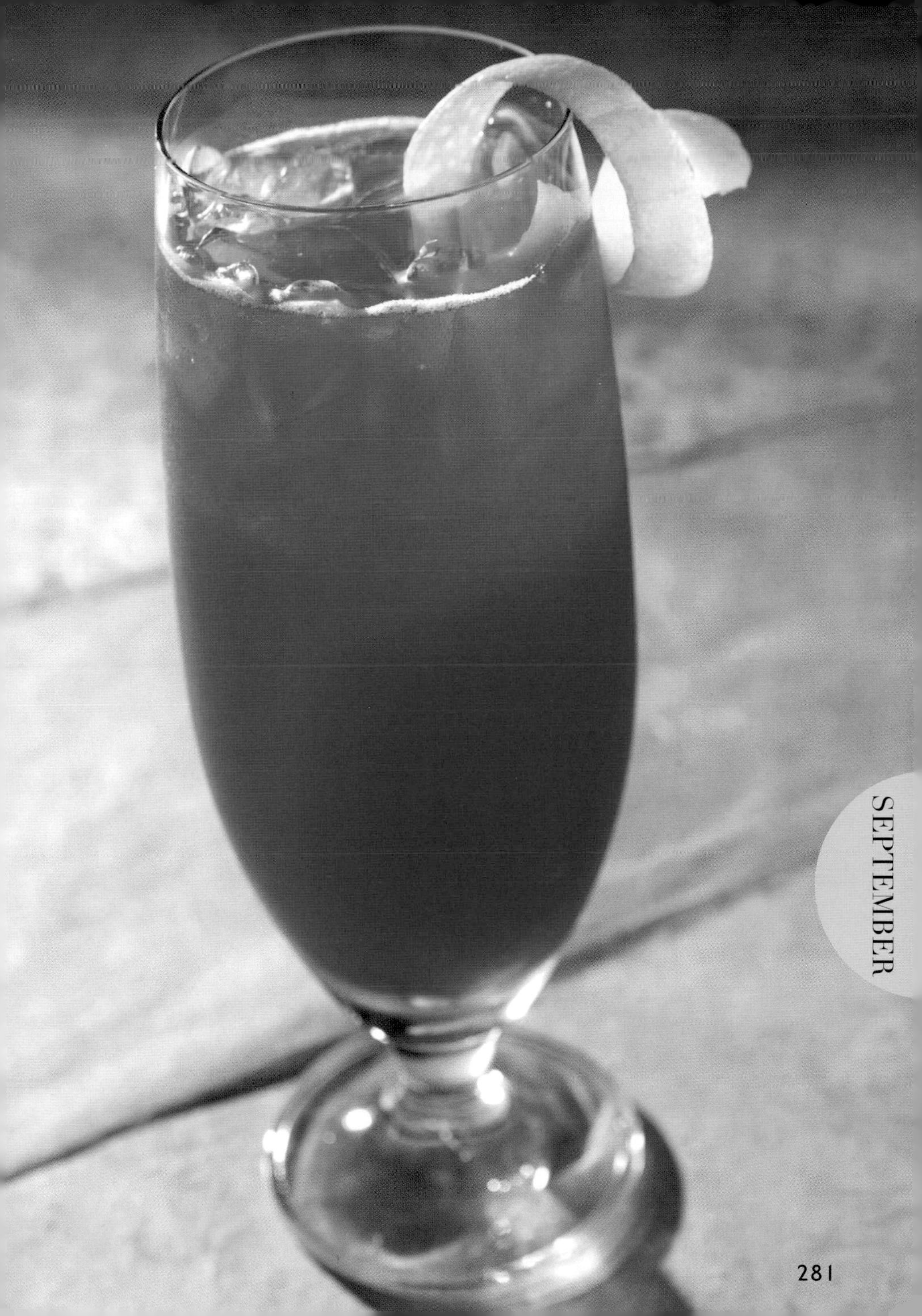

22

On September 22, 1975, Sara Jane Moore failed in an attempt to assassinate President Gerald R. Ford outside a San Francisco hotel. Rattling as it was, it was actually the second attempt on the president's life during that trip to California. Days before, Squeaky Fromme, a member of Charles Manson's cult, also tried unsuccessfully to kill the president (the gun wasn't loaded). So we're going to go out on a limb and say that President Ford is a survivor! Not only did he survive assassination attempts, he survived several well-publicized falls down the stairs leaving *Air Force One*, and wife Betty's very public fall from the bottle. In honor of Gerry, shake up a few batches of this cocktail and see how many of them you can survive.

SURVIVOR

- 2 oz cognac
- $1/2$ oz peach Schnapps
- $1/2$ oz Jägermeister herbal liqueur

Pour all the ingredients into a mixing glass or cocktail shaker half-filled with ice cubes. Stir well to combine, strain into a chilled cocktail glass and serve.

23

On September 23, 1969, The *London Daily Mirror* became a rumormonger when it printed a story proclaiming that Beatle Paul McCartney was dead. It was the first, but not the last, time that rumor would make the rounds. Following the release of his duet "Say, Say, Say" with Michael Jackson, and "Ebony and Ivory," which he recorded with Stevie Wonder, it's clear to us that what the Mirror meant to say was that it was his career that had died.

DEAD MAN WALKING

- $1/2$ oz absinthe herbal liqueur
- $1/2$ oz Goldschlager cinnamon Schnapps

Pour both ingredients, in equal parts, into a shot glass, and shoot.

24

Pull out the polyester cruise wear and clear the shuffleboard! On this day in 1977, *The Love Boat* set sail on ABC-TV. Weekly cruises to Mexico were staffed by cruise director Julie, bartender Isaac, Gopher the steward, and the sensitive and wise Captain Stubing. The series served as CPR for the careers of many Hollywood has-beens, who surfaced briefly for guest stints on the show before finally sinking permanently to the ocean floor. (Has anybody seen Georgia Engel recently?) One regular guest star who got much more than her 15 minutes out of the show was Charo, who, strangely enough, is still riding *The Love Boat* wave of fame to this day. Truth is stranger than fiction, people. Cuchi cuchi.

CRUISER COCKTAIL

1 1/4 oz coconut rum
 3 oz orange juice
 2 oz pineapple juice

Pour all the ingredients into a cocktail shaker half-filled with ice cubes. Shake well, strain into a Collins glass filled with ice cubes, and serve.

> "You can't drown yourself in drink. I've tried. You float."
>
> —JOHN BARRYMORE

SEPTEMBER

25

On this day in 1890, Mormon president Wilford Woodruff issued a manifesto formally renouncing the practice of polygamy. We can only imagine the awkward weeks and months that followed that announcement. "All right, ladies, I'm thinking of a number between one and ten . . . "

MORMON SURPRISE

1	part vodka
2 ½	parts white grape juice
	ginger ale

Add the vodka and grape juice to a Collins glass over ice and fill with ginger ale.

26

You know how we mentioned before that sometimes there are those days in history when not a lot happened? Well, we're not saying that September 26 was a complete wash, but it was on this day in 1985 that Shamu, America's favorite killer whale, was born at SeaWorld in Orlando, Florida. Not the first Shamu, nor the last Shamu, but one of the Shamus was born on this day. Since absolutely nothing else was happening . . . anywhere . . . ever, that seems like a good enough reason to drink!

BLUE WHALE

1	part vodka
1	part blue curaçao
1	part orange juice
1	part pineapple juice
1	part sweet and sour mix

Pour all the ingredients over ice and mix in a shaker. Strain into a cocktail glass, and serve.

> "There's nothing wrong with sobriety in moderation."
>
> —JOHN CIARDI

The first pair to go over Niagara Falls in a barrel and live to tell about it did so on this day in 1989. Actually, Jeffrey Petkovich and Peter DeBernardi went over 167-foot-high Horseshoe Falls on the Canadian side. When asked why they did it, they said that their goal was to show kids there are better things to do than drugs. Riiiiiiight . . . We're pretty sure they were on drugs when they did it. We say, stick to drinking, it's safer.

BOYS ARE STUPID

- 2 oz Bacardi 151 proof rum
- 2 oz Smirnoff vodka
- 2 oz Bailey's Irish Cream
- 2 oz Kahlùa

Pour all the ingredients in equal parts into a margarita glass over ice. Serve unstirred.

28

This day in 1850 saw the abolishment of flogging as a form of punishment in the U.S. Navy. However, grounding, television restrictions, and being sent to bed without dessert are still very much in play.

MONKEY SPANKER

3 oz Tennessee whiskey
8 oz ginger ale

Pour the whiskey over ice into a beer mug and fill with ginger ale.

"I don't have a drinking problem. I drink. I get drunk. I fall down. No problem."

–UNKNOWN

29

Elizabeth Taylor, undergoing rehabilitation at the Betty Ford Clinic (we've been over this one before, and if you've made it this far in the book, you may need to check yourself in there soon enough) and overcoming a nagging weight problem, was voted the world's most beautiful woman in a Louis Harris poll released on this day in 1984. We don't think there's anything we can add to this little factoid; we feel it really speaks for itself, don't you?

◀ LIZZY SOUR

- 1 oz Alize liqueur
- 1 1/2 oz apricot liqueur
- 1 oz fresh lemon juice
- 1 slice lemon

Shake the liquid ingredients well with ice and strain into a cocktail glass. Garnish with a lemon slice, and serve.

30

Teenage girls (and several teenage boys) everywhere went into shock and mourning on this day in 1955, when actor James Dean was killed in a two-car collision near Cholame, California, at age 24. Dean, an avid racer, died when another car turned into the path of his Porsche Spyder on a California highway. Officers estimated he was driving between 70 and 75 mph. Despite his brief Hollywood career—only three major films—Dean's image as rebel antihero still resonates with teens around the globe. His image as a hottie still resonates with everybody.

REBEL YELL COCKTAIL

- 2 oz bourbon whiskey
- 1/2 oz Cointreau
- 1 oz lemon juice
- 1 egg white
- 1 slice orange

Combine the bourbon, Cointreau, lemon juice, and egg white in a shaker half-filled with ice cubes. Shake well and pour into an old-fashioned glass. Garnish with an orange slice, and serve.

SEPTEMBER

1

Congested highways, potholes, high gas prices—we can thank Henry Ford for all of these things. Well, sort of, because on this date in 1908, Ford started selling the first successful mass-market car, the Model T. For the better part of the next two decades, 15 million cars with the Model T engine were sold, making Ford's company the industry leader. Because of Ford's innovative approach—using mass production—he became known the world over. Almost as famous is the drink listed here! Try the Sidecar and toast Mr. Ford, but not while driving your Ford.

SIDECAR

$3/4$ oz Triple Sec
$1/2$ oz cognac
$3/4$ oz lemon juice
 I twist lemon peel

Combine the liquid ingredients with ice, shake and strain into a chilled cocktail glass. Garnish with a twist of lemon peel.

2

It is rare that a well-known movie director "lowers" his standards to do television. But Alfred Hitchcock enjoyed a challenge, and he enjoyed being the focus of things. He agreed to produce a weekly TV series called *Alfred Hitchcock Presents*, which aired for the first time on this date in 1955. At first, each episode was 30 minutes, and then, due to the popularity of the series, the shows became an hour each. Apparently, the American public couldn't get enough terror and mystery in their lives! The series remained on television for 10 years, but also continues in reruns to this day. Also noteworthy: several well-known actors and directors had their careers boosted by their affiliation with the show, among them Robert Redford, Joanne Woodward, Steve McQueen, Robert Altman, and Sydney Pollack. Have a Thriller, described here, and think about what scares you!

THRILLER

 I $1/2$ oz Scotch whisky
 I oz green ginger wine
 I oz orange juice

Pour the ingredients into a shaker half-filled with ice. Shake! Strain into a cocktail glass.

3

At the end of World War II, Germany found itself divided, literally and figuratively. Everything in the east fell under the control of the Soviet Union, and West Germany was jointly controlled by Great Britain, France, and the United States. Nothing lasts forever, however, and Communism became a failed experiment for the Soviets and the rest of the former Easter Bloc. (After all, no one was trying to defect to East Germany!) The Berlin Wall came down (see November 9) and, after years of separation, the two Germanys reunited. This reunification happened on this date in 1990, a date known as Unity Day in Germany. Have an East West Cocktail to celebrate!

EAST WEST COCKTAIL ▶

    1   oz vodka
    1   oz bourbon whiskey
 $^{1}/_{4}$ oz peach Schnapps
 $^{1}/_{4}$ oz lemon juice

Mix the ingredients in an old-fashioned glass with a few ice cubes.

OCTOBER

4

On this date in 1970, Janis Joplin was found dead in a hotel room in Hollywood. She was only 27 years old, but had lived the rock-and-roll lifestyle hard for several years. For example, she wrote the song "What Good Can Drinkin' Do" when she was 19. The first two lines are:

What good can drinkin' do, what good can drinkin' do?
Lord, I drink all night but the next day I still feel blue

Then she goes on to mention whiskey, bourbon, gin, and beer. That combination would make anyone feel blue! Have a Death Star, described here, but not too many of them. And remember: you can't drink your blues away. Just ask Janis!

DEATH STAR

- 1 oz Jägermeister
- 1 oz Jack Daniels
- 1 oz Triple Sec
- 2 oz cola
- 1 oz vodka
- 2 oz sour mix

Mix all the ingredients in an old-fashioned glass over ice; stir and serve.

5

On this date in 1969, six very funny men launched a very funny comedy series on not-very-funny BBC television. Yes, yes, *Monty Python's Flying Circus* made its debut in Great Britain. Who says the British don't have a sense of humor? Well, probably the Monty Python crowd, that's who! The show was zany from the beginning, with invisible television announcers, interesting uses of cartoons, and an irreverent approach to topics such as the Queen and the Stock Exchange. And we can't forget Spam. Lots of Spam! One restaurant in the Monty Python world served everything with Spam. More than three decades later, *Spamalot* opened on Broadway to rave reviews and won the 2005 Tony for Best Musical. Celebrate their comedic success with a Monty's Coffee, described here.

MONTY'S COFFEE

- 1 oz butterscotch Schnapps
- 8 oz coffee
- 1 oz milk
- 1 tsp sugar
- 1 oz Kahlùa

Pour the Schnapps, then the coffee, into a mug. Add milk and sugar to taste. Top off with the Kahlùa and stir.

6

In the early 1990s, the name Anita Hill became synonymous with workplace hanky-panky. Hill had served as an assistant to Clarence Thomas, first at the Department of Education and then at the Equal Employment Opportunity Commission. According to Hill, Thomas tried many opportunities to "employ" her outside of a normal working relationship. This happens in workplaces all the time, of course, but the difference here is that Thomas was nominated by the first President Bush to serve on the Supreme Court. On this date in 1991, the previously undisclosed details of Hill's harassment allegations were reported by the press, jolting the country and jeopardizing Thomas's nomination. Hill testified before the Senate Judiciary Committee five days later. Thomas testified, too, defending himself and denying the charges. Reaction to Hill ran the gamut from supportive ("That poor woman!") to extremely negative ("She's trying to ruin that man!"). As we know, Thomas was con-firmed; the vote was 52 to 48. Hill's testimony was not for naught, however. Sexual harassment in the workplace became something people could talk about, and the number of reported cases—and monetary awards to victims—skyrocketed. Have a Hillinator, described here, as you think about the last time you used the copy machine in that not-so-appropriate way.

HILLINATOR

1	oz cinnamon Schnapps
2	oz spiced rum
6	oz Mountain Dew
4	tbsp sugar

Pour the schnapps into a shot glass. Pour the remaining ingredients into a Collins glass. Remove any errant hairs. Toss back the shot and follow it up quickly with the mixed drink.

> "The telephone is a good way to talk to people without having to offer them a drink."
>
> —FRAN LEBOWITZ

7

"Hmm . . . I have an idea for a musical. Let's dress actors like cats, put them in a set that looks like a back alley full of garbage, and make them sing T.S. Eliot poems. That'll sell millions of tickets!" Sounds ridiculous, right? Wrong! On this date in 1982, *Cats* had its first show on Broadway, and then went on to become an institution. It became the longest-running show in Broadway history, with 7,485 performances. It won seven Tony Awards, including best musical, and grossed $380 million on Broadway by the time it closed on September 10, 2000. Hats off to Andrew Lloyd Webber, who wrote the music; he was eventually knighted by the Queen. Have a Famous Pussy, described here, as you celebrate this fantastic feline feat.

FAMOUS PUSSY ▶

1 oz watermelon Schnapps
1 oz cinnamon Schnapps
1 pinch sugar
1 oz chilled cranberry juice
1 splash lime

Pour both Schnapps into a shot glass; add the sugar, cranberry juice, and the lime. Drink a few—till you have no "memories."

8

A cow kicks over a lantern and a city goes up in flames! Once again, truth is stranger than fiction. What we didn't know, until we had to do research for a drinks book, is that Chicago should have been known as the Fire City, not the Windy City, back in the day. Apparently, for the year leading up to the Chicago Fire that started on this date in 1871, Chicago had suffered an average of two fires per day! Mother Nature had helped by holding off on significant amounts of rainfall. So, now we have it— cow, lantern, fire. Three hundred people were killed and four square miles were burned, destroying $200 million in property value in all. Have a Kicking Cow, described here, and make sure your fire extinguisher is fully operational. You never know when bovine arsonists may move into the neighborhood!

KICKING COW

1/3 oz maple syrup
1/3 oz cream
2/3 oz whiskey

Mix all the ingredients with ice; strain into a cocktail glass. Be thankful you don't own a cow!

9

Now we know we just wrote about the perils of fire, but we still can't resist reporting on today's main event. On this date in 1946, in Petersburg, Virginia, the electric blanket went on sale for the first time. Okay, we know it's not as ironic as reporting on the "first ashtray attached to a bedpost" invention, but you get it, don't you? We must, of course, reveal that the majority of electric blankets are perfectly safe; thousands of us snuggle under them each year when snowflakes first fly. Have an Electric Relaxation, and let the cognac warm you up instead of a hundred little wires full of electricity coursing through flammable cotton. Not that that's a bad thing!

ELECTRIC RELAXATION

1 oz cognac
1 1/2 oz Triple Sec
4–5 oz pineapple juice

This will warm you up! Pour the cognac into a Collins glass over ice. Add the Triple Sec and juice and stir. Feels cold and warm all at the same time.

10

As products of the 1980s, we know all about hair bands. These are the ones with frontmen who have longer, frizzier hair than Madeleine Kahn in *Young Frankenstein*. One of the first and most successful of these bands was Van Halen, with lead singer David Lee Roth. Roth was born on this date in 1955 and grew up in Massachusetts, but moved to L.A. He met the Van Halen brothers, the band was formed, and they released one of the most successful debut albums in rock history. As we've said before, however, all good things must come to an end. Roth and Eddie Van Halen, after producing six albums, each more successful than the last, called it quits. Have a Hair Dryer, described here, and celebrate Roth's birthday.

HAIR DRYER

12 oz Vanilla Coke
2 oz hazelnut liqueur

Mix both ingredients in a margarita glass and serve.

"An intelligent man is sometimes forced to be drunk to spend time with fools."

—ERNEST HEMINGWAY

11

Who likes to spend time in the closet, other than those people from California who install shelving systems? On this date in 1987, half a million people marched on Washington to demand equal rights for gays and lesbians. We applaud these brave souls, not just because they were fighting bigotry, but also because many of them were doing it in high heels—and we're not talking about the ladies! Due to the success of the march, the following year October 11 was designated National Coming Out Day, a day when previously closeted homosexuals were urged to declare their orientation to the world. Millions of men and women have come out since, including Ellen DeGeneres, Candace Gingrich, Chastity Bono, professional baseball player Billy Bean, and the guy who cuts your hair. Oops—didn't know that yet? Well, make your next haircut appointment for October 11, and drink a Jolly Homo in his honor.

◀ JOLLY HOMO

1 1/2 oz DeKuyper Buttershots liqueur
1 1/2 oz spiced rum
   4 maraschino cherries

Pour the liqueur and rum into an old-fashioned glass filled with ice cubes. Garnish with four maraschino cherries, and serve.

OCTOBER

12

On this date in 1920, the Holland Tunnel began construction. The tunnel links Jersey City to New York City under the Hudson River. It took seven years to build, and the cost, in today's dollars, was $1.4 billion. The tunnel was named for Clifford Milburn Holland, chief engineer for the project, who passed away from exhaustion on the night before the work crews from either side were supposed to break through the last few feet of earth. A later engineer, Ole Singstad, is credited with devising the ventilation system for the tunnel, a feat never accomplished until then. Eighty-four fans pump fresh air into the tunnel every 90 seconds, making air in the tunnel actually cleaner than the air above the surface of the Hudson River. Of course, it's probably not too difficult to find air that's cleaner than New York City air in just about any place. Have an Urban Jungle as you plan your next trip to the Big Apple. If you pass through the Holland Tunnel—all 8,000-plus feet of it—breathe deeply. It's the last clean air you'll get for a while!

URBAN JUNGLE

3/4 oz blackberry brandy
3/4 oz dry sherry
1/2 oz Triple Sec
1 tbsp vanilla ice cream

Blend all the ingredients with a tablespoon of crushed ice and serve in a champagne saucer. Fly through your commute with ease!

13

Faithful readers of this book have learned a lot about the inhabitants of the White House, from Thomas Jefferson to William Jefferson Clinton. How much do you know about their place of residence, however? Welcome to October 13! On this date in 1792, the cornerstone for the White House was laid. The oldest federal building in the capital, it became home to all of the American presidents since John Adams, the country's second president, who occupied it in 1800. The home has 132 rooms, with 28 fireplaces, eight staircases, and three elevators. Although it takes 570 gallons of paint to cover the outside surface, the choice of color is never difficult! Have a drink, the El Presidente Cocktail, to celebrate the home of our nation's leader.

EL PRESIDENTE COCKTAIL

1 1/2 oz light rum
   1   tsp grenadine
   1   tsp pineapple
       juice from 1 lime

Mix the ingredients with ice; strain into a cocktail glass. Order people around like you're The Man!

"If your doctor warns that you have to watch your drinking, find a bar with a mirror."

–JOHN MOONEY

OCTOBER

14

In the years following World War II, advances in military technology were kept highly secret. The Air Force was working on increasing the speed of its fighter planes. One brave man with a proven flight history, Chuck Yeager, was chosen to fly a new type of plane. The Bell XS-1, nicknamed the Glamour Glennis after Yeager's wife, broke the sound barrier, flying Mach 1.06 (that's 700 miles per hour for us laypeople), on this day in 1947. Yeager took the plane to 43,000 feet over Victorville, California. The achievement was kept secret until June of 1948. This leads us to two questions: didn't the residents of Victorville hear the sonic boom above their heads as Yeager reached such a high speed? And when Yeager was flying faster than the speed of sound, could he still listen to the radio in the cockpit? Think about it as you try the High Speed, described here.

HIGH SPEED

- 1 oz gin
- 2 oz lemon-flavored rum
- 8 oz Red Bull

Mix the gin and rum in a Collins glass with some ice. Add the Red Bull and stir. Make loud noises.

15

Margaretha Zelle was born in Holland in 1876. She was dark-skinned, almost exotic, in a country of people with blond hair and blue eyes. She and her family lived in Java and then Sumatra. Upon her return to Europe at the start of World War I, she began a new life as an exotic dancer in Paris under the name Mata Hari, which means "eye of the day" in Malay. Men flocked to her, and she was equal opportunity in her trysts—German, French, and Russian men of different ages and status were wooed—so some viewed her suspiciously. Was she a German spy? Was she a French spy? Some say she was both, some say she was neither. The French intercepted a German communiqué implicating Mata Hari. She was arrested, tried, and then executed on this date in 1917. Have a Spy Catcher as you think of secrets you'd rather not have people know about.

SPY CATCHER ▶

- 1 oz Canadian whisky
- 1/2 oz sambuca

Pour both ingredients into a shot glass, and serve.

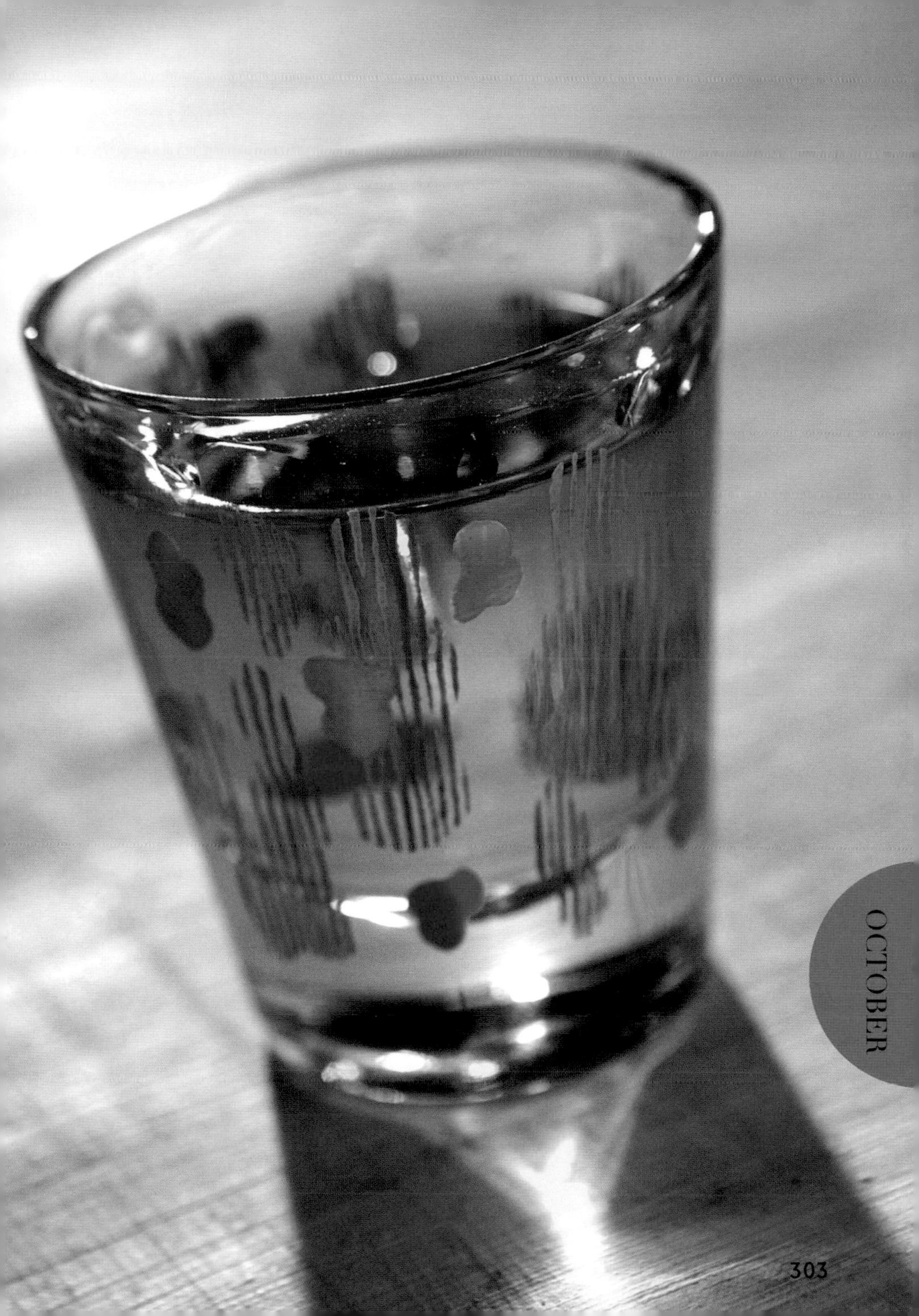

16

Fame and fortune can be fleeting, as was found by one Oscar Fingal O'Flahertie Wills Wilde, born in Dublin on this date in 1854. His father had been a successful doctor, and his mother was a writer who spoke several languages. Wilde must have inherited her gifts, because he was recognized at an early age as being an exceptional writer. He wrote and produced several popular plays in his lifetime, among them *A Woman of No Importance, An Ideal Husband, and The Importance of Being Earnest.* He also wrote poetry, yet it was his one novel, *The Picture of Dorian Gray,* that gained him notoriety due to its homosexual undertones—a no-no in Victorian England. Although this may have seemed scandalous at the time, the novel wasn't his undoing. Despite his seven years of marriage and the fact that he had fathered two children, it was Wilde's affair with the college-aged son of the Marquis of Queensberry that got him into trouble. Wilde sued the Marquis for libel when the Marquis called him a homosexual. Wilde eventually withdrew the charges—for obvious reasons—but was subsequently arrested for gross indecency. He was found guilty and sentenced to two years of hard labor. His wife left him, and Wilde relied on the kindness of friends as he drifted during the remaining few years of his life. We do have a few questions about the whole affair: if you are going to hold the title of Marquis of Queensberry, what lifestyle do you think your son is going to lead? Why not dress the lad in pink chiffon and call it a day?! Try the Wild Irish Buttery Squirrel, described here, as you wonder about the impact your dad's title had on your upbringing.

WILD IRISH BUTTERY SQUIRREL

1 oz vodka
1 oz butterscotch Schnapps
¹/2 oz amaretto
¹/2 oz Bailey's Irish Cream

Shake all the ingredients over ice until the drink is ice cold. Pour into an old-fashioned glass over ice.

17

Oil and gas prices going through the roof, people wondering about how they'll be able to heat their homes in the winter, lines of cars at the gas pumps. Sound familiar? Well, yes, we could be talking about post-Katrina 2005, but we're really talking about the early 1970s. You see, on this date in 1973, OPEC began an embargo of oil to Western countries and Japan. Why would these mostly Arab countries do such a thing? Because the United States and its allies had helped Israel rebuff an attack by Egypt and Syria in October of 1973. Although it suffered losses initially, Israel soon was on the offensive and vanquished the intruders. Members of OPEC were disgruntled and began the embargo. Oil prices eventually quadrupled, causing an energy crisis in the United States. For the first time, Americans were forced to realize the implications of their dependence on foreign sources of energy. Thankfully, we learned our lesson and began to develop nat-ural and renewable resources to replace oil and gas. Just kidding! We love oil and gas from foreign countries! But we know that these other countries would never take advantage of our dependence on them. Ha, just kidding again! Have a drink, the Motor Oil, described here, and be thankful you drive that huge gas-guzzling SUV sitting in your driveway.

MOTOR OIL

 1 oz Jägermeister
 $1/2$ oz peppermint Schnapps
 $1/2$ oz cinnamon Schnapps
 $1/2$ oz coconut rum

Pour the liquors in the order listed above into a large shot glass. Serve. Consider buying a hydrogen-powered vehicle or at least a hybrid.

OCTOBER

18

West Side Story is a modern-day Romeo and Juliet romance, set in New York City. Instead of the Montagues and the Capulets, we have rival gangs—a Puerto Rican group, known as the Sharks, and a white American group, the Jets. Despite their affiliations with different gangs, Tony and the beautiful Maria can't help but fall in love. On this date in 1961, the movie, based on the play, which was based on the book, premiered at the Rivoli Theater in New York City. How successful could such a movie be? Don't ask Madonna, who tried it with *Evita!* *West Side Story* won 10 Academy Awards, more than any other movie except *Ben-Hur* and *Titanic*. Wow! Celebrate this terrific take on an old story by trying the Juliet, described here.

JULIET

1	oz tequila
1	oz Pisang Ambon liqueur
1 1/2	oz pineapple juice
1/2	tsp grenadine
1	slice pineapple
1	maraschino cherry

Mix together the liquid ingredients and strain into a cocktail glass. Garnish with a slice of pineapple and a cherry. As you drink, choke back your tears for the unfortunate lovers!

19

We can't figure out what surprises us most about the Concorde, the world's fastest commercial plane. Is it the fact that the British and French actually worked together on a successful project? Is it the fact that the Americans let the title of fastest anything go to another nation? Or is it the fact that the planes flew for so many years despite their cramped seats and lack of first-class extras? On this date in 1977, the first Concorde landed in New York City. Daily flights were scheduled from London and Paris to New York and Washington, DC. Travel time to New York was reduced to a remarkable 3 1/2 hours. The Concorde flew until 2003, when the commercial fleet was finally grounded. The causes of its demise? The expense of upkeep and the drop in consumer demand. All good things come to an end, as we know. Celebrate the Concorde's long and speedy run as you try the Concorde, described here.

CONCORDE

$1/2$ oz coffee liqueur
$1/2$ oz Bailey's Irish Cream
 1 splash rum

Gently pour the ingredients into a
shot glass in the order listed so that
they are layered. Light the rum on
fire. Please put the flame out
before drinking!

"A man is a fool if he drinks before he reaches the age of 50, and a fool if he doesn't afterward."

–FRANK LLOYD WRIGHT

OCTOBER

20

One of the most famous buildings in the world, the Sydney Opera House in Sydney, Australia, opened on this date in 1973 to the tune of $102 million. Those of us familiar with Boston's Big Dig financial woes can appreciate the rise in costs experienced by the Opera House builders: it was originally projected to cost $7 million. Ha! It was designed by Jorn Utzon and took 16 years to build. Utzon had taken into consideration acoustics and the importance of interior design. However, when a change in Australian government took place, Utzon was replaced by officials who redesigned some aspects of the project, impacting acoustics. Utzon described the fiasco as "Malice in Blunderland." His design was redeemed when plans were made to redesign the interior and he was designated as the supervisor. Sometimes it takes governments a while to make the right decision, huh, Jorn? Have a Sydney Sling as you celebrate the famed Sydney Opera House.

SYDNEY SLING ▶

1 1/2 oz light rum
1 oz cherry brandy
1/2 oz Triple Sec
1/3 oz Yellow Chartreuse
3/4 oz lime juice
2 oz pineapple juice
1 1/2 oz orange juice
1 dash bitters
1 sprig mint
lime, lemon, and orange slices
1 maraschino cherry

Mix the liquid ingredients in a shaker and strain over ice into a Collins glass. Garnish with a sprig of mint, and slices of lime, lemon, and orange. Add a cherry and an umbrella. Sing an aria like a fat Italian fellow.

21 The world's oldest commissioned warship still afloat is the *USS Constitution*, based in Charlestown, Massachusetts. A three-masted frigate, she was launched on this date in 1797 in Boston Harbor as the fledgling nation tried to build a navy. During the War of 1812, she earned the nickname "Old Ironsides" when an opposing sea captain noticed his cannonballs making no impact on the 7-inch-thick oak planks of her hull. Rumor has it he was heard to say, "Frigate!" Try the Navy Grog as you toast this lady of the sea.

◄ NAVY GROG

- $^1/_2$ oz light rum
- $^1/_2$ oz gold rum
- $^1/_2$ oz dark rum
- $^1/_2$ oz orange liqueur
- 1 oz grapefruit juice
- 1 oz orange juice
- 1 oz pineapple juice
- 1 orange wedge
- 1 pineapple chunk

Pour the liquors into a Collins glass over ice and add the juices. Garnish with a wedge of orange and a pineapple chunk.

22

"Our missiles are bigger than your missiles." Such is the essence of the Cuban Missile Crisis, which began on this date in 1962. Spy planes over Cuba, which had become the cozy Communist comrade of the Soviet Union after the rise to power of Fidel Castro (see August 13), communicated the construction of what appeared to be missile silos. President John F. Kennedy was faced with the choice of allowing a potential nuclear threat to be located 20 or so miles off the U.S. coastline or demanding that the missile base be closed. The real difficulty was the involvement of the Soviets. The United States and the USSR were in the throes of the Cold War, and any misstep could result in nuclear warfare. Kennedy decided that an air and naval blockade of the island would be the best route in handling the threat; he communicated this to the American people and the Soviet government on television. The Soviets backed down—they promised to dismantle the missile base if the United States promised not to invade Cuba. The Soviets also demanded that the missile site that had been established in Turkey aimed at the eastern half of their country be dismantled. The United States secretly agreed to this demand, because the Turkish site had been secret as well. The world had come to the brink of war—perhaps nuclear, perhaps worldwide—and had survived. Try a Cuba Libre, below. We assume the libre, which means "free" in Spanish, stands for "free of missiles."

CUBA LIBRE

    ½ oz fresh lime juice
    2 oz light rum
       cola

Pour the lime juice into a Collins glass over ice. Add the rum and then the soda, stir, and serve. Salute Fidel, JFK, fine cigars, or whatever you feel like!

OCTOBER

23

"I can't die until the government finds a safe place to bury my liver."

—PHIL HARRIS

On this date in 1925, Johnny Carson was born. Carson was the king of late-night television and a beloved fixture of American culture. He was known for making guests feel at ease with his casual interviewing style, and he also handled nervous performers with aplomb, ensuring their best work. Carson earned six Emmy Awards, won a George Foster Peabody Award, and a Congressional Medal of Freedom, and entered the Television Hall of Fame in 1987. Celebrate his life with a Johnny Bravo, described here.

JOHNNY BRAVO

- 1 oz vodka
- 1 oz peach Schnapps
- 1 oz watermelon Schnapps
- 1 oz blue curaçao
- 2 oz cranberry juice

Mix all the ingredients in a Collins glass over ice and serve.

24

On this date in 1861, ponies across the United States breathed a huge sigh of relief. Why? Because Western Union completed the first transcontinental telegraph line. Now, instead of sending messages via horseback, er, ponyback, from one end of the country to the other, Samuel Morse's combination of dots and dashes could send messages in mere moments. Of course, some ponies were jealous of the new technology, and could be seen smoking cigarettes and drinking whiskey in cafes and saloons. Others tried to find work in parades and carnivals. We won't even discuss the increase in glue production in this new era of the telegraph. Well, we'll try: - -
- - -   . - .   . / - - .   . - . . .
. -   !! Use Morse code to figure this one out as you try a Telegraph, described here.

TELEGRAPH

1 $^1/_2$ oz rum
$^3/_4$ oz vodka
　　 ginger ale

Mix the rum and vodka over ice in a Collins glass. Top off with ginger ale, stir, and serve.

"He who laughs last, hasn't passed out yet."

–UNKNOWN

"Let's all drink gin and make wry faces.

−BOB HOPE,
THE CAT AND THE CANARY

By October 25, 1944, at the culmination of the battle of Leyte Gulf in the Philippines, the Allied Forces had experienced a frightening new tactic employed by the Japanese forces. The kamikaze pilots, who flew suicide missions with airplanes loaded with explosives into the decks of Allied ships, were definitely unexpected. The Japanese military never had a problem in recruiting volunteers for kamikaze missions; in fact, there were three times as many volunteers as there were aircraft. Even more surprisingly, the average kamikaze pilot was a 20-something studying at a university. Their motives in volunteering varied from patriotism to a desire to bring honor to their families, or simply to prove themselves personally. Maybe they should have considered taking up the cello. Just a thought . . .

KAMIKAZE ❯

- 1 oz vodka
- 1 oz Triple Sec
- 1 oz lime juice

Mix all the ingredients with ice and strain into an old-fashioned glass over ice.

315

26

The gunfight at the O.K. Corral was an event of legendary proportions that took place on October 26, 1881, in a vacant lot, behind the corral in Tombstone, Arizona. For such a historically lauded event, it was surprisingly short: only 30 shots were fired in just 30 seconds. Wyatt Earp, Morgan Earp, Virgil Earp, and Doc Holliday fought against Billy Claiborne, Frank McLaury, Tom McLaury, Billy Clanton, and Ike Clanton. To this day, pro-Earp followers view the gunfight as a struggle between law-and-order and outlaw forces, while pro-Clanton/McLaury followers view it as a political vendetta and abuse of authority. We view it as the stuff of good movie makin'!

DOC HOLLIDAY

- 2 oz whiskey
- 6 oz citrus soda
  orange juice
  sugar

Pour the whiskey and soda into a Collins glass. Stir in the orange juice and sugar to taste.

27

On October 27, 1914, Dylan Thomas, one of the greatest poets of the twentieth century, was born. His most famous poems include "Do Not Go Gentle into That Good Night" and "And Death Shall Have No Dominion." In honor of Thomas and his amazing work, we've decided to write a poem for you. Here's what we came up with:

Roses are red
Violets are blue
For tonight's cocktail hour
How about this brew!

DARING DYLAN

- 4 oz Mexican hot cocoa
- 2 oz tequila
- 1 oz Kahlùa

Make the cocoa and let it cool. Combine over crushed ice with the remaining ingredients in a coffee mug. Stir and serve.

28

On October 28, 1636, Harvard College was founded. You know Harvard—it's the place your parents tell their acquaintances you went to school. The place you'd like to tell most people you went to school. The place where, if you've been paying careful attention, you would realize we did not go to school. A community of the uber-smart. Since 1974, 19 Nobel Prize winners and 15 Pulitzer Prize winners have served on the Harvard faculty. Rumor has it that, like osmosis, the more time you spend near Harvard, the smarter you become. But that's just a rumor. We're going to stick with what we know: the more of these Harvard Cocktails you have, the smarter you will definitely become. You'll know it when you get there, as will everybody else.

HARVARD COCKTAIL

    1   oz dry vermouth
    3/4 oz brandy
    1   dash bitters

Pour all the ingredients over ice in a shaker. Shake well and strain into a chilled cocktail glass. Drink until you feel smart.

"My nerves could stand a drink."

–GRACE KELLY, *TO CATCH A THIEF*

"Gosh, I just love gambling in Vegas. Sure, I may lose $100,000, but the drinks are free so it evens out!"

–MEGAN MULLALLY,
WILL & GRACE

The phrase Black Tuesday refers to October 29, 1929, five days after the U.S. stock market crash, when general panic set in and everyone with investments in the stock market tried to pull out en masse. The week and its aftermath marked the start of the Great Depression. But while Black Tuesday is often cited as the worst day in stock market history, Black Monday of 1987 was much worse in terms of percentage loss. See, when you put it in perspective, its not really that bad at all. Wonder how it'll seem after a few Run for Your Money shots?

RUN FOR YOUR MONEY

$^1/_2$ oz sour apple Schnapps
$^1/_2$ oz strawberry Schnapps

Pour both Schnapps into a shot glass. Have it go down like your retirement nest egg.

30

On October 30, 1938, Orson Welles aired his *War of the Worlds* program over the radio waves across the United States. The broadcast was a contemporary retelling of the events of Welles' novel of the same name, presented as a series of news bulletins in documentary style. Funny for us—but not for them—many people missed or ignored the opening credits of the program, as well as the several disclaimers scattered throughout, and took it to be an actual news broadcast of extraterrestrials attacking the Earth. Needless to say, *War of the Worlds* caused nationwide panic. This was very similar to the nationwide panic we ourselves experienced when it was announced that it would be made into a modern-day movie starring Tom Cruise, who believes, incidentally, that we're all aliens from another planet.

"It is the wise man who stays home when he's drunk."

–EURIPIDES

A LITTLE GREEN MAN FROM MARS

1	mint green maraschino cherry
$^1/_2$	oz Jagermeister
$^1/_2$	oz Rumple Minze

After removing the stem, place the cherry in a shot glass. Add the liquors and serve.

31

Boo! It's Halloween. Pull out the white sheet for your ghost costume and cut the two eyeholes, and, of course, the mouth hole for drinking. All Hallow's Eve is celebrated the night before the Day of the Dead. According to Celtic beliefs, it is when the spirits supposedly rise from the dead. To pacify them, people placed food at the doors of their houses, which is why candy is distributed today. To scare off the evil spirits, the Celts wore masks. Stir up today's featured drink, the Witch's Brew, and rouse a few spirits of your own.

WITCH'S BREW

    2 oz Yellow Chartreuse
1 $^1/_2$ oz blue curaçao
  $^1/_2$ oz spiced brandy
  $^1/_4$ tsp ground cloves
    1 dash nutmeg
    1 dash allspice

Combine all the ingredients over ice and shake. Pour into a chilled cocktail glass and garnish with eye of newt or snake's brains.

"Alcohol may be man's worst enemy, but the Bible says love your enemy."

—FRANK SINATRA

OCTOBER

1 NOVEMBER

Everybody loves an art opening. The wine, the cheese, the critical judgments, the back-stabbing . . . a good time for everybody! On this day in 1512, Michelangelo had an art opening of his own when his paintings on the ceiling of the Sistine Chapel were first exhibited to the public. We're sure there was the usual fanfare, raised eye-brows, whispers, you know the drill. Following the opening reception, several critics were rumored to have said they thought the hand of man touching the hand of God was a nice touch, but now they needed the hands of a chiropractor to touch their necks. All just rumors, of course.

ANGEL'S WING

$^1/2$ oz white crème de cacao
$^1/2$ oz brandy
  1 tbsp light cream

Pour the ingredients carefully, in the order given, into a cordial glass so that they do not mix. Serve.

2

On this date in 1947, the largest and widest airplane ever built—with a wingspan of 319 feet, 11 inches—made its only flight. Its pilot, owner, and designer, Howard Hughes, flew the huge wooden plane over Long Beach Harbor, California, at an altitude of 70 feet. The flight lasted just one minute. Hughes named the plane "Hercules," but it was later renamed the "Spruce Goose." Largest plane? Made out of wood? Only one minute in the air? We're going to file this one in the category of: People with too Much Time and Money on Their Hands.

LONG BEACH ICED TEA

1 shot vodka
1 shot light rum
1 shot gin
1 shot tequila
1 shot Triple Sec
1 splash cranberry juice
1 lemon wedge

In a Collins glass, pour the shots over ice and top off with the cranberry juice and lemon wedge. Stir, and wish you had money to burn.

These days, it seems like the qualifications for getting a government job have veered toward the silver screen—or at least the television screen. Former actor Ronald Reagan went on to be a governor and eventually the president of the United States. Sonny Bono, variety show entertainer and ex-husband of Cher, settled into a U.S. Congressman position before that fateful skiing trip, as did Fred Grandy, the loveable Gopher from TV's *The Love Boat*. Arnold Schwarzenegger has his meaty hands around California's equally meaty neck, and on this day in 1998, former pro wrestler Jesse "The Body" Ventura was elected governor of Minnesota. Mix up a Wild Thing, below, and ponder how you might wrestle yourself up a government job when your current career heads down the drain.

WILD THING

1 ¹/₂	oz	tequila
1	oz	cranberry juice
1	oz	club soda
¹/₂	oz	lime juice
1		slice lime

Pour the liquid ingredients over ice into an old-fashioned glass. Garnish with a lime wheel.

"Let there be dancing in the streets, drinking in the saloons, and necking in the parlor."

—GROUCHO MARX,
A NIGHT AT THE OPERA

NOVEMBER

Laura Lane Bush was born November 4, 1946, and is the wife of U.S. President George W. Bush and therefore the First Lady of the United States. We don't subscribe to most of her family's political hoo-ha, and frankly, we don't subscribe to most politicians' political hoo-ha . . . but we do like to say "hoo-ha!" Regardless, we think Laura is all right. She's stylish and witty, has the cutest little Texas twang, and is a champion for literacy nationwide. Being as this is a book and we're the authors of it, we're a big fan of reading, too. However, we suspect that by now, if you've been trying a few of the libations we've recommended so far, reading is something you definitely cannot do. You also probably can't write your name and definitely shouldn't be driving a car, so mix up a smooth and creamy Bailey's Bush, kick back, and relax.

BAILEY'S BUSH

1 ½ oz Bailey's Irish Cream
1 ½ oz Irish whisky

Pour both ingredients over ice into an old-fashioned glass, and serve.

> "Meet me down in the bar! We'll drink breakfast together."
>
> –W. C. FIELDS,
> *THE BIG BROADCAST OF 1938*

5

On November 5, 1872, Susan B. Anthony cast a vote in the U.S. presidential election, which earned her a fine of $100—a whopping sum at the time. Why would somebody be fined for voting in an election, you might ask? Well, we'll tell you. Ms. Anthony was a woman, and in those days, women weren't allowed to vote. Apparently, it would seem the menfolk thought the ladies would be better served havin' babies and makin' pie. Susan, a staunch suffragist, didn't agree. She never paid the fine, and little more than 100 years later, her likeness graces the Susan B. Anthony dollar, a coin still in circulation to this day.

HEARTY SUSAN

1 1/2 oz blended whiskey
1/2 oz cherry brandy
1 maraschino cherry

Pour the whiskey and cherry brandy into a mixing glass half-filled with ice cubes. Stir well, and strain into a cocktail glass. Garnish with a maraschino cherry, and serve.

6

On November 6, 2002, a jury in Beverly Hills, California, convicted actress Winona Ryder of stealing $5,500 worth of merchandise from Saks Fifth Avenue. It seems Ms. Ryder, regardless of her hefty movie-makin' paychecks, didn't feel as though she needed to pay for that which caught her fancy in the high-end department store. Do you think the 37 different illegal prescriptions she had had filled using 20 different doctors and 6 aliases might have had something to do with it? We're going to go out on a limb and say . . . probably. In honor of Winona, indulge in your own Guilty Verdict, as outlined below.

GUILTY VERDICT

1 oz Bacardi 151 proof rum
6 oz orange juice

Pour the Bacardi 151 into a Collins glass half-filled with ice. Add orange juice, and serve.

7

The cigarette-manufacturing machine was patented by Albert H. Hook of New York City on November 7, 1876. Ironic name for the man who certainly helped millions of nicotine addicts take one giant leap forward on the path to social ostracism. Yes, Hook made it easier for generations of people to take up smoking, thereby creating a global community of the Us-es versus the Thems-es.

SMOKY MARTINI

2 1/2 oz gin
1 splash Scotch whisky
1 twist lemon peel

Stir the gin and whisky together in a cocktail glass with ice to chill. Garnish with a twist of lemon peel, and serve.

"I distrust a man who says "when." If he's got to be careful not to drink too much, it's because he's not to be trusted when he does."

—SYDNEY GREENSTREET,
THE MALTESE FALCON

NOVEMBER

> "The whole world is drunk and we're just the cocktail of the moment. Someday soon, the world will wake up, down two aspirin with a glass of tomato juice, and wonder what the hell all the fuss was about."
>
> —DEAN MARTIN

The Louvre, arguably the greatest museum in the world, opened its doors in Paris on this day in 1793. Home to thousands and thousands of lesser-known works of art, it is also home to some of the world's most famous art, including the Mona Lisa and the Venus de Milo. Why should this armless, ancient Greek statue of the goddess Aphrodite have gained such fame? It was apparently all a propagandist coup on the part of the French government, which was trying to convince its citizens, still cranky from the loss of a beloved statue to Italy following the downfall of Napoleon, that the Venus de Milo was a much greater treasure. The French bought it—and so did we; we think she's stunning. As a matter of fact, the more of these Venus on the Rocks we drink, the more beautiful she gets! Who needs arms?

VENUS ON THE ROCKS ▶

1 oz amaretto
2 oz peach Schnapps
3 oz club soda
1 twist lime peel

Pour the liquid ingredients into an old-fashioned glass with five ice cubes. Garnish with a twist of lime, and serve.

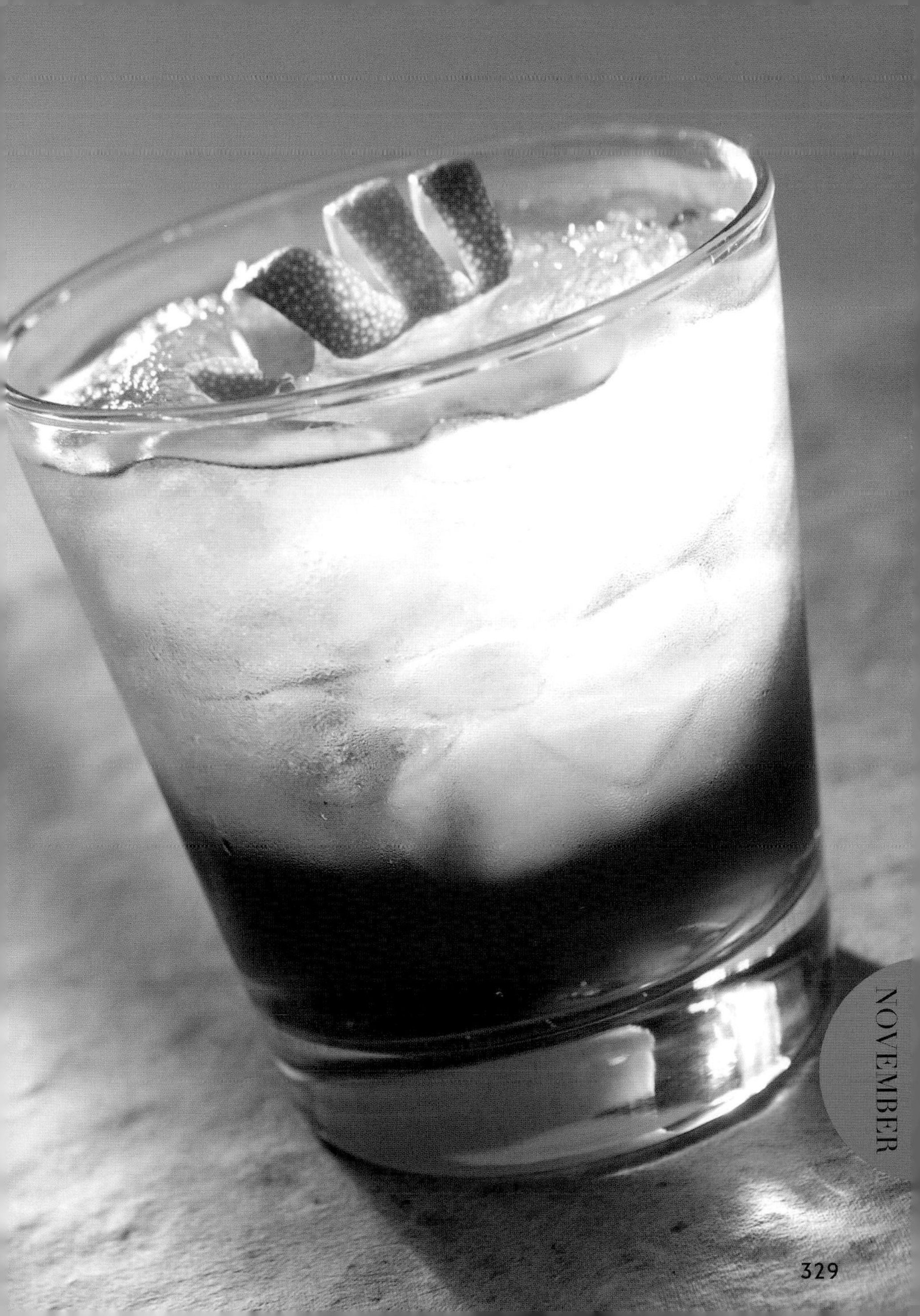

9

Arguably one of the most historic events to take place during our lifetime occurred on this day in 1989, when the 27.9-mile-long Berlin Wall was opened and thousands of East Germans poured into the West, prompting a nationwide party and reuniting countrymen who had been kept apart for nearly 30 years. Nationwide party? Long-overdue reunions? You know what that means: plenty of hooch to go around. God bless the end of the Cold War and the beginnings of a cold drink!

HARVEY WALLBANGER

    1   oz vodka
    4   oz orange juice
    1/2 oz Galliano herbal liqueur

Pour the vodka and orange juice into a Collins glass over ice cubes and stir. Float the Galliano on top and serve.

10

Monsters who are afraid of monsters? A large yellow bird with a hairy, elephant-like friend that only he can see? Two men who live in the same house, share the same room, but are "just friends"? Sounds like 1969 to us, and no, we're not smokin' the whacky tobaccy. It was on this day in the year of brotherly love and peace signs that *Sesame Street* made its debut on PBS television, to the delight of millions of American children and several stoned adults. Now normally, we would turn up our noses at associating an alcoholic drink with a children's television program. However, we didn't invent the Big Bird recipe below, but we certainly imbibed it!

BIG BIRD

    1   oz banana Schnapps
    2 1/2 oz pineapple juice
    2 1/2 oz orange juice

Pour the banana Schnapps into a Collins glass filled with ice cubes. Fill the rest of the way with the pineapple and orange juices, and serve.

11

Not having lived through a world war, we're not sure, but we can only imagine that it's awfully nice when one comes to an end. And so it was on this day in 1918 when the fighting of World War I came to an end with the signing of an armistice between the Allies and Germany. During the war, more than 9 million people died on the battlefield, and nearly that many more died on the home front due to food shortages, genocide, and ground combat. It's a good thing that it came to an end—with numbers like that, there wouldn't have been anybody left to fight in the Second World War! Shake up an Allies Cocktail, below, and thank your lucky stars there hasn't been a third.

ALLIES COCKTAIL

    1   oz dry vermouth
    1   oz gin
    $^1/_2$ tsp caraway liqueur

Stir all the ingredients with ice, strain the contents into a cocktail glass, and serve.

"Alcohol is the anesthesia by which we endure the operation of life."

–GEORGE BERNARD SHAW

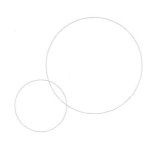

12

"I never should have switched from Scotch to Martinis."

–HUMPHREY BOGART'S
LAST WORDS

November 12 marked the breaking point in a dark period of history for the American gay man. It was on this day in 1996 that Jonathan Schmitz was convicted of second-degree murder for shooting Scott Amedure, a gay man who'd revealed that he had a crush on Schmitz during a taping of *The Jenny Jones Show* in 1995. Schmitz was lured onto the show with promises that a secret crush would be revealed, only to discover that the amorous one was his gay neighbor, Amedure. We're outraged that anybody would kill another human being, especially for something as innocuous as a crush, but we do question Amedure's thought process. Did he really believe he was going to win his man by spilling his heart out on *The Jenny Jones Show*? They don't have onstage bodyguards for nothing!

DEEP DARK SECRET ▶

1 ¹/₂ oz dark rum
¹/₂ oz Anejo rum
¹/₂ oz coffee liqueur
¹/₂ oz heavy cream

In a shaker half-filled with ice cubes, combine all of the ingredients. Shake well, and strain into a cocktail glass.

13

On this day in 1940, Walt Disney Pictures released their third animated film, *Fantasia*. A technical dream at the time, the film met with a lackluster reception and played mostly at B-movie houses. Frankly, we're shocked by this. How could a movie that included a mouse dressed up as a magician cajoling a herd of brooms to perform a choreographed dance not be a smash hit? Oh, right. Well, luckily, Disney's next film, *Dumbo*, was a big hit. Drink a Magic Flute, below, while you ponder the nature of popularity.

MAGIC FLUTE

  2 oz chocolate liqueur
  1 oz amaretto

Shake the ingredients well in a shaker. Strain into a cocktail glass over three or four ice cubes, and serve.

14

Moby Dick, which was published on this day in 1851, follows the hardy crew of the Pequod, led by Captain Ahab, on a whaling expedition that takes them around the world. The expedition soon degenerates into a monomaniacal hunt for the legendary "Great White Whale," as Ahab seeks revenge on the animal that cost him a leg. Revenge is a spiteful thing, as we can attest. Many a power-mad bartender who dared to cut us off has suffered a whalelike harpooning at our hands. Thar she blows!

THE CAPTAIN'S MARTINI

  1 1/2 oz gin
  1 tsp vermouth
  1/2 oz white crème de menthe

Combine the gin, vermouth, and crème de menthe in a shaker with ice. Shake and serve in a cocktail glass.

Where to begin with the deliciously trashy case of Joey Buttafuoco and Amy Fisher, his "Long Island Lolita"? On this day in 1993, following a media circus complete with metaphorical clowns and hoops of fire, a judge in Mineola, New York, sentenced Joey Buttafuoco to six months in jail for the statutory rape of Amy Fisher, who shot and wounded Buttafuoco's wife, Mary Jo, in a jealous attempt to win her man. Fisher apparently met Joey Buttafuoco in May of 1991, when she took her car to his auto shop for repairs.

A sexual affair began, and when Fisher needed money, Joey set her up to work with an escort agency. The affair continued while Fisher was working as a prostitute. We've said it before and we'll say it again: truth is stranger than fiction. These days, Buttafuoco is producing a movie that encompasses his famous saga and the battle to recover from his very public humiliation. Of course he is! It's the American way, after all.

BUTTAFUOCO

  2 oz light tequila
  ¹/₂ oz Galliano herbal liqueur
  ¹/₂ oz cherry liqueur
  ¹/₂ oz fresh lemon juice
      club soda
  I maraschino cherry

In a cocktail shaker, combine all the ingredients except the club soda and the cherry with cracked ice. Shake well. Strain into a Collins glass over ice cubes and fill with club soda. Stir, then add the cherry.

NOVEMBER

16

Theater junkies and anybody who's ever watched nonfootball-related television on Thanksgiving afternoons can rejoice in celebration on this day. It was on November 16, 1959, that the Rodgers and Hammerstein musical *The Sound of Music* opened on Broadway. Not too long after, it was made into a movie starring the lovely Julie Andrews as an Austrian singing-nun-turned-nanny-turned-stepmother. We can thank Rodgers and Hamm for such catchy jingles as "Doe a Deer" and "Climb Every Mountain." We'd be remiss not to admit that more than one drunken night has found us whaling those two numbers as well as the rest of *The Sound of Music* score (in falsetto, of course) as we sipped a Hot Nun down at the local piano bar.

"The trouble with jogging is the ice falls out of your glass."

—MARTIN MULL

◀ HOT NUN

1 ¹/₂ oz Frangelico hazelnut liqueur
1 tbsp honey
3 whole cloves
1 twist lemon peel
hot water

Pour the hazelnut liqueur into a brandy snifter. Add the honey, cloves, and lemon peel, and then fill the snifter with hot water.

17

As we look back upon California's colorful political history, we can't help but ask ourselves and everybody around us: what happened to California? It was on this day in 2003 that Austrian bodybuilder Arnold Schwarzenegger, who had already melted into many of our pots, was sworn in as the thirty-eighth governor of the state. But this isn't the first time that the California Governor's Mansion has played host to an off-the-beaten-path tenant. Remember, before he made it to the White House, Ronald Reagan spent time in Sacramento as well. I guess California just goes to prove that, in the United States, anyone really can be a politician. Hey, I think we've learned this lesson before . . .

TERMINATOR

¹/₂ oz 151 proof rum
¹/₂ oz Rumple Minze peppermint liqueur

Pour the rum first, then fill the shot glass with the peppermint liqueur.

18

On November 18, 1978, two metal buckets of grape-flavored Kool-Aid laced with Valium and cyanide were brought into the assembly hall of the People's Temple Cult, which was headed by Jim Jones in Jonestown, Guyana. The mixture was dispensed to the entire congregation in small paper cups, and they were urged to kill themselves by drinking the grape punch. Surprisingly, they all did, more than 1,000 of them, as a matter of fact. And the really shocking thing is that they weren't even drunk! We understand how you might be skeptical of the grape stuff after reading that, but try ours anyway—it has more of the good stuff and less of the bad. We promise.

GRAPE PUNCH ▶

1 oz rum
2 oz grape Schnapps
1 tsp powdered sugar
2 oz fresh lemon juice
1 lemon wedge

Pour the rum, grape Schnapps, sugar, and lemon juice into a cocktail shaker half-filled with ice. Shake well, and strain into a Collins glass filled with ice. Garnish with a lemon wedge, and serve.

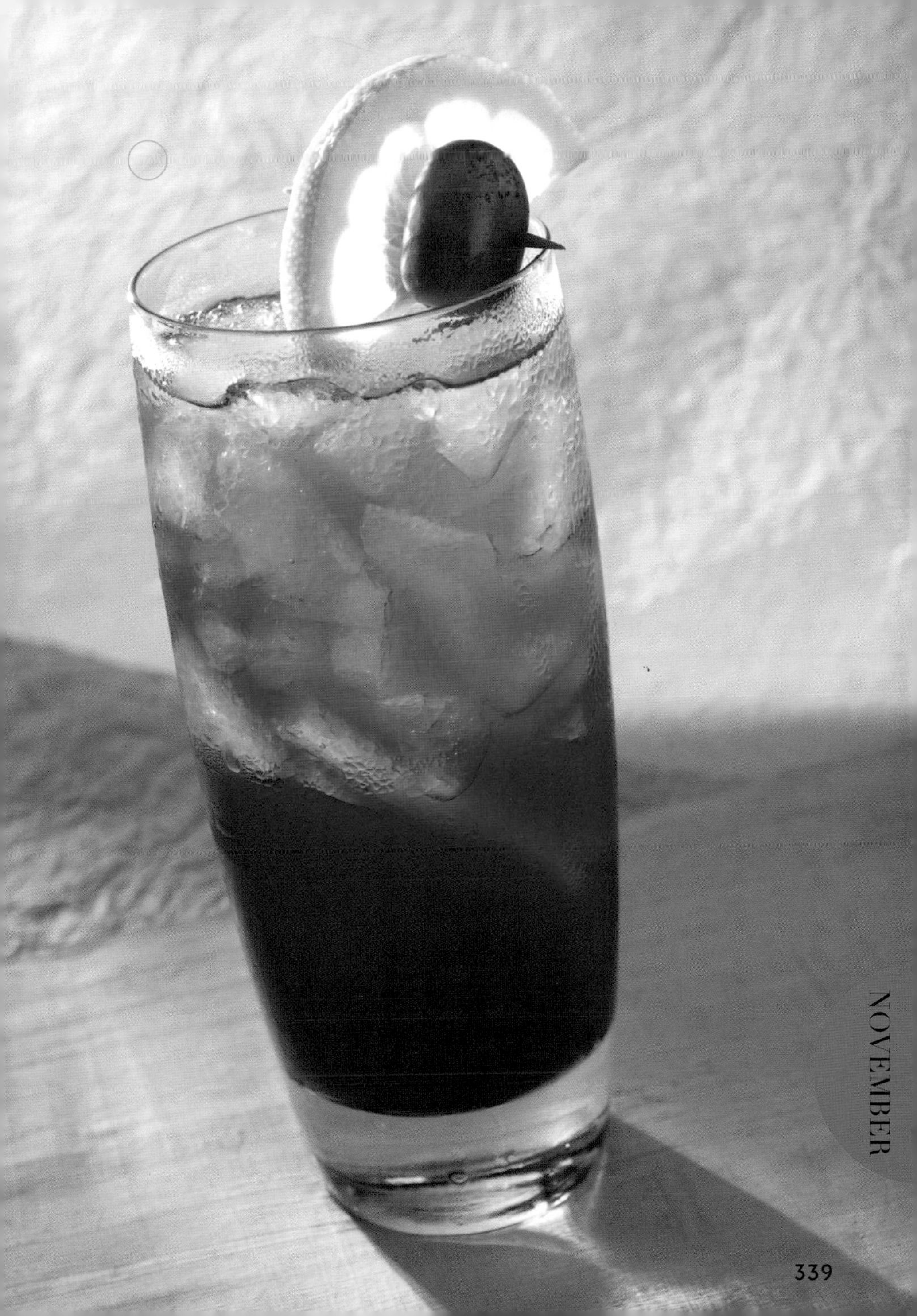

19

On this day in 1990, the pop duo Milli Vanilli was stripped of its Grammy Award after it was revealed that neither performer sang on the group's album "Girl You Know It's True." Oops. Bummer for the boys, but we don't know what the big deal is: in our opinion, half the pop and rock albums out there today have no singing at all on them, just a lot of yelling. Back in our day, when we walked to school 10 miles in the snow with no shoes, uphill both ways, musicians really knew how to sing. Mix up a Milli Vanilli and hum a few bars.

MILLI VANILLI

2 oz vanilla Schnapps
1 oz coffee liqueur
milk or cream

Pour the vanilla Schnapps and coffee liqueur into an old-fashioned glass with ice. Finish with cream or milk to taste, and serve.

20

During an interview broadcast on BBC television on this day in 1995, Princess Diana admitted that she had been unfaithful to her husband, Prince Charles. Shocking, we know. But don't turn your noses up at the late great princess just yet: it turns out that Prince Charles himself had also been unfaithful to her with his longtime gal pal Camilla. What?! The public, of course, drank in each and every intoxicating new twist, proving that royal scandal is a spectator sport. We ourselves simply drew comfort in knowing that the royals have faults of their own and are just like the rest of us . . . except for the fabulous wealth, the numerous castles, the yachts, the cars, the titles . . . but other than that they're exactly like us. Don't you think?

INFIDELITY

1 oz vodka
1/2 oz Triple Sec
1/2 oz whiskey sour mix
4 oz fruit punch
6 oz grape punch

Pour all the ingredients into a shaker half-filled with crushed ice and shake well. Strain into a Collins glass half-filled with crushed ice, and serve.

21

The mother of all television cliffhangers came to an end on this day in 1980, when the largest TV audience to date, an estimated 82 million people, watched as Sue Ellen's sister, Kristin Shepard, shoot J.R. Ewing on *Dallas*. The jilted mistress was finally seen holding the smoking gun after viewers were left hanging for an entire summer, asking the question that is emblazoned into our gray matter for eternity: "Who shot J.R.?" Emblazoned, we tell you, right next to that other unnerving TV question that we wish we could forget: "Where's the beef?"

DALLAS STARS

$^1/_2$ oz green crème de menthe
$^1/_2$ oz cinnamon Schnapps

Layer the ingredients in a shot glass. Drink up. Try to find the beef.

"The important thing is the rhythm. Always have rhythm in your shaking. Now a Manhattan you always shake to fox-trot time, a Bronx to two-step time, a dry martini you always shake to waltz time."

—WILLIAM POWELL,
THE THIN MAN

NOVEMBER

We've all heard the question: where were you when President Kennedy was shot? Those who were around all have an answer, and it's usually preceded by the statement "I'll never forget it." But the only one it really mattered to was Kennedy himself, unfortunately. He was in Dallas on this day in 1963, when he was assassinated while riding in a motorcade beside his wife Jackie. The nation mourned the beloved president, and the shooting still mystifies the nation. Have a Presidential Margarita to commemorate JFK.

◖ PRESIDENTIAL MARGARITA

1 $^{1}/_{2}$ oz brandy
1 $^{1}/_{2}$ oz orange liqueur
1 $^{1}/_{2}$ oz tequila
    juice of 1 lime
1 slice lime

Pour the brandy, liqueur, and tequila into a large glass and add ice. Rim a margarita glass with lime juice and salt, fill with ice, and garnish with a lime slice. Carefully pour the contents of the large glass into the salted margarita glass, leaving the salt undisturbed.

"A lush is a lush is a lush."

—GERTRUDE STEIN

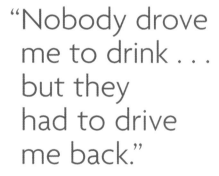

23

It was on this day in 1887 that Boris Karloff was born. Although he was a very distinguished actor, it is for his roles in the horror genre that we know him best, most specifically for his roles in *Frankenstein* and *The Mummy*. He also narrated the famous made-for-television animated feature *How the Grinch Stole Christmas*— a piece of television trivia that many people don't know. In honor of the scariest actor ever born, shake up a Vampire and pray that the sun doesn't go down.

VAMPIRE

- 1 oz raspberry liqueur
- 1 oz vodka
- 1 oz cranberry juice

Combine the ingredients in a shaker with ice. Serve as shots in an old-fashioned glass.

"Nobody drove me to drink . . . but they had to drive me back."

–JOHN BARLEYCORN

24

On November 24, 1859, British naturalist Charles Darwin published *On the Origin of Species*, which explained his theory of evolution. Man from monkey is widely debated to this day, with many simply not believing that we could have evolved in such a manner. But we ask you to look around at some of your friends, neighbors, and fellow countrymen before you make your decision. And when you're opening the bottle of brandy to make the Funky Monkey below, thank God for those opposable thumbs!

FUNKY MONKEY

- 2 oz brandy
- 2 oz Kahlùa
- 1 oz milk
- 1 banana
- 5 oz ice cream

In a blender, add all the ingredients and blend. Serve in a beer mug.

"One tequila, two tequila, three tequila, floor." —GEORGE CARLIN

NOVEMBER

"I'll have what the man on the floor's having!"

—UNKNOWN

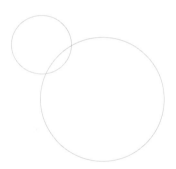

Speaking of underage drinking in college (which we absolutely do not promote or condone), it was on this day in 1825 that the first college social fraternity, Kappa Alpha, was formed at Union College in Schenectady, New York. We're guessing that since there were no cars to turn over then or televisions to toss out of bedroom windows, things were much tamer for the Kappa Alpha brothers. Luckily, there was alcohol, though, so tip your glass to the original party boys at Union College. If not for them, generations of college students that followed might have actually gotten some school work done.

PARTY BOY

1	slice lemon
1	tsp sugar
1 1/2	oz pink lemonade
1	dash sweet and sour mix
1	oz Bacardi 151 proof rum
1/2	oz Triple Sec
1/2	oz citron vodka

Rub a lemon slice on the edge of a whiskey sour glass. Dip the edge of the glass in sugar. Add the pink lemonade and a dash of sweet and sour mix. Then add rum, Triple Sec, and vodka. Stir. Lick around the edge of the glass, then take the shot.

26

Hey, it's not just the man in the Oval Office who can bring scandal to the White House. Presidential offspring have been popping up in the news and causing their parents to see red since the very beginning. Jenna and Barbara Bush, who were born on this day in 1981, have certainly done their share of causing sleepless nights for the beleaguered President Bush. Both daughters have had well-publicized incidents of underage drinking in college, causing a media uproar. Everybody has an opinion about it, and they've been dubbed "bad girls" more than once. But we ask you, dear reader, before you shake your head and point an accusing finger at the Bush twins, to remember that you were once in college, too.

NAUGHTY ANGEL

    3 oz white chocolate liqueur
    1 oz Bacardi 151 proof rum

Combine both ingredients in a
cordial glass and stir.

"Drunk is feeling sophisticated when you can't say it."

–UNKNOWN

NOVEMBER

> "Here's to bein' single . . . drinkin' doubles . . . and seein' triple!"
>
> –UNKNOWN

27

On this day in 1978, San Francisco Mayor George Moscone and City Supervisor Harvey Milk were shot to death inside City Hall by former supervisor Dan White. It was a horrifying crime, but as our mothers used to say, search for the cream filling, which, believe it or not, this assassination actually had! As a key piece of his defense, White's uncharacteristic diet of Twinkies and Coca-Cola was used as evidence of depression leading to the crime. Thus the infamous "Twinkie defense" was born, causing many to misinterpret it and believe they were saying that Twinkies caused the crime. Evil, evil Twinkie!

TWINKIETINI ▶

- 1 tsp sugar
- 2 oz vanilla vodka
- 1/4 oz sweet vermouth

Dip the rim of the cocktail glass in sugar. Combine the vodka and vermouth in a shaker with ice. Shake, strain into the glass, and serve.

28

In the category of What Goes Around Comes Around, on November 28, 1994, serial killer Jeffrey Dahmer was murdered in a Wisconsin prison by a fellow inmate. Dahmer, whose claim to fame was that he ate parts of his victims following their murders, had been sentenced to 936 years in prison without parole. We've thought about it, and decided we don't even want to do something fun for 936 years! Besides, there's no way our livers are going to last that long.

THE CANNIBAL

$^3/_4$ oz Jägermeister herbal liqueur
$^3/_4$ oz Tennessee whiskey
$^3/_4$ oz amaretto
1 $^3/_4$ oz cherry cola

Combine all the ingredients in a cocktail glass with ice. Stir and serve.

29

Who doesn't love the opera? The dressing up, the glamorous opera house, the catchy tunes that you'll be singing for a week. Okay, face it, most of us have never been to an opera, but they really are the epitome of high culture, huh? On this day in 1825, Rossini's *Barber of Seville* was presented in New York City. It was the first Italian opera to be presented in the United States. Although we ourselves have never seen it, we have seen the Bugs Bunny parody called the *Rabbit of Seville*. You go, Bugs!

OPERA HOUSE SPECIAL

1 oz tequila
1 oz gin
1 oz light rum
1 oz vodka
1 oz pineapple juice
1 oz orange juice
1 oz sweet and sour mix

Combine all the ingredients in a blender with ice. Blend and serve in a cocktail glass.

30

"Lucy! You got some 'splainin' to do!" It was on this day in 1940 that America's favorite fiery redhead, Lucille Ball, married Cuban musician Desi Arnaz. With the success of their television sitcom, *I Love Lucy*, the two quickly became one of America's favorite couples, performing vaudeville-style shtick on each episode. Sadly, the pressures of trying to maintain successful careers and a healthy marriage became too much for them, and they were divorced in 1960. Wha, wha, whaaaaa . . . We feel Lucy's own words best describe the Juicy Lucy below: "Do you pop out at parties? Are you unpoopular? Well, the answer to all your troubles is in this bittle lottle! And, it's so tasty too!"

JUICY LUCY

- 2 shots vodka
- 1 shot gin
- 2 shots blue curaçao
  orange juice
  lemon/lime soda

Pour the vodka, gin, and blue curaçao into a Collins glass. Fill with equal parts orange juice and Sprite, and serve.

"Never buy a drink for the road, because the road is already layed out."

–FLIP WILSON

1 DECEMBER 2

It was on this day in 1955 that Rosa Parks, an African-American seamstress, was jailed for refusing to give up her seat on a bus to a white man. Her arrest sparked the Montgomery bus boycott, which lasted for 381 days and forced the government to repeal the law legalizing segregation on public buses. Parks has been dubbed by many the "Mother of the Civil Rights Movement" and is widely considered to be one of the most important citizens of the twentieth century. When Parks died in October 2005, Oprah Winfrey paid tribute to her by saying, "I would not be standing here today, nor standing where I stand every day, had she not chosen to sit down."

VICTORY COLLINS

- 1 1/2 oz vodka
- 3 oz lemon juice
- 3 oz unsweetened grape juice
- 1 tsp powdered sugar
- 1 slice orange

Shake all the ingredients (except the orange slice) with ice and strain into a Collins glass over ice cubes. Add the slice of orange and serve.

One of the Ten Commandments can best be summed up as "Thou shalt not covet thy neighbor's goods." In this day and age we might say, "Touch my stuff and I'll smack you upside the head." On this date in 1823, however, it was stated entirely differently: No European powers would be involved in the goings-on of the Americas, and likewise, the United States wouldn't be involved in European affairs. Although this creed was called the Monroe Doctrine, it was actually put forth by John Quincy Adams, the nation's sixth president. The principle guided American foreign policy for decades, isolating America from potentially entangling alliances with European countries at war.

HOME ALONE

- 2 oz vodka
- 2 tsp blueberry-flavored drink
- 1 tbsp sugar
- 4 oz Gatorade energy drink
- 1/2 oz Mountain Dew

Stir the ingredients together in a Collins glass almost filled with ice cubes, and serve.

3

Ozzy Osbourne, the granddaddy of heavy metal, was born on this day in 1948. If his mother had only known! Among his more notable stunts: Ozzy bit the head off of a dove during a meeting with record execs (he was kicked out of the building), bit the head off of a bat during a concert (he was hospitalized for rabies vaccinations), and was arrested for urinating on the Alamo while wearing one of his wife's dresses (he was banned from San Antonio, Texas, for ten years). Newer generations know Ozzy best as the bumbling, spaced-out dad on his family's reality TV series, and most recently he's been busy writing a Broadway musical. Really, we kid you not.

BAT BITE

2 shots spiced rum
  cranberry juice
1 splash grenadine syrup

Pour the spiced rum over ice cubes in a Collins glass. Fill with cranberry juice, and add a splash of grenadine. Stir and serve.

"My grandmother is over eighty and still doesn't need glasses. Drinks right out of the bottle."

—HENNY YOUNGMAN

DECEMBER

4

Frank Zappa died on this day in 1993. Zappa is widely known to have been an eccentric musician . . . okay, crazy, we know. But we find that the most interesting things about Zappa occurred post-mortem. For example, he has two asteroids named in his honor, as well as a gene, a goby fish, a jellyfish, an extinct mollusk, and a spider with an abdominal mark resembling Zappa's mustache. In 1995, a series of Intel PC motherboards were named after him. We are in awe of such a wide and odd collection of namesakes. Therefore, we didn't want to be left out of the naming game, and have named our very own cocktail after him. Shake up a Zappa Cocktail, below, and feel the love.

ZAPPA COCKTAIL

    1   oz vodka
    3/4 oz dry vermouth
    1/2 oz apricot brandy
    1   tsp Triple Sec
    1   maraschino cherry

Stir all the ingredients (except the cherry) with ice and strain into a cocktail glass. Add the cherry and serve.

5

A day for true celebration! December 5, 1933, saw the end of American Prohibition! We know we don't have to explain what Prohibition is to you, dear readers, for of all the villains we have written about in this book, it is the most evil of them all. We're sure you will agree! Imagine, 14 years of repression—very bleak, bleak years indeed. We thank the gods that we weren't alive to experience the pain and angst of the Prohibition years, and we serve up the Nectar of the Gods here as a peace offering to ensure we never see the evil P-word again.

NECTAR OF THE GODS

    1 1/2 oz vodka
    1 1/2 oz coffee liqueur
    5–6   oz iced tea

Stir the ingredients together in a cocktail glass half-filled with ice cubes, and serve.

6

The good news is that on this day in 1921, the Anglo-Irish treaty was ratified, thereby freeing Ireland of British rule. The bad news is that it caused a massive civil war that pitted brother against brother, cousin against cousin, and worst of all, drinking buddy against drinking buddy. While we recognize that war is never a dream, we realize that freedom is, so tip your glass to the Irish today and thank your lucky stars for freedom.

IRISH DREAM ▶

- 1/2 oz hazelnut liqueur
- 1/2 oz Bailey's Irish Cream
- 3/4 oz brown crème de cacao
- 4 oz vanilla ice cream
- 1 1/2 oz whipped cream
  chocolate sprinkles or shavings

Combine the hazelnut liqueur, Bailey's, brown crème de cacao, and vanilla ice cream in a blender with 1 cup of crushed ice. Pour into a frosted pilsner glass. Top with whipped cream. Garnish with chocolate sprinkles or shavings and serve.

7

December 7, 1941, was called by American President Franklin D. Roosevelt "a day that will live in infamy," as it was on this day that Pearl Harbor was bombed by Japanese forces, embroiling the United States in the Second World War. The attack damaged or destroyed 12 U.S. warships and 188 aircraft, and killed 2,403 American servicemen and 68 civilians. The United States declared war on Japan the very next day, which confuses us, frankly. Wasn't it pretty much a given that the United States and Japan were at war when the Japanese jumped Hawaii? War things generally confuse us. Let's drink.

PEARL HARBOR

- 2 oz vodka
- 2 oz melon liqueur
- 2 oz orange juice

Pour the ingredients over ice into a cocktail glass and serve.

8

It was on this day in 1980 that John Lennon was shot and killed outside of his New York City apartment by deranged fan Mark David Chapman. When asked if he knew what he had done, Chapman said, "I just shot John Lennon." He then took out a copy of J.D. Salinger's *Catcher in the Rye* and began reading. Chapman was, at various points in his life, a drug addict, a born-again Christian, and a hospitalized mental patient. He was expected to enter an insanity plea, but instead he pleaded guilty. Chapman has been denied parole several times in recent years and has received death threats should he ever be released. No surprise there—those Beatles fans don't mess around!

JOHN STALKER

- 2 oz tequila
- 1 oz grenadine
- 4 oz 7-Up

Combine the tequila and grenadine in a Collins glass, top with 7-Up, stir briefly, and serve.

9

Lech Walesa became Poland's first directly elected leader on this day in 1990. During his presidency, he started the "war at the top," which meant shaking up the government almost annually. He was responsible for completely changing Poland from an oppressive Communist country under strict Soviet control with a weak economy to an independent and democratic country with a fast-growing free-market economy. Previous to that small accomplishment, he won the 1983 Nobel Peace Prize and was chosen as *Time* magazine's "Man of the Year" in 1982. By comparison, in 1982 and 1983, we were struggling with acne and wrestling with the teenage-boy angst of boxers versus briefs. We're sure *Time* will be calling us any day now.

POLISH BUTTERFLY

$2/3$ oz blue curaçao
$1/3$ oz Polish vodka

Mix the ingredients in a shot glass and serve.

"The cocktail party is a device for paying off obligations to people you don't want to invite to dinner."

–CHARLES MERRILL SMITH

DECEMBER

357

> "Let the chips fall where they may, but when the alcohol wears off tomorrow there's gonna be one hell of a mess to clean up."
>
> –DAVID MUENCH

10

It was on December 10, 1965, that the Grateful Dead played their first concert at Fillmore Auditorium in San Francisco. The band quickly became one of the most loved bands of all time, touring almost continuously for 30 years. Many of their fans, who happily accepted the moniker "Deadheads," would follow the band on tour, much like Jimmy Buffet's "Parrotheads," who follow him around from concert to concert. We wonder: would a devoted fan of both be a Dead Parrothead?

GRATEFUL DEAD PUNCH ▶

- 3 cups light rum
- 3 cups vodka
- 3 cups Triple Sec
- 3 cups cranberry juice
- 3 cups sweet and sour mix
  2-liter bottle Sprite soda
  grapes

Combine all the ingredients in a pitcher or punch bowl and mix. The punch should be dark red with a fizz to it, but the alcohol shouldn't be completely diluted. Adjust to taste and you're ready to go!

11

We just can't get enough royal scandal! One of the first modern-day scandals for Britain's royals happened on this day in 1936, when King Edward VIII abdicated the throne and married American divorcée Wallis Warfield Simpson. It seems Buckingham Palace and the crown couldn't compete with true love for the king, and in a chivalrous move that frankly makes us sigh and melts our hearts, he stepped down and sailed off into the proverbial sunset with Ms. Simpson. We bet the palace wishes the more recent scandals that have plagued them had such poetic endings. Of course, they wouldn't be half as juicy if they did!

DEEP DARK LOVE

  1   oz vanilla vodka
  $^1/_2$ oz Kahlùa
  $^1/_2$ oz crème de cacao
      2 or 3 whole coffee beans

Shake all the ingredients (except the coffee beans) with ice and then strain into a cocktail glass. Garnish with a couple of whole coffee beans and serve.

12

Come on dooooown! Bob Barker, the host of television's longest-running game show, The Price Is Right, and a staunch animal-rights activist, was born on this day in 1923. Barker has become the most visible figure in the animal-rights movement. The "Fur Flap" surrounding the 1987 Miss USA Pageant attracted tons of publicity when Barker took his chances, spun the wheel, and refused to participate in the program if the models wore real furs as planned. The game show host won, and fake furs were used. In honor of Barker's love of animals, we offer The Purple Squirrel for today's refreshment. Neutered, of course.

THE PURPLE SQUIRREL

  $^1/_2$ oz light rum
  $^1/_2$ oz dark rum
  $^1/_2$ oz blue curaçao
  $^1/_2$ oz grenadine
  $^1/_2$ oz fresh lime juice
  $^1/_2$ oz club soda
      almonds
  1   slice lime

Pour the light rum, dark rum, blue curaçao, grenadine, and fresh lime juice into a cocktail shaker half-filled with ice cubes. Shake well and strain into a cocktail glass with a small amount of crushed ice. Add the club soda. Garnish with an almond-embedded slice of lime, and serve.

13

Who doesn't love to see the truly evil get what's coming to 'em? After all, it's what shows like *Dallas* and *Dynasty* are all about—waiting for the slap in the face, the fall from the glass window, or the shove into the pool. Well, on this day in 1989, Leona Helmsley, the "Queen of Mean," finally got shoved into the pool—figuratively, at least. She was sentenced to four years in prison and 750 hours of community service, and forced to pay a $7.1 million fine for mail fraud and tax evasion. She is widely reported to have once said to an employee: "We don't pay taxes. Only the little people pay taxes," and she named her pet dog Trouble. Try the Nasty Cocktail; we think it sums up Mrs. Helmsley nicely . . . or nastily!

NASTY COCKTAIL

1 ¹/4   oz vodka
³/4   oz Kahlùa
³/4   oz bourbon
³/4   oz brown crème de cacao
¹/2   oz cream

Pour the ingredients into a cocktail shaker half-filled with cracked ice. Shake well, strain into a cocktail glass, and serve.

"The problem with the world is that everyone is a few drinks behind."

–HUMPHREY BOGART

14

On December 14, 1503, Nostradamus, possibly the world's most famous psychic connection (next to Dionne Warwick, of course) was born. He is often referred to as the "Prophet of Doom" because of his many predictions of death and war. His followers say he predicted the French Revolution, the birth and rise to power of Hitler, the assassination of John F. Kennedy, the Challenger shuttle disaster, the terrorist attacks of September 11 in the United States, and almost every other major tragic event throughout history. We figured if he could do it, we'd give it a shot as well. Our prediction: more than three Good Fortunes (below) and you will be suffering Bad Fortune in the morning. Please let us know whether our predictions are true.

◀ **GOOD FORTUNE**

  1 1/4 oz citron vodka
    3/4 oz passion fruit liqueur
    6 oz lemonade
    1 slice lemon

Shake the liquid ingredients and strain into an ice-filled hurricane glass. Garnish with a lemon wheel.

"When people drink, then they are successful and win lawsuits are happy and help their friends. Quickly, bring me a beaker of cider, so that I may wet my mind and say something clever."

—ARISTOPHANES, 424 B.C.E.

"It's not whether you win or lose . . . it's how drunk you get while playing the game."

—HOMER SIMPSON

15

We're guessing that James Brown, the "Godfather of Soul," wasn't feeling so good on this day in 1988 when he began his prison sentence in South Carolina for resisting arrest following a high-speed car chase, threatening pedestrians with a firearm, and abuse of PCP. Yikes, James, that's quite a rap sheet! He only served three years of his six-year prison sentence. Somewhat of a tortured soul, Brown had several other arrests for drug possession. I guess we know why he was feeling so good after all. Try the Godfather, below; it's guaranteed to make you feel good, too.

GODFATHER

1 ¹/₂ oz whiskey
³/₄ oz amaretto

Pour both ingredients over ice into an old-fashioned glass. Drink until you "feel good."

16

Remember the tea parties from when you were a little kid? Miniature teacups, teapots, little cakes? Well, when Boston threw its very own Tea Party on this day in 1773, it was a lot like that. Okay, not really; as a matter of fact, it was nothing like that. You see, it was all about taxation and the British importers undercutting the prices of local merchants. Fed up, the Bostonians boarded ships loaded with incoming tea and destroyed 342 crates of it by dumping it into Boston Harbor. This was all done without the loss of a single life, so it was all very civilized, just like a tea party!

BOSTON TEA PARTY

- $1/2$ oz gin
- $1/2$ oz rum
- $1/2$ oz vodka
- $1/2$ oz Triple Sec
- $1/2$ oz amaretto
- $1/2$ oz coffee liqueur
- $1/2$ oz orange liqueur
- 2 oz sweet and sour mix
- 5 oz cola
- 1 lemon wedge

Combine all the ingredients (except the cola and lemon wedge) in a Collins glass with ice and shake. Top with cola, garnish with a lemon wedge, and serve.

"I drink too much, way too much; when my doctor drew blood he ran a tab!"

—RODNEY DANGERFIELD

DECEMBER

365

17

December 17, 1903, is the day in history that changed the way the world travels. It was on this day that Orville and Wilbur Wright became the first people to successfully fly a motorized airplane. As we're sure you recall, their triumph took place at Kitty Hawk, North Carolina. They made four flights that day, which were witnessed by four lifeguards from the beach and a young boy from the village. We imagine that when the boy reported what he'd seen later in the evening to his parents, he was told something along the lines of "if God had intended for man to fly, he would have given us wings." Oh, if they only knew then what we know now. So shake up an American Flyer, described here, and take a flight of your own.

AMERICAN FLYER

1 ½ oz light rum
1 tbsp lime juice
½ tsp sugar syrup
Champagne

Shake the rum, lime juice, and syrup with cracked ice. Strain into a chilled white wine glass and fill with Champagne.

18

On this day in 1865, the Thirteenth Amendment to the U.S. Constitution was proclaimed, abolishing slavery and putting an end to a very bleak time in American history. As it turned out, President Lincoln's Emancipation Proclamation of 1863 had only freed slaves held in the Southern states, while it was the Thirteenth Amendment that hammered the nail in the coffin for Northern slave owners two years later. But wait, wasn't it the soldiers in the North who were fighting against slavery in the Civil War? And if slavery was simply a red herring, what was the whole Civil War about anyway? What every war is about: the Benjamins, the Jacksons, the Lincolns, and the Washingtons. Bling, bling.

SOUTHERN COMFORT SOUR ▶

1 oz Southern Comfort Peach Liqueur
2 oz sour mix
1 slice orange
1 maraschino cherry

Mix the peach liqueur and sour mix with ice and strain into a whiskey sour glass. Add an orange slice and a cherry on a pick as a garnish.

> "I go from stool to stool in singles bars hoping to get lucky, but there's never any gum under any of them."
>
> –EMO PHILLIPS

19

Canadians have this day to thank for their national sport. It was on this day in 1917 that the first games of the newly formed National Hockey League were played. Toronto, Ottawa, Québec, the Montréal Canadiens, and the Montréal Wanderers were the five teams who made up the league. Of course, by the end of the season, after piecing together the leftover body parts, they were only able to make up about three and a half teams. It's all fun and games until somebody loses a tooth.

ICE FROST

   4 oz Frangelico hazelnut liqueur
   4 oz milk
       ground cinnamon

To start, make sure the ingredients are chilled. Mix the liqueur and milk in a Collins glass, and sprinkle some ground cinnamon over your icy concoction.

20

On December 20, 1803, the Louisiana Purchase was completed and the territory was formally transferred from France to the United States during ceremonies in New Orleans. No small real estate deal, the Louisiana Purchase included nearly 530 million acres, or to put it in perspective, roughly one-third of the mainland United States. That is some serious square footage, and it came at a bargain, only $3 per square mile! Boy, don't we all wish we saw real estate prices like that these days? Of course, it also came with a downside, as Hurricane Katrina proved once and for all. Until you can make it back to Bourbon Street for Mardi Gras, jazz and Zydeco, jambalaya and beignets, have a Louisiana Lullabye and dream of happy days.

LOUISIANA LULLABY

1 ½ oz dark rum
2 tsp dry vermouth
3 drops Grand Marnier
1 Slice lemon

Stir the rum, Dubonnet, and Grand Marnier together with ice in a mixing glass. Strain into a cocktail glass, garnish with a sliver of lemon, and serve.

> "I'm for anything that gets you through the night, be it prayer, tranquilizers, or a bottle of Jack Daniels."
>
> —FRANK SINATRA

DECEMBER

369

"The problem with the designated driver program, it's not a desirable job. But if you ever get sucked into doing it, have fun with it. At the end of the night, drop them off at the wrong house."

–JEFF BRIDGES

On this day in 1980, the fabulously wealthy high-society maven Sunny von Bulow was found comatose on the floor of her Newport, Rhode Island, bathroom. When investigators began sniffing around that bathroom, they smelled a lot more than hair products and expensive perfume—they smelled foul play. It seems Sunny had been injected with a lethal dose of insulin, leading to the eventual conviction of her husband, Claus, for attempted murder. But he was later acquitted at a second trial and hightailed it back to Europe. Poor Sunny has remained in a vegetative state in a New York City hospital ever since, and her case remains open. Ponder who you think is guilty as you sip on a Sunny Delight cocktail.

SUNNY DELIGHT ▶

1 shot Triple Sec
3 shots lemon vodka
1 slice lemon
  orange juice
1 shot club soda

Pour the Triple Sec and vodka into a Mason jar. Gently squeeze the lemon into the mix, then place on the rim as a garnish. Fill almost to the top with the orange juice, and then add the shot of club soda.

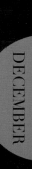

On this date in 1964, Lenny Bruce, a well-known American comedian, was arrested on obscenity charges (not for the first time) in New York City. The highly publicized trial lasted six months and resulted in a conviction and a sentence of four months in a work house, but he was released on bail during the appeals process. When asked what his thoughts were on the trial, we're guessing Bruce said something like: "The whole ____ thing ____ ____ and I ____ hope they ____ my ____ for ____. You ____ hear that you ____ ____ ____ ____!"

DIRTY BASTARD

1 1/2 oz vodka
1/2 oz blackberry brandy
5 oz cranberry juice
1 lime wedge

Pour the vodka, brandy, and juice into a Collins glass over ice. Add one squeeze of lime, and serve. If you spill a little, try not to swear.

We've all experienced the struggle: what is the perfect gift for my one true love? Does she want chocolates or flowers? Is it the tie or the cuff links that will warm his heart? When trying to impress Rachel, a Dutch brothel employee (yes, we all know what that made her: popular), on this day in 1888, the artist Vincent van Gogh was clearly struggling with the same indecision and chose mistakenly, as men often do. He must have thought that it's not the flowers or the diamonds that would make a real difference; instead, he should give her something special, something of his very own. So he went down to the brothel and delivered his right ear to her. Police went to his home the next day and delivered him to the hospital. What sort of card says "Thanks for the body part. I will treasure it forever"?

SUNFLOWER HIGHBALL

1 oz vodka
1 oz Licor 43 liqueur
5 oz orange juice
nutmeg

Mix the vodka, liqueur, and juice with ice in a Collins glass. Sprinkle with nutmeg and serve.

24

Only one day left to finish the decorating, complete the shopping, get the turkey into the brine, make the cookies, write the last of the cards, chop the firewood, prepare the guest room for the extended family, write your letter to Santa, and finally, make the eggnog. It's Christmas Eve, a time for family and loved ones to come together, let bygones be bygones, and try not to think about the credit-card bills that will be arriving just after the New Year! Not your cup of eggnog? Bear in mind that Christmas isn't just for Christians anymore. Because most places are closed, it's for everybody these days, so cozy up, grab an eggnog or three, and fall asleep dreaming of sugar plums and dancing fairies. Santa Claus will be here before the hangover sets in.

EGGNOG

12 eggs, separated
1 cup bourbon whiskey
1 cup cognac
1/2 tsp salt
3 pints heavy cream
1 cup granulated sugar
   nutmeg

Beat the egg yolks until light in color. Slowly add the bourbon and cognac, while beating at a slow speed. Chill for 3 hours. Add the salt to the egg whites, and beat until peaks form. Whip the cream until stiff peaks form. Fold the whipped cream into the yolk mixture, then fold in the beaten egg whites. Chill for 1 hour. Serve with nutmeg sprinkled on top. For a thinner drink, add 1 or 2 cups of milk. Serve in a punch bowl or another large bowl.

25

Christmas Day. The gifts are unwrapped, the tinsel is falling off the tree, the fire is making the whole house hot, and Grandpa is snoring in the Barcalounger. Nothing left to do but pick up where you left off last night with the eggnog while you pick at the turkey bones still sitting on the counter. But instead of eggnog, we thought you might appreciate going a little more hard-core today; after all, the sooner you pass out, the sooner it's all behind you and you can hit the stores and start the returns. Try a Drunk on Christmas, below; it delivers on its promise and tastes delicious, too.

DRUNK ON CHRISTMAS

    3 oz Midori
    2 oz whiskey
    1 oz apple Schnapps
    4 oz sour mix
       maraschino cherries

Mix first three ingredients with ice and strain into an old-fashioned glass over ice. Fill with the sour mix and garnish with a few cherries.

26

Kwanzaa is a weeklong holiday observance held from December 26 to January 1 to honor African-American heritage, primarily in the United States. It was founded in 1966 by Ron Karenga. It is not a religious holiday but a cultural one, a syncretic festival, based on various elements of the first harvest celebrations widely celebrated in Africa. The timing is meant to offer people an alternative to the growing commercialism of Christmas, but a recent survey shows that only 1.6 percent of the African-American community celebrates Kwanzaa. It doesn't matter what color you are: nobody wants to give up Santa!

CELEBRATION

    2 1/2 parts gold rum
        1 part brandy
        1 part Triple Sec
        1 part lemon juice
        5 drops orange bitters
        1 twist lemon peel

Pour the liquid ingredients over ice and mix in a shaker. Strain into a cocktail glass, garnish with a lemon peel, and serve.

DECEMBER

375

27

Radio City Music Hall, known as the "Showplace of the Nation," opened to the public in New York City on December 27, 1932. Although a host to awards shows galore, the Radio City Christmas Spectacular, and any number of other presenting organizations, it is somehow impossible to think about Radio City without calling to mind their in-house precision dance team, the Rockettes. So why is it that these dancing ladies stick out so much in our minds? Well, legs, silly. What else? So dance your way into the kitchen and stage the creation of a Radio City, as listed here. It will help you kick off your evening just right.

RADIO CITY

    1   oz sweet sherry
    1   oz dry sherry
   1/2 oz gin
    1   oz 7-Up

Pour the ingredients over crushed ice and serve in an old-fashioned glass.

28

We want to dislike her, we really do, she stood against everything we lean drunkenly on the bar for, but we can't help but admire the chutzpah of Carry A. Nation, who attacked a saloon in Kansas on this day in 1900 in her fight against alcohol. She eventually did this more than 30 times. A large woman, at 6 feet tall and 175 pounds, she liked to describe herself as "a bulldog running along at the feet of Jesus, barking at what he doesn't like." Alone or accompanied by hymn-singing women, she would march, singing and praying, into a bar while smashing bar fixtures and bottles of alcohol with a hatchet. That's one feisty, booze-hatin' granny! She was slightly before her time, however, as Prohibition in the United States didn't kick in until 1919, but eventually Nation's mission was accomplished . . . thankfully, for only a short while.

MISSION ACCOMPLISHED ▶

    4   oz vodka
    2   oz Triple Sec
    2   splashes lime juice
    2   splashes grenadine

Mix the ingredients in a shaker with ice. Shake well and serve in an old-fashioned glass.

29

The struggle between church and state has been a long one, involving powerful popes and murderous monarchs. One of the best-known tales of such disagreement resulted in the assassination of Archbishop Thomas Becket on this date in 1170. Becket had previously been a staunch supporter of the English monarchy and King Henry II; at one time, Henry had even sent his son to live with Becket. Upon his installation as the Archbishop of Canterbury in 1162, Becket did a 180-degree turn. He wanted the church to have complete autonomy over its own proceedings and, further, to make the church immune from taxation by the monarchy. Henry was so vexed by this about-face and the subsequent demands that he purportedly stated, "Will no one rid me of this troublesome priest?" Several of his knights overheard their leader, and so rid him they did; Becket was murdered in Canterbury Cathedral. Henry was reviled throughout Christendom, faced rebellion led by his wife and three of his sons, and eventually paid penance at Becket's tomb. What a real-life game of chess this seems! Try an Archbishop, the drink listed here, or we'll have some of our knight friends stop by your place, too!

ARCHBISHOP

- 2 oz gin
- 1 oz green ginger wine
- 1 tsp Benedictine herbal liqueur
- 1 lime wedge

Pour the gin, wine, and herbal liqueur over ice and stir. Garnish with a lime wedge and serve in an old-fashioned glass.

30

On December 30, 1965, Ferdinand Marcos was inaugurated president of the Philippines, a nation he led for 20 years before he was unseated. The most interesting thing about Marcos, however, was his wife, Imelda. After they had fled into exile in Hawaii, it was revealed that Imelda had amassed a stunningly large collection of shoes and lingerie, including more than 3,000 pairs of shoes, 500 brassieres, 200 girdles, and a bulletproof bra. Bang, bang!

EASY MONEY

1	oz light rum
1/2	oz dark rum
1/2	oz coconut rum
1	oz orange juice
1/4	oz lime juice
2	tbsp mango sherbet
1	tsp grenadine

Blend all the ingredients except the grenadine and fruit garnish with crushed ice. Pour into a Parfait glass; sprinkle with grenadine, and serve.

"I drink too much. Last time I gave a urine sample there was an olive in it."

–RODNEY DANGERFIELD

31

"I hope Mom behaves at this cookout. Last time she started drinking margaritas, she wandered off in the woods for 18 hours and woke up to a deer licking salt off her lips." —DAVID LETTERMAN

You've made it! You've been with us for a full year. Congratulations! We thought maybe we'd take you out and get you drunk to celebrate, but really, haven't we done that every day this year already? And besides, if you're anything like us, your liver is probably crying mercy. But don't give in just yet, there's still one final cocktail to shake up and send the year out with a bang. The best news is, if you're a real trooper—and we know you are—tomorrow you get to start all over again from page 1. Happy New Year!

HAPPY NEW YEAR ▶

1/4	oz brandy
3/4	oz ruby port
3/4	oz orange juice
4	oz Champagne

Shake the brandy, port, and orange juice well over ice cubes in a shaker. Strain into a Champagne flute, fill with Champagne, and serve.

SHOPPING LIST

Spirits
Brandy
Apricot brandy
Blackberry brandy
Calvados apple brandy
Cognac
Pisco brandy

Gin
Plymouth gin
Sloe gin

Rum
Anejo rum
Bacardi 151 dark rum
Bacardi Limon rum
Captain Morgan Original
  spiced rum
Coconut rum
Gold rum
Jamaican dark rum
Light rum
Mount Gay Barbados
  rum
Orange rum
Silver rum

Tequila
Light tequila

Vodka
Blavod vodka
Citrus vodka
Cranberry vodka
Peach vodka
Polish vodka
Raspberry vodka
Russian vodka
Vanilla vodka

Whiskey/Whisky
Blended whiskey
Bourbon whiskey
Canadian whisky
Crown Royal Canadian
  whiskey
Irish whiskey
Jack Daniel's Tennessee
  whiskey
Rye whiskey
Scotch whisky

Grain alcohol
Everclear alcohol

Cordials
Absinthe herbal liqueur
Aftershock
Alize Bleu liqueur
Alize liqueur
Amaretto
Amer Picon
Anise liqueur
Anisette
Apricot liqueur
Aquavit
Bailey's Irish Cream
Benedictine herbal liqueur
Bianco vermouth
Black sambuca
Blue curaçao
Butterscotch liqueur
Cachaça (Brazilian liquor)
Caraway liqueur
Chambord raspberry
  liqueur
Cherry liqueur
Cherry heering
Chocolate liqueur
Citrus liqueur
Cointreau orange liqueur
Crème de bananes
Crème de cacao
  (brown/dark/white)
Crème de cassis
Crème de menthe
  (green/white)
Crème de noyaux
DeKuyper Buttershots
  liqueur
Drambuie Scotch whisky
  liqueur
Framboise raspberry
  liqueur
Frangelico hazelnut
  liqueur
Galliano herbal liqueur
Grand Marnier orange
  liqueur
Green Chartreuse
Irish Cream
Jägermeister herbal
  liqueur
Kahlúa coffee liquor
La Grande Passion
  liqueur
Licor 43 liqueur
Kirschwasser cherry
  brandy
Maraschino liqueur

Midori melon liqueur
Orange curaçao
Passoa liqueur
Pear liqueur
Pernod licorice liqueur
Pisang Ambon liqueur
Raspberry liqueur
Rock and Rye liqueur
Rum Tree liqueur
Sabra chocolate-orange
  liqueur
Rumple Minze
  peppermint liqueur
Sambuca, black
Sambuca, white
Schnapps, apple
Schnapps, banana
Schnapps, blackberry
Schnapps, butterscotch
Schnapps, cinnamon
  (Goldschlager)
Schnapps, grape
Schnapps, peach
Schnapps, peppermint
Schnapps, raspberry
Schnapps, root beer
Schnapps, sour apple
Schnapps, strawberry
Schnapps, vanilla
Schnapps, watermelon
Southern Comfort
  peach liqueur
Sour apple liqueur
Strega herbal liqueur
Triple Sec
White chocolate liqueur
Yellow Chartreuse

Flavorings
Allspice
Bloody Mary mix
Brown sugar
Campari bitters
Celery salt
Cinnamon
Ground cloves
Nutmeg
Orange bitters
Pepper
Salt
Sugar
Sweet and sour mix
Whisky sour mix
Worcestershire sauce
Tabasco sauce

Syrups
Banana syrup
Chocolate syrup
Grenadine syrup
Maple syrup
Raspberry syrup
Simple syrup
Strawberry syrup

Beers
Bass ale
Guinness stout
Rolling Rock lager

Wines
Champagne
Claret
Cream sherry
Dubonnet French
  vermouth
Dubonnet Rouge
  vermouth
Gekkaikan sake
Green ginger wine
Madeira
Port, ruby
Port, tawny
Red wine
Rosso vermouth
Sherry, dry
Sherry, sweet
White wine

Juices
Apple cider
Apple juice
Clamato juice
Cranberry juice
Fruit punch
Gatorade
Grapefruit juice

Grape punch
Lemon juice
Lemonade
(regular/pink)
Lime juice
(regular/sweetened)
Mandarin
Mango juice
Maraschino cherry juice
Olive juice
Orange juice
Passion-fruit juice
Peach orchard punch
juice
Pear cider
Pineapple juice
Strawberry juice
Tomato juice
White grape juice

Sodas

7-Up
Bitter lemon soda
Cherry cola
Coca-Cola
Cola
Ginger ale
Grapefruit-lemon soda
Lemon-lime soda
Mountain Dew
Limeade
Orange soda
Vanilla cola

Miscellaneous Mixers

Black tea
Blueberry flavored
drink
Chocolate milk
Club soda/soda water
Coffee
Espresso
Iced tea
Mexican hot cocoa
Milk
Red Bull
Tonic water

Garnishes and Assorted Ingredients

Almonds
Apples
Apricots
Bananas
Celery
Cherries
Circus peanuts
Cinnamon sticks
Chocolate shavings or
sprinkles
Coffee beans
Cream
(double/light/heavy)
Eggs
Fresh mint
Grapes
Honey
Ice cream (vanilla)
Limes
Lemons
Mango sherbet
Olives
Oranges
Paper umbrellas
Pickled peppers
Pickle spears
Pineapple
Strawberry puree
Strawberry sorbet
Whipped cream

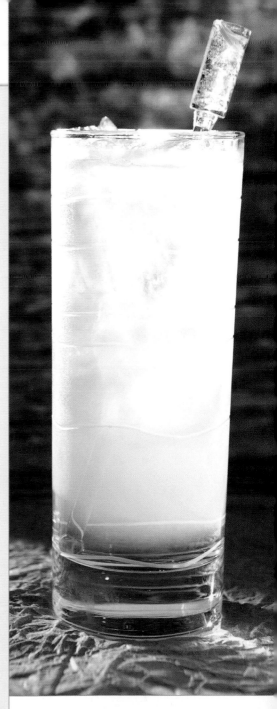

DRINKS INDEX

LIQUOR INDEX

390

ACKNOWLEDGMENTS

Thanks to the Fair Winds Press staff beginning with publisher Holly Schmidt who knowingly announced during a staff meeting that we would be the perfect authors for this book because, although we weren't professional bartenders, we were professional drinkers. We thank our editor Ellen Phillips who whole-heartedly agreed and managed to keep us sober enough to finish the book yet urged us to stay drunk enough to enjoy it. Thanks to managing editor John Gettings who put up with the abuse without having a single drink...at least during working hours. And special thanks to Fair Winds' president Ken Fund who has rolled his eyes and groaned but still greenlighted the project.

We'd like to thank every bartender who's ever said to us: "Here try this, you'll love it!" and we'd like to especially thank every bartender who's ever said the words: "This one's on me."

We'd like to thank all of our long-standing, tried-and-true drinking friends who enthusiastically helped us test the drinks and not so enthusiastically held our hair back when we'd tested too much. They are: Jason Southerland, Annie Damphousse, Catherine Caswell, Steve Katnack, Karen Rosenhoover, Kimberly Samaha, and Kelly and Mikael Backman. We hope you have such great friends to drink with as well.

ABOUT THE AUTHORS

LARRY DONOVAN

Larry Donovan drank as an amateur early in his 20s and then professionally from the moment he could get through the entire night and still remember it the next day. Though a resident of the Boston area and a lifelong New Englander, he has taken his drinking to over 20 states, Washington, D.C., and countries in North America, Europe and Africa. Like a parent with his children, he cannot choose his favorite drink - but it knows! As stated in The Daily Cocktail, he hopes to be able to manage his alcoholic intake carefully so that he may continue to drink for the rest of his life. Cheers!

DALYN A. MILLER

Dalyn A. Miller began his drinking in the Southwestern state of New Mexico where he was broken-in early on wine coolers, tequila and cheap Mexican beer. Once he'd moved to the Northeast and regained his taste buds he refined his drinking habits and expanded his repertoire to include cocktails from all over the world (except Norwegian Aquavit which he still can't stomach following an unsavory crab fishing trip in the North Sea in the late 80s). Like James Bond he likes his martinis shaken and not stirred, but is the first to admit that the similarities come to a screeching halt there. His liver is alive and well and resides in Boston.